Semiconductors

Elgar Practical Guides

Rich in practical advice, *Elgar Practical Guides* are handy, concise guides to a range of legal practice areas.

Combining practical insight and step-by-step guidance with the relevant substantive law and procedural rules, the books in this series focus on understanding and navigating the issues that are likely to be encountered in practice. This is facilitated by a range of structural tools including checklists, glossaries, sample documentation and recommended actions.

Elgar Practical Guides are indispensable resources for the busy practitioner and for the non-specialist who requires a first introduction or a reliable turn-to reference book.

For a full list of Edward Elgar published titles, including the titles in this series, visit our website at www.e-elgar.com.

Semiconductors

Law, Strategy and Tax

IAIN SHERIDAN
MBA (Oxon), Legal Consultant, Barrister, London, UK

Elgar Practical Guides

Edward Elgar
PUBLISHING

Cheltenham, UK • Northampton, MA, USA

Published by
Edward Elgar Publishing Limited
The Lypiatts
15 Lansdown Road
Cheltenham
Glos GL50 2JA
UK

Edward Elgar Publishing, Inc.
William Pratt House
9 Dewey Court
Northampton
Massachusetts 01060
USA

Authorised representative in the EU for GPSR queries only: Easy Access System Europe – Mustamäe tee 50, 10621 Tallinn, Estonia, gpsr.requests@easproject.com

A catalogue record for this book
is available from the British Library

Library of Congress Control Number: 2025932490

This book is available electronically in the **Elgar**online
Law subject collection
https://doi.org/10.4337/9781035357024

MIX
Paper | Supporting responsible forestry
FSC® C013604

ISBN 978 1 0353 5701 7 (cased)
ISBN 978 1 0353 5702 4 (eBook)

Printed and bound by CPI Group (UK) Ltd, Croydon, CR0 4YY

To my late father, an exceptional IBM engineer of Da Vincian ingenuity. For the many lessons he taught me about problem solving.

Content overview

Contents

About the author

Iain Sheridan is a legal consultant with experience in all aspects of regulation and technology, including fundraising, structuring, contracts, dispute resolution, policy documentation, intellectual property, regulatory risk framework reviews and taxation.

Before becoming a consultant, he was head of legal Europe and Asia for the financial sector dedicated investment bank Fox-Pitt, Kelton. His consulting projects have included advising ABN AMRO, Bank of America, Bank of China, Barclays, Citadel, Citigroup, CQS, Deutsche Bank, Fidelity International, Fox-Pitt Kelton, and Société Générale. He has also been a consultant to the OECD and the United Nations.

Over two decades his articles on regulation and cutting-edge technology have been published by Butterworths, Kluwer, Oxford University Press, and Sweet & Maxwell. His scientific research on GNSS and drones was published by the Royal Society. His first book, *Financial Regulation and Technology* (Edward Elgar), is relied on by practitioners throughout Asia, Europe and North America.

A qualified barrister (England and Wales) and solicitor (NSW), Iain has also studied data science at Oxford University and machine learning at Cambridge University. Originally from Stratford upon Avon, he has lived in Beijing, Brisbane, London, Paris, Sydney, and Vienna.

Preface

This first edition of *Semiconductors – Law, Strategy and Tax* concentrates on the key issues in the global semiconductor sector with particular focus on the UK. I am a regulatory lawyer who's been tackling technology issues for more than 20 years. My first practitioner-angled article, published in 2001, whilst practising as an associate at A&O Shearman, involved collaborating with IBM engineers and UK regulators to examine prosecuting fraud over the Internet.

I have since contributed a wide range of financial regulation and technology articles, produced by Butterworths, Kluwer Law International, Oxford University Press, and Sweet & Maxwell. Additionally, my scientific research on GPS, other GNSS and drones was published by the Royal Society. My earlier practitioner book, *Financial Regulation and Technology* (2022), has provided me with current insights on advances in both machine learning and quantum computing.

The seed of this book was planted in 2015. In that year I had the benefit of attending a strategy briefing in Seoul that formed part of an international investment event organised by the state-funded Korean Trade Promotion Corporation (KOTRA).[1]

For 30 minutes the strategy director of SK Hynix presented slide after slide on the projected demand to 2030 for logic, memory and sensor semiconductors. Two messages were simultaneously delivered to the audience. First, semiconductors were essential to the growth of AI, the automotive sector, drones, the Internet of Things and robotic applications. Second, Korean ambition, commitment, and government support would sustain their competitiveness to supply this future demand.

1 See www.kotra.or.kr.

This book is a one-stop reference guide for CEOs, strategy directors, lawyers, and government policy makers. For all readers its contents will be illuminating, also saving time on research and analysis. The wider readership includes entrepreneurs, innovators seeking intellectual property protection, all relevant senior management functions, risk specialists and semiconductor engineers. In sum it is written to benefit professionals as well as anyone seeking to expand their knowledge on opportunities and risks in this most dynamic sector.

From a form and style viewpoint, nearly all statute and case law citations are confined to the footnotes. Thus, any chapter can be fluidly read. An initial perusal of each chapter does not get slowed down because of long titles to multifarious legislation and case law names. Each chapter assumes no advanced knowledge of semiconductors and related technology topics, and, when necessary, encapsulates the essential aspects.

Any reader should come away with an understanding of the key case law regulation and authoritative guidance and international standards governing multiple specific themes. Many comparisons are made between the UK, Asia, the EU and the US. Given even the most formidable memories can be forced to pause for thought to make an impromptu application of all the salient aspects of what can often be complex topics, this book also attempts to make memorable the essential features of each topic by including diagrams and graphs.

For public service officials and government ministers, some of my viewpoints are constructive criticism. I have dedicated myself to providing succinct explanations on how to grow our semiconductor sector, saving you months of hard work to ascend this steepest of learning curves. Omitting to act, to make ambitious, long-term decisions, is totally wrong. The opportunities lost by failing to sufficiently understand, then heavily invest in the UK semiconductor sector are incalculable. As mentioned in Chapter 5 Strategic issues, engineers educated in British universities should be making careers in the UK, not the US.

Finally, I would like to acknowledge my gratitude to the team at Edward Elgar who made all this happen. This is my second outing with them. A special thank you to Anthony Hawitt for sharing the vision.

The law is stated as of 6 January 2025.

Abbreviations

Group III-V	Group III elements and group V elements
5G	Fifth Generation network of cellular mobile communications
6G	Sixth Generation network of cellular mobile communications
ADAS	Advanced Driver Assistance Systems
AI	Artificial Intelligence
ALD	Atomic Layer Deposition
AP&T	Assembly, Packaging & Testing
AQI	Air Quality Index
AR	Main Corporate Tax Rate
ASIC	Application Specific Integrated Circuit
ASP	Average Selling Price
BEPS	Base Erosion Profit Sharing
BOM	Bill of Materials
CAD	Computer Aided Design
CEO	Chief Executive Officer
CFIUS	Committee on Foreign Investment in the United States
CHIPS Act	Creating Helpful Incentives to Produce Semiconductors for America Act
CIA	Central Intelligence Agency
CISM	Centre for Integrative Semiconductor Materials
CLO	Chief Legal Officer

CMOS	Complementary Metal Oxide Semiconductor
COO	Chief Operating Officer
CPO	Co-Packaged Optics
CPU	Central Processing Unit
CSA	Compound Semiconductor Applications
CSO	Chief Strategy Officer
CTO	Chief Technology Officer
CUDA	Compute Unified Device Architecture
DARPA	Defense Advanced Research Projects Agency
DBT	Department of Business and Trade
DC	Defined Contribution
DORA	Digital Operational Resilience Act
DPU	Data Processing Unit
DRAM	Dynamic Random Access Memory
DSIT	Department of Science, Innovation and Technology
EDA	Electronic Design Automation
EEA	European Economic Area
EPO	European Patent Office
EPSRC	Engineering and Physical Sciences Research Council
EU	European Union
EUV	Extreme Ultraviolet
EV	Electric Vehicle
FaaS	Fab-as-a-Service
FDI	Foreign Direct Investment
FET	Field Effect Transistor
FPGA	Field Programmable Gate Array
FRAND	Fair, Reasonable, And Non-Discriminatory
FTC	Federal Trade Commission
GAA	Gate All Around

Ga	Gallium
GaN	Gallium Nitride
GC	General Counsel
GDP	Gross Domestic Product
Ge	Germanium
GNSS	Global Navigation Satellite Systems
GPS	Global Positioning System
GPU	Graphics Processing Unit
GSA	Global Semiconductor Alliance
HCF	Hollow Core Fibre
HPU	High Performance Computing
HTVI	Hard to Value Intangibles
IC	Integrated Circuit
ICBM	Intercontinental Ballistic Missile
ICS	Institute for Compound Semiconductors
IDM	Integrated Device Manufacturer
IEEE	Institute of Electrical and Electronics Engineers
IP	Intellectual Property
IPO	Intellectual Property Office
IPO	Initial Public Offering
IPR	Intellectual Property Rights
IPU	Intelligence Processing Unit
IKC	Innovation and Knowledge Centre
IMEC	Interuniversity Microelectronics Centre
IoT	Internet of Things
ISA	Instruction Set Architecture
ISU	Investment Security Unit
KOTRA	Korea Trade Investment Promotion Agency
LED	Light Emitting Diode
LSEG	London Stock Exchange Group
LSTC	Leading-edge Semiconductor Technology Center

MAC	Material Adverse Change
MEMS	Micro Electro-Mechanical Systems
METI	Ministry of Economy, Trade and Industry
MIT	Massachusetts Institute of Technology
ML	Machine Learning
MOD	Ministry of Defence
MOS	Metal Oxide Semiconductor
MOSFET	Metal Oxide Semiconductor Field Effect Transistor
MoU	Memorandum of Understanding
MSTAR	Michigan Semiconductor Talent and Technology for Automotive Research
NAND	Non-volatile flash memory
NASA	National Aeronautics and Space Administration
NDAA	National Defense Authorization Act
NED	Non-executive Director
NMI	National Microelectronics Institute
NMOS	N-channel Metal-Oxide Semiconductor
NSIA	National Security and Investment Act
NSTC	National Semiconductor Technology Center
NWF	Newport Wafer Fab
NYSE	New York Stock Exchange
OECD	Organization for Economic Cooperation and Development
PAE	Patent Assertion Entity
PCSEL	Photonic Crystal Surface Emitting Laser
PE	Private Equity
PFC	Perfluorocarbon
PIN	Personal Identification Number
PMIC	Power Management Integrated Circuit
PMOS	P-channel Metal-Oxide Semiconductor
PV	Photovoltaics

QC	Quality Control
RAM	Random Access Memory
R&D	Research and Development
RDEC	Research and Development Expenditure Credit
RF	Radio Frequency
RISE	Research Institute in Secure Hardware and Embedded Systems
RP	Relevant IP Profits
SAMR	State Administration for Market Regulation
SEP	Standards Essential Patent
Si	Silicon
SIA	Semiconductor Industry Association
SiC	Silicon Carbide
SmartNIC	Smart Network Interface Card
SME	Small- and Medium-sized Enterprise
SMMT	Society of Motor Manufacturers and Traders
SNU	Seoul National University
SoC	System on Chip
SSD	Solid State Drive
SSO	Standard Setting Organisation
STEM	Science, Technology, Engineering and Mathematics
TFEU	Treaty on the Functioning of the European Union
TIGBT	Trench Insulated Gate Bipolar Transistor
TSMC	Taiwan Semiconductor Manufacturing Company
UAV	Unmanned Aerial Vehicle
UDA	Unified Driver Architecture
UKRI	United Kingdom Research and Innovation
VC	Venture Capital
WTO	World Trade Organization
WTP	Willingness to Pay

WTS	Willingness to Sell

Table of cases

United Kingdom (UK)

Other Jurisdictions

Judgement of the European Court of Justice

Netherlands

US Judgments

Table of legislation

Agreements, conventions and treaties

EU legislation

Other legislation

China

Japan

South Korea

United Kingdom

United States

1. Introduction to semiconductors

All things are ready, if our minds be so.[1]

1.1 Law, strategy, and tax

Competition in semiconductors and securing supply chain resilience across the sector are two of the most important challenges of this era.[2] Given in such a competition any advantage, no matter how marginal, can make a difference, this practical book provides guidance on English law, strategy, and taxation. Every Chief Executive Officer (CEO), strategy director, general counsel, and government policy maker may benefit from reading it.

My motivation to produce this book is based on a belief that the growth of the UK semiconductor sector matters. For any other country already possessing or ambitious to grow a semiconductor sector the strategic thinking equally applies. Further, many legal points also include comparative insights from Asia, the EU and North America.

As a lawyer my skillset and experience can support all participants and influential stakeholders to make more of an incremental difference in this pivotal sector. If innovation is the equivalent of gold particles in the

---

1 Shakespeare, W. (1599) *Henry V*, Act 4, Scene 3, https://shakespeare.mit.edu/henryv/henryv.4.3.html.

2 *Financial Times* (2022) 'Account of the global chip battle wins FT book prize – Chris Miller's "Chip War" digs into the fight for semiconductor supremacy', 5 December 2022.

stream of semiconductor challenges, my hope is that this book becomes a reliable pan for swirling new ideas, opportunities, and risks.

The 12 chapters provide independent analysis on strategic competitive advantages and options that factor in multiple tactical variables, especially law, regulation, and tax. Whether a start-up, an established SME, or a multinational, business strategy requires legal astuteness. By which is meant, the ability of a top management team and legal counsel to collaboratively solve problems.[3]

CEOs, and all other board members, need to stay at a higher level of analysis, and lawyers must delve into the details of case law, and many rules. Therefore, it would be accurate to describe the structure of the book as starting with the background contexts of the global semiconductor sector, then the specific situation in the UK. Thereafter, it presents strategic frameworks and strategic issues of global application.

The remainder of the book covers the legal detail. Bearing in mind that law is always an opportunity and a risk, it would, in my view, be a mistake for any board member to ignore these seemingly dry legal chapters. To find gold dust requires swirling the pan.

This book has relevance to readers across the main products and services. These products are classified in Table 1.1, accepting that some 'Other' can qualify in both the Logic and Memory categories. Semiconductor services covered include Assembly, Packaging & Testing (AP&T), Electronic Design Automation (EDA), equipment providers, foundries, and semiconductor designers.

The strategy chapters provide analysis of corporate strategy supported by the tactics of law and tax. There are also tactical sections covering future regulatory reform. Semiconductors are a lucrative component of numerous dynamic sectors, but how to change UK regulations to make the sector even more successful has not to date been covered from the three angles of law, strategy, and tax.

[3] Bird, R.C., 'Law, Strategy, and Competitive Advantage', 7 February 2011, available at SSRN: https://ssrn.com/abstract=1327795 or http://dx.doi.org/10.2139/ssrn.1327795.

Table 1.1 *Main semiconductor products and services*

Product type	Function	Example firms
Logic	Central Processing Unit (CPU) or Graphics Processing Unit (GPU) or equivalent - logic processing	*AMD, Graphcore, Intel, Lattice, Nvidia, Qualcomm, SMIC*
Memory	Dynamic Random Access Memory (DRAM)	*Infineon, Samsung, SK Hynix*
Memory	Non-volatile flash memory (NAND)	*Kioxia, Micron Technology, Samsung, SK Hynix*
Other	Discrete and analog sensors	*Broadcom, IBM, Infineon, Intel, Nexperia, Paragraf, Pragmatic Semiconductor, ST Microelectronics, Texas Instruments, Vishay*

Source: © Iain Sheridan (2025)

The legal detail throughout is English law and United Kingdom (UK) legislation. However, since 2022, several leading jurisdictions have enacted or planned significant changes aimed at regulating and supporting semiconductor growth, so these are logically covered as important comparators. What is implemented or imminent in the European Union (EU), South Korea, Taiwan, and the United States (US), all provide valuable options on where a UK firm may choose to incorporate foreign subsidiaries.

Further, for semiconductor sector lobbyists and policy makers there are also an array of proposed changes to consider for the future. In sum, this book can earn its keep in not only short-term planning meetings, but also for medium- and long-term scenario analysis.

The benefits of expanding the UK semiconductor sector are clear. For example, the gross domestic product (GDP) per capita strength of South Korea or Taiwan are significantly based on their respective successful expansion of semiconductor sectors. Neither of these countries have abundant natural resources nor large populations. The principal drivers behind their successes are ambition, science, technology, engineering

Table 1.2 *Main semiconductor services*

Services	Function or process	Example Firms
Design and EDA	Design of semiconductor architecture or software that facilitates their design and testing	*AMD, ARM Holdings plc, Cadence, Huawei, Imagination Technologies, Keysight Technologies, MTK, Nordic Semiconductor, Pulsic, Siemens, Silicon Labs, Synopsis*
Foundry	Fabrication of semiconductors	*TSMC*
Equipment	Etching, deposition, and lithography	*AMEC, Applied Materials, ASML, LAM Research, Oxford Instruments*
Materials	Advanced epitaxial wafers, films and inks	*IQE, Dycotec*
AP&T		*Amkor Technology, ASE Technology, JCET*

Source: © Iain Sheridan (2025)

and mathematics (STEM) talent, and long-term industrial policies. With sensible levels of government funding[4] and an increase in domestic or immigrant STEM talent, the UK can strengthen its current market share and develop new semiconductor sub-sector specialisations.

[4] In May 2023 the UK Government published its 'National semiconductor strategy' along with a commitment to provide up to £1 billion funding over a ten-year period. That is a modest sum of money compared with other technology areas, for example quantum computing which has no established commercial proof of concept. For long-term growth, the UK semiconductor sector annually needs many billions of pounds. Available at www.gov.uk/government/publications/national-semiconductor-strategy.

Specifically in the UK, this book will be of significant value to a multi-disciplinary range of civil servants and advisers engaged by the Department for Science, Innovation and Technology,[5] (DSIT), the Department for Business and Trade (DBT)[6], the Ministry of Defence, and HM Treasury. It may also be of interest to strategists serving the Ministry of Housing, Communities and Local Government that seek to understand how high-skilled semiconductor manufacturing jobs can potentially grow in areas that are experiencing structural decline.

The importance of civil servants as a key part of the semiconductor strategic equation cannot be overlooked. For instance, a 2024 study found that 59 per cent of citizen respondents from 28 countries believed government regulators lack an adequate understanding of emerging technologies to effectively regulate them. The same survey revealed that in the UK this lack of trust was notably higher at 66 per cent.[7] Policy makers may not agree with all my specific conclusions on how they can support semiconductor growth. Nevertheless, the combination of summaries and detailed footnotes should support some of their choices.

Regionally, what is relevant to the UK is often applicable to policy decision makers elsewhere. Economies as diverse as Austria, Czechia, Estonia, France, Germany, and Ireland all have accomplished STEM talent. All these EU member states have ambition to compete at greater levels of success in the semiconductor sector, albeit at different scales. Therefore, this book provides many jurisdictions with possibilities for the future. Some of the proposals may miss the mark or for timing reasons just do not fit into what some readers envisage as achievable. Other ideas would work but require a cold towel on the head in a quiet room to reflect on.

The EU is pivotally important to the UK given the history of industrial collaboration, short geographical distance, and lower geopolitical risks.

---

5 DSIT leads the UK Semiconductor Strategy.

6 DBT is responsible for the allocation of research funding, and all policies for supporting industry. Further, DBT is the owner of the broader UK Innovation Strategy, and also the UK Quantum Strategy.

7 Edelman (2024) *2024 Edelman Trust Barometer* at 16. The Edelman Barometer survey was based on 28 countries, 32 000 respondents, and each sample size varied between 1 109 and 1 500. Available at www.edelman.com/trust/2024/trust-barometer.

Unfettered access to supply chains is especially important. I recall Hermann Hauser, one of the founders of ARM Holdings plc (hereafter 'ARM'), commenting at a conference in London, 'there is no chance in hell that the UK can have semiconductor sovereignty without a close relationship with Europe'.[8]

1.2 My background and experience

I'm a dual qualified lawyer, originally trained as a barrister at One Crown Office Row in the Inner Temple, and then at Allen & Overy.[9] Later I qualified as a solicitor in Sydney. Additionally, I practised for two years in Vienna, which provided insights into the different approaches applied in an EU civil law jurisdiction. My in-house experience has extensively covered both Europe and Asia. My private law firm experience includes attempting to build two China law practices focused on the high-technology and financial services sectors.

From 2013, specific semiconductor physics insights have come from attending annual semiconductor and electronic engineering conferences in the UK and South Korea. Then in 2018, with the aim of better understanding engineering and science, a sabbatical at Cambridge University provided the opportunity to research drone GPS/GNSS navigation systems, including how artificial intelligence (AI)/machine learning can be applied to unmanned aerial vehicles (UAVs).[10] I'm a member of the Alan Turing Institute Artificial Intelligence Multi-Agent Systems Research Group, and the Institute of Electrical and Electronics Engineers (IEEE) Solid-State Circuits Society. Further, as a Chatham House member any limited time spent there is dedicated to promoting the importance of semiconductors with ministers visiting London from the Global North and Global South.

---

8 Economist Events (2023), Commercialising Quantum Global Conference, 17 May 2023, London.

9 Allen & Overy has merged with Shearman & Sterling to become A&O Shearman.

10 Scientific results from my research were published by the Royal Society. See Sheridan, I. (2020) 'Drones and global navigation satellite systems: current evidence from polar scientists', available at https://royalsocietypublishing.org/doi/10.1098/rsos.191494.

My legal experience and semiconductor insights are not anchored in the UK, but are international in nature, predominantly influenced by the successful concentration of manufacturing centres in Asia and the US. When you travel abroad you often feel enriched with fresh ideas, new possibilities. Simultaneously you have greater clarity on the advantages of your home country. This book is not only built on visits to Newcastle, Newport, Sheffield, and Swansea. There were also meetings with ambitious minds in Bethlehem, Boston, Daegu, Detroit, Fukuoka, Shenyang, Shenzhen, Seoul, Silicon Valley, and Tokyo.

1.3 Recurring questions

Increasingly semiconductors are pivotal components in the aerospace, automotive, defence, retail goods and telecommunications sectors. Intel's former CEO, Pat Gelsinger, explains this based on the digitisation of everything and four super drivers, namely AI, cloud-to-edge infrastructure, pervasive connectivity, and ubiquitous compute. In the automotive sector, Gelsinger has predicted that the share of semiconductors in the total high-end vehicle bill of materials (BOM) will increase to more than 20 per cent by 2030. This automotive industry prediction would represent a fivefold change in growth compared with 2019.[11]

Whatever the level of future demand for semiconductors, there are five recurring questions:

- What relevant legal or regulatory rules apply?
- Which semiconductor specialisms are rational to focus on?
- Where should semiconductor firms choose to operate?
- How can tax laws and policies facilitate semiconductor growth?
- How can central and local government decision makers support semiconductor growth?

For CEOs, Chief Strategy Officers (CSOs), other board members, and government policy makers, there are strategic decisions to be made concerning what to concentrate on, where to operate, as well as levels of funding. This is all, to varying degrees, bedazzlingly diverse in nature.

[11] See www.intel.com/content/www/us/en/newsroom/news/intel-mobileye-iaa-mobility.html.

For instance, at a UK national level there is a growing concentration of semiconductor talent and infrastructure in South Wales that presents opportunities for new entrant firms.[12] However, there are many other growing clusters, including Glasgow and Newcastle.

Moving to a wider regional level, given the established global supply chain of semiconductor fabrication includes Intel's fabrication plant in Ireland, for the right types of semiconductor firms there may be synergistic benefits in building additional semiconductor infrastructure in Northern Ireland. So, all readers can envisage a triangle of activity between Belfast, Leixlip and South Wales.[13] That would not be the conclusion of every CEO or other directors responsible for strategy, but it is valuable to explore what the future could look like.

More broadly, factoring in the different product specialisms, and the locations of relevant STEM talent across Europe requires joining as many synergistic resource dots as possible – from County Kildare to the State of Saxony. Any group-think tendencies or an unwillingness to explore new possibilities, are unlikely to provide innovative long-term advantages. Evidence-based reflection and new thinking are required.

1.4 Power structures and frameworks

The global semiconductor sector has four issues that require careful ongoing assessment: (a) global supply chains that vary with each sub-sector; (b) high barriers to entry; (c) fierce competition; and (d) an increasing concentration of leading firms in Asia. While each sub-sector has varying degrees of challenge to cope with (a) to (d), they are the four significant peaks to conquer.

In my view, these four challenges can be addressed by applying a structural power analysis borrowed from international relations research. An added

[12] UK House of Commons (2022) *The Semiconductor Industry in the UK*, HC 291, at 40.

[13] Since 1989, Intel has invested more than €30 billion in its Leixlip fab. A further EUR €17 billion has been committed for a new fab development that will incorporate Intel's most advanced process technology. See www.intel.ie/content/www/ie/en/company-overview/intel-in-ireland.html.

benefit here is that governmental policy makers are used to analysing at the nation-state level, so this model especially suits their way of thinking. In summary, structural power can be determined by four inter-related elements, namely finance, knowledge, production, and security.

For each semiconductor firm, these four structures interact and change over time.[14] First, the financial structure refers to the ways in which credit is provided, distributed, and managed. For semiconductor firms, access to capital-raising on stock exchanges or via venture capital firms is an equally important part of the finance structure.

Second, knowledge is principally manifested in access to STEM staff with relevant hardware, software, and sub-sector market experience. The semiconductor sector can be distinguished as reliant on knowledge as its principal raw material, because highly creative engineers and scientists are the ongoing catalysts of technological innovation.[15] Further, intellectual property and trade secrets are also important aspects of knowledge power.

Third, for each semiconductor firm the means of production and access to production facilities will vary based on the location, scale of orders, bargaining position, and many other factors.

Fourth, firms are affected by security in the sense of political authority and policy influences. For a nation-state that has a clear direct governmental power setting, but for any individual semiconductor firm that is narrower. It can be characterised as control over their supply chains, immigration rules, the availability of government research and development (R&D) support, tax policies, and other legislative measures.

---

14 In the 1990s, the LSE's pioneering Professor Susan Strange illustrated the finance, knowledge, production and security structures as four sides of a 3D pyramid. In the twenty-first century digital era, my adaptation of that model to a semiconductor firm is to depict these structures as a 3D graph. However, legal power structures are not represented as a quantitative x, y, or z variable, but as an omnipotent qualitative strategic component within the other three structures. See Strange, S. (1998) *States and Markets*, A&C Black.

15 Henderson, J. (1989) *The Globalisation of High Technology Production*, Routledge, at 4.

Collectively, common law UK High Court precedents, primary legislation, statutory instruments, and other forms of regulation are termed 'law'. More broadly, all law and regulation influencing each jurisdiction, or, in the case of the EU, its supranationally implemented regulations. This legal power structure influences choice of factory locations, access to critical materials, options to hire foreign nationals, and myriad other variables.

Applied to semiconductor firms these power structures provide insights into the fact that any business will be influenced by varying degrees of finance, knowledge, production and law. As Figure 1.1 illustrates, three quantitative elements are finance (x), knowledge (y) and production (z), the business application of a 3D Cartesian coordinate system. Law is an omnipresent fourth form of qualitative structural power presenting risk and opportunity in every 3D square. Law is not only a cost of doing business, but it is also a qualitative strategic variable.[16] In the future, we can imagine a CEO having the quality and quantity of data, enabling daily guidance on the elements of finance, knowledge, production and law.

Most, but by no means all, CEOs realise that there is a strategic value in knowing how existing and future legal rules affect finance, knowledge, and production. This valuable mindset has been characterised as 'legal astuteness'. By which is meant the ability of board members to skilfully anticipate future regulations and collaborate with legal counsel. To manage lawyers as strategic partners in decision making.[17]

Lawyers often refer to anticipating what future rules will affect business as horizon scanning. With commercial technical innovation a more appropriate metaphor is professional ice hockey. Fans of that sport would generally agree that one of the most outstanding players to influence how the game is played was a Canadian called Wayne Gretzky. While Gretzky had many qualities, he was most famous for constantly anticipating the position where the puck would slide to. In semiconductors the vector of

---

16 My past in-house activity included a 'time and complexity' billing algorithm that facilitated significant control of legal costs. See Sheridan, I. (2008) 'Daring George to slay the dragon – alternative legal billing algorithm' *New Law Journal*, 158(7324), 802–3.

17 Bird, R. (2011) 'Law, Strategy, and Competitive Advantage', *SSRN Electronic Journal*, at 7.

change requires constant anticipation by both board members and legal counsel.

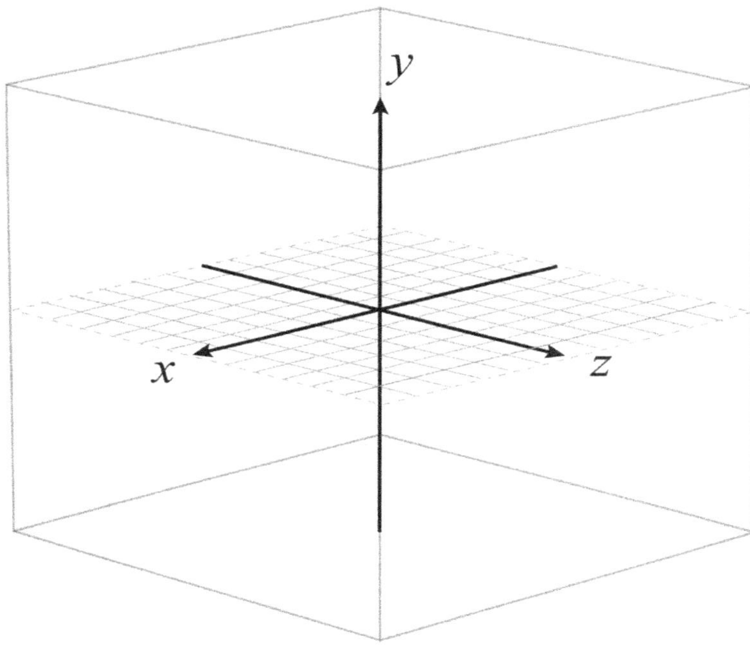

Source: © Iain Sheridan (2025)

Figure 1.1 *Firms manage Finance (x), Knowledge (y), Production (z) quantitative structures within the omnipresent factor of qualitative law*

1.5 Supply chain understanding

Fundamentally, semiconductor law and strategy also requires establishing a full picture of the supply chain landscape for every relevant specialist sub-sector product. Dr Andrew Rickman OBE, founder of Bookham Technology and Chairman and CEO of Rockley Photonics, has succinctly observed that this mapping allows understanding of:

> each step of the supply chain associated with them from the specific wafer that you might use for that process right the way through to the IP element, the design, the test, how that gets built up and the value chain that is on top of that. You can represent that across each particular sector, and you can analyse it in terms of this country's strengths and weaknesses.[18]

My legal, strategic and tax analysis attempts to factor in the complex supply chain landscape.

1.6 Risks and opportunities in the defence sector

This book is of equal relevance to the demand for semiconductors in aerospace, AI, automotive, consumer wearable, and the Internet of Things (IoT). However, no rational government can ignore that the supply chain of semiconductors for its defence procurement needs adds a significant extra dimension to government policies and laws.

A former UK Chief Scientific Adviser for National Security has remarked that the semiconductor sector can be characterised as a market of 'hyper complex products exhibiting a vast number of dependencies'.[19] During the Covid-19 pandemic the global economy experienced the consequences of supply chain disruption. It can be imagined that an extended armed conflict at any point in a global supply chain may cause disruption over several years even with permanent loss of fabrication infrastructure.

The added complexity of creating long-term effective strategies for semiconductor sector growth for defence contracts is that strategy encompasses (a) national security with clear military relevance, (b) the consequences of industrial policy choices for firms, and (c) corporate strategy applied by individual firms. To manage this strategy, defence procurement require three key aspects, namely reliability of components, reliability of supply and, in some instances, assurance that hostile actors do not receive certain advanced products. All three procurement aspects

[18] UK House of Commons (2022) *The Semiconductor Industry in the UK*, Fifth Report of Session 2022–23, HC 291, at 27.

[19] Professor Sir Anthony Finkelstein (2022) 'Advanced Technology: Made in Britain or Made Insecure', RUSI Seminar, 16 December 2022.

present extra costs and risks for UK firms, but also opportunities in terms of high-value, long-term contracts.

1.7 Dedicated government policy focus

For businesses, the consequences of industrial policy choices for firms requires highly effective central and local government strategic leadership. In my view, for industrial policy makers an effective blend of strategic approaches can be learnt from General Stanley McChrystal. As most readers will recall, Stanley McChrystal is a retired US Army four-star general with more than three decades of strategic experience. Currently a senior fellow at Yale's Institute for Global Affairs, in his book *Team of Teams*, McChrystal proposes that, to achieve a superior outcome, not to think like a chess player, but like a good gardener.[20]

McChrystal sums up the leadership required, that can equally apply to government actors that supervise semiconductor policy, in this way:

> First, I needed to shift my focus from moving pieces on the [chess] board to shaping the ecosystem...Creating and maintaining the teamwork conditions we needed – tending the garden – became my primary responsibility... Gardeners plant and harvest, but more than anything, they tend. Plants are watered, beds are fertilized, and weeds are removed... Regular visits by good gardeners are not pro forma gestures of concern – they leave the crop stronger.[21]

From a semiconductor sector perspective, DBT and DSIT civil servant leadership contributions don't end when a policy is approved via Parliament or at a ministerial level. The role is an ongoing one that can only be achieved by meeting Chairman, CEO and other board leaders and the workers committing their lives to this most pivotal sector. Many sections of this book will support policy makers tending to the needs of individual entrepreneurs and the whole semiconductor landscape.

---

[20] McChrystal, S. (2015) *Team of Teams, New Rules of Engagement for a Complex World*, Penguin.

[21] Ibid at 2269.

1.8 Summary of chapters

For humanity there is no tougher business competition than semiconductors. My hope is that these 12 chapters aid entrepreneurial decision making and lead to even greater success. Chapter 2 focuses on the current global semiconductor sector. This is a succinct coverage of the main economies contributing to or dominating substantial market share in each product or service market.

There are several highly readable accounts of why the semiconductor sector functions and is shaped as it is today.[22] These publications all provide an accurate account of the landscape. However, Chris Miller's recent contribution entitled *Chip War – The Fight for the World's Most Critical Technology* (*Chip War*) deserves special attention. This important and highly readable account won the FT Business Book of the Year 2022.[23]

Chapter 2 attempts to concertina the *Chip War* tome into about 4 000 words. Not only is *Chip War* based on thoroughly researched original authoritative sources, but is it also enriched by over 100 interviews with key industry figures, including CEOs, engineers, government officials, and scientists. Further, it makes memorable that the semiconductor sector has been shaped by driven, entrepreneurial personalities across the decades, from Gordon Moore, Robert Noyce, Andy Grove, Morris Chang, Akio Morita, Jensen Huang, and Ren Zhengfei.

Chapter 3 provides an overview of the UK semiconductor sector, discussing not only the increasing importance of South Wales as a semiconductor hub, but also the success stories in Bristol, Cambridge, Oxford, and Scotland. The diversity of UK expertise is discussed, including its strengths in semiconductor design, GPUs and photonics. With supportive government policies and investment-friendly law, it is a sector with massive potential for the UK economy.

---

[22] Goldstein, A. and W. Aspray (1997) *Facets – New Perspectives on the History of Semiconductors*, IEEE Centre for the History of Electrical Engineering; Nenni, D. and P. McLean (2013) *Fabless: The Transformation of the Semiconductor Industry*, Semiwiki.com Project.

[23] Miller, C. (2022) *Chip Wars – The Fight for the World's Most Critical Technology*, Simon & Schuster.

Chapter 4 concentrates on semiconductor strategic frameworks, examining long-term commercially successful approaches to growing all viable sub-sectors. Its sections can be applied to not only the UK, but also any similar dynamic middle power economy. The proposed frameworks also include risk- and evidence-based elements.

For the founders of small- and medium-sized enterprises (SMEs), the strategic frameworks provide an invaluable tool that is portable and scalable. It has the added advantage that it presents a time-efficient opportunity to quickly work out what a competitor is doing.

Chapter 5 covers numerous strategies. My analysis covers diverse cities in which I have first-hand, ground truth experience. The due diligence includes American, Austrian, Belgian, British, Canadian, Chinese, Czech, Dutch, Finnish, French, German, Irish, Italian, Japanese, Korean, Norwegian, and Swedish locations.

Given that the UK is no longer part of the EU, the extra challenges that presents are addressed, especially the scenarios of collaboration opportunities and supply chain costs. At a conference I attended in London, Hermann Hauser, co-founder of Acorn Computers and ARM, sagely observed that 'there is no chance that the UK can control its semiconductor sector without a close relationship with Europe'.[24] Politically, it is evident that whatever the detail of the UK's semiconductor strategy under the Labour Party, they are dedicated to rebuilding closer European relations.[25]

Chapter 6 investigates how the UK semiconductor sector can integrate sustainability into its business models. Environmental considerations may seem a relatively new area of concern, but in fact corporate environmental management in the sector was rigorously assessed nearly two

[24] Hermann Hauser: Economist Events (2023), Commercialising Quantum Global Conference, 17 May 2023, London.

[25] Before the UK General Election of 2024, David Lammy, the current British Foreign Minister, underlined at a Chatham House presentation entitled 'The UK's role in the world', that key priorities for a Labour Party in power included both closer European business relations and a semiconductor strategy. See www.chathamhouse.org/2022/07/david-lammy-mp-uks-role-world.

decades ago.[26] Going forward, there is increasing detail on climate change regulation, including transition planning of semiconductor manufacturing. Further, greater energy efficiency and the recycling of materials present competitive advantages.

Chapter 7 provides a comparison of competition laws in the EU, Japan, South Korea and the US. Given the semiconductor sector can be global in nature, it is beneficial to have a broader understanding of the reasons for one or more of these actors taking enforcement action or blocking a planned acquisition or merger.

Legal counsel can find themselves working to support an acquisition or a merger. That can occur at the mature firm level as witnessed by the UK regulatory scrutiny over Nvidia's attempt to acquire ARM from SoftBank.[27] In either scenario, they need to have some understanding of current and likely future competition law that may affect expansion plans with different time scales, risk management choices and strategy up to board level.[28]

Chapter 8 addresses contract law. The reliance on international supply chains vulnerable to regional and global geopolitics makes *force majeure* and material adverse change (MAC) clauses of particular importance.[29] In the near future, legal counsel will be able to cost-effectively combine satellite and machine learning technology to improve the management of both *force majeure* and MAC clauses in contracts.[30]

---

26 Howard-Grenville, J. (2007) *Corporate Culture and Environmental Practice*, Cheltenham, UK and Northampton, MA, USA: Edward Elgar Publishing.

27 *Financial Times* (2022) 'SoftBank's $66bn sale of chip group Arm to Nvidia collapses', 8 February 2022.

28 An authoritative and in-depth work on all aspects of competition is Scott, A. et al (2021) *Encyclopaedia of Competition Law*, London: Sweet & Maxwell.

29 *Travelport Ltd & Ors v WEX Inc* [2020] EWHC 2670 (Comm), at [171]. While there are not too many English cases on MAC clauses, this decision summarises English cases, and also references an illuminating US case. See www.bailii.org/ew/cases/EWHC/Comm/2020/2670.html.

30 My research on satellite imagery and machine learning covers *force majeure* scenarios. See Kerrigan, C. (2022) *Artificial Intelligence: Law and Regulation*, Cheltenham, UK and Northampton, MA, USA: Edward Elgar Publishing, Chapter 7 Commercial Contracts, at 109–32.

Given that *force majeure* case law is well established, it is a discrete area of law that illustrates how machine learning works and how it changes both legal obligations and drafting relevant to semiconductor agreements. Under English law, a *force majeure* event is undefined in statute, but generally treated under case law as a broad concept of 'events beyond the control' of the parties that entitles the cancellation or suspension of the contract.[31] For example, parties to a commercial contract may agree on a *force majeure* clause that includes a pandemic such as Covid-19 as a qualifying *force majeure* event.

Chapter 9 revolves around intellectual property law as the main way to manage innovation protection. Semiconductor revenues are principally created by innovative engineering where not only patents and copyright have to be protected. Approaches in Asia, the EU and the US are compared with the UK. This chapter suggests a broader mindset for legal counsel to adopt, namely to think in terms of (a) confidentiality, (b) intellectual property and (c) trade secrets – three key ways to either licence or protect products.[32]

Chapter 10 considers the UK's national security law. Cutting edge technologies, including semiconductors, are affected by the introduction of the National Security and Investment Act 2021 (NSIA 2021).[33] In sum, NSIA 2021 created a new regime for vetting both foreign and national investment in the UK. While the main political driver behind NSIA 2021 is national defence and security, it will certainly play a role in the make-up of actors supplying technology to not only established larger firms, but also start-up ventures.

---

[31] See Beale, H. et al, *Chitty on Contracts* (2024), 35th edn, London: Sweet & Maxwell, 15–152. The effect of a *force majeure* clause is a matter of construction. See Treitel, G. (2014) *Frustration and Force Majeure*, 3rd edn, London: Sweet & Maxwell, at 12-026.

[32] Of course, most intellectual property simultaneously performs both functions. By which is meant it is licensed to others and protected by law against unlicensed use. An authoritative and in-depth work on all types of intellectual property with extensive case law referencing is Cornish, W., D. Llewelyn and T. Aplin (2023) *Intellectual Property: Patents, Copyright, Trade Marks and Allied Rights*, 10th edn, London: Sweet & Maxwell.

[33] NSIA 2021 came into effect on 4 January 2022.

Covering 17 sectors including artificial intelligence, general computing hardware, cryptographic authentication, data infrastructure and quantum technologies, NSIA 2021 introduces a mandatory notification regime. Therefore, international firms in the semiconductor sector will all be scrutinised by the Secretary of State. If a proposed acquisition or merger is considered to pose an unacceptable risk to national security, NSIA 2021 provides the power to block the transaction. Chapter 10 uses Nexperia's sale of a large majority of its shareholding in Newport Wafer Fab (now Nexperia Newport Ltd) (NNL) as a case study to illustrate how the NSIA 2021 regime is applied and the legal risks it presents.[34]

Chapter 11 analyses UK corporate taxation. While the main coverage is current and future UK corporate tax, that coverage is supported by fiscal benefits offered in other highly successful semiconductor jurisdictions, especially Japan and South Korea. In short, Asian approaches to tax have something to offer the UK and other ambitious economies.

Finally, Chapter 12 sums up the future of semiconductor law and regulation as a blueprint of rules to steer opportunities and risks across the sector for the foreseeable future. While AI is often hyped, it is evident that machine learning, powered by semiconductors, is an increasingly important application across the globe.[35]

Generative AI, a mix of generative models with deep learning methods, runs on large quantities of GPUs, so there is ongoing market demand for these specific types of semiconductors in various areas. First, the automotive sector increasingly allocates a considerable percentage of total costs to semiconductors. With electric vehicles (EVs) and hybrids, even more so.

---

[34] Department for Business, Energy & Industrial Strategy (2022), Publication of notice of Final Order.

[35] My own research on satellite imagery and machine learning underlined how the hardware of the future will need to cope with increasingly vast quantities of data to achieve more accurate predictions on the trajectory of hurricanes and typhoons. See Kerrigan, C. (2022) *Artificial Intelligence: Law and Regulation*, Cheltenham, UK and Northampton, MA, USA: Edward Elgar Publishing, Chapter 7, at 109–32.

Cars and trucks will require progressively more sophisticated AI systems, especially machine learning ones, powered by semiconductors to:

1. improve fuel efficiency in hybrids switching from battery to fuel and vice versa;
2. provide camera sensor technology to increasingly improve the safety level of both driver lane and road position;
3. self-diagnose current or imminent maintenance issues.

Second, mobile phone are increasingly important devices requiring more powerful, smaller semiconductors, and the ability to facilitate AI-related applications, such as ChatGPT. Third, the likely demand for wearables that provide the ability to purchase goods and services, monitor health and open cars and other secured vehicles presents opportunities to develop AI semiconductors.

Fourth, drones increasingly require greater numbers of and more sophisticated semiconductors. For instance, to incorporate navigation systems relying on machine learning to classify the degree to which GNSS is distorted by atmospheric phenomena, such as scintillation. Additionally, in an era of geopolitical instability there is increasing demand for robust drones able to operate in hostile environments and at night without line of sight (LOS) piloting and avoid defence jamming systems.

Given the significant game-changing competitive advantage that AI is predicted to be, there is an inevitable trend of firms seeking to develop their own semiconductors with the intellectual property protection. While intellectual property laws will evolve to address AI, not all regulation will be sensitive to the confidentiality and strategic advantages of each firm.

In sum, the future global contribution of semiconductors to AI has memorably been put in this way:

> For all the talk of Moore's Law ending, there's more money than ever before flowing into the chip industry. Startups designing chips optimized for AI algorithms have raised billions of dollars in the past few years, each hoping that they can become the next Nvidia...Google, Amazon, Microsoft, Apple,

> Facebook, Alibaba, and others – are now pouring money into designing their own chips. There's clearly no deficit of innovation.[36]

This is the first edition, but it would be valuable to improve subsequent volumes with adjusted approaches and new references. With this hope in mind, if you have any proposed future additions, no matter how marginal, I would be very grateful for you to contact me.

[36] Miller, C. (2022) *Chip Wars – The Fight for the World's Most Critical Technology*, Simon & Schuster, at 349.

2. The global semiconductor sector

What does the global semiconductor sector look like today? Starting from the design phase, the United Kingdom (UK)-based ARM Holdings (ARM) dominates in mobile computing to the extent that 95 per cent of smartphones are based on its intellectual property. Two United States (US) firms, Cadence and Synopsis, hold 80 per cent of the design software used. In logic processor manufacturing, Taiwan provides 92 per cent of cutting-edge sub-10nm semiconductors, predominantly produced by Taiwan Semiconductor Manufacturing Company (TSMC). South Korea is the global leader in the manufacturing of memory semiconductors, led by Samsung and SK Hynix.

In Japan and the Netherlands their strengths in specific chemicals and optical equipment used in semiconductor manufacturing amount to a virtual duopoly. China and Taiwan are responsible for 65 per cent of semiconductor packaging.[1] In my view, if you keep all these firms, their country of origin, and the percentages at the forefront of your mind, they provide a helpful snapshot of the current global semiconductor sector. However, the sector's development, its multi-dimensional tapestry, requires analysing as to how it got to this point.

2.1 Introduction

This chapter summarises the global semiconductor sector's origins and development.[2] In the maelstrom of daily competition in the semicon-

[1] Department for Digital Culture, Media and Sport (DCMS) (2022), Written Evidence to BEIS Select Committee Inquiry *The Semiconductor Industry in the UK*, at para.13.

[2] A semiconductor can be defined as a solid, such as silicon, with an electrical conductivity intermediate between that of a conductor and an insula-

ductor sector, it is easy to forget how the industry has evolved. For policy makers the background detail can be time consuming, especially if tasked at short notice to 'get up to speed'. Insights from industry practitioners are often biased to their own country of origin, research, and corporate experiences, so my attempt is to provide an independent synopsis.

The sources that have most influenced this chapter are conversations with leaders from Massachusetts Institute of Technology (MIT), publications from the Institute of Electrical and Electronics Engineers (IEEE) Center for the History of Electrical Engineering[3] and Chris Miller's *Chip War* first published in 2022.[4] Many readers will have read Miller's incisive contribution. Since its publication, Miller has also contributed to several *Nikkei Asia* online seminars with Chinese, Japanese and Taiwanese journalists. Additionally, an FT podcast entitled 'Who is winning the chip wars?' provides his observations on the US CHIPS Act,[5] covered in Chapter 5 on strategic issues.

2.2 Origins of the semiconductor sector

From 1925, patents and laboratory notes are evidence of research into the behaviour of electrons in semiconductors in several countries.[6] However, from 1945 it is the long-term extensive investment by Bell Labs in its

tor. Source: *Oxford University Dictionary of Physics* (2019) at 60. If you are reading this chapter with absolutely no knowledge about the historic technical development of semiconductors, an authoritative account is provided by Grundmann, M. (2010), *The Physics of Semiconductors – An Introduction Including Nanophysics and Applications*, Springer at Chapter 1. See also Goldstein, A. and W. Aspray (1997) *Facets – New Perspectives on the History of Semiconductors*, IEEE Publishing, at 7.

3 IEEE (2024) History Center, available at www.ieee.org/about/history-center/index.html.

4 Miller, C. (2022) *Chip Wars – The Fight for the World's Most Critical Technology*, Simon & Schuster; and Goldstein and Aspray (1997); and Nenni, D. and P. McLellan (2013) *Fabless: The Transformation of the Semiconductor Industry*, Semiwiki.com Project.

5 *Financial Times* (2024) 'Who is winning the chip wars?' Podcast, 25 August 2024.

6 For example, in 1925, Julius Edgar Lilienfeld, an Austro-Hungarian physicist and electrical engineer, filed the first patent on the field-effect transistor (FET).

New Jersey laboratory that allowed electronic engineering researchers to explore many avenues of research that achieved two catalyst breakthroughs in 1947–48.[7] At the highest level of abstraction, competitive spirit, finance, and knowledge all combined to accelerate US advances in semiconductors. Namely, starting in 1947 with the John Bardeen and Walter Brattain point-contact transistor,[8] followed very soon after in early 1948 with William Shockley's *p-n* junction transistor.

First, the long-term financial investment by Bell Labs was a core factor. For solid state physicists dedicated to research Bell Labs was, in effect, the only choice if the researchers preferred to work in business rather than academia. As Philip Seidenburg, a founder of several electronics firms has observed, 'the management at Bell Labs were intent on attracting talented researchers and creating an atmosphere of fellowship and the result was a research facility which could be confirmed favourably with those of the leading universities in the United States'.[9]

Second, knowledge existed in the form of an immense concentration of electronic engineering talent. In 1947, in the Bell Labs semiconductor group there were multiple high-level science, technology, engineering and maths (STEM) talents dedicated to advancing technology. In Philip Seidenberg's words:

See US patent number US1745175 (A), Method and apparatus for controlling electric currents.

7 Established in 1925, Bell Labs was officially called Bell Telephone Laboratories, was a research and development (R&D) company. Its parent company between 1925–96 was AT&T Corporation. Legacy Bell Labs knowledge and resources still exist under the ownership of Nokia Bell Labs headquartered in Murray Hill, New Jersey. Many talented former Bell Labs researchers have grown successful semiconductor start-ups. For a solid historical account that covers its technological innovations see Gertner, J. (2012) *The Idea Factory: Bell Labs and the Great Age of American Innovation*, Penguin Books.

8 The British Science Museum used to have a display of the point-contact transistor invented by Bardeen and Brattain. In an era of electronic vehicles (EVs), drones and smartphones, it is a still an exciting object. While it was not commercially significant, it represents the beginning. An invention so symbolic that it might well be one of the most important of the twentieth century.

9 Goldstein and Aspray (1997) at 41.

> the quality and quantity of the researchers at Bell Labs, operating in an atmosphere of easy communication and unfettered disclosure, contributed considerably to the semiconductor industries high rate of growth during the 1950s. The strategy of the management to encourage the researchers to be independent promoted basic solid-state research.[10]

No pressure was placed on researchers to give up on semiconductor research even after several years of negligible progress. Maintaining a quality pool of researchers required considerable long-term investment.

Third, the competitive pressure drove both individual and team ambitions. When you combine the financial resources, the STEM talent, the chemistry to market a product comes from competitive pressure. What made each game-changing breakthrough was competition, both internally within Bell Labs and externally with the threat of others beating 'them', meaning individually and collectively as a semiconductor group, to it.[11]

Here are just two examples of how much competitive spirit contributed to birth of the pioneering US semiconductor sector. First, to cite an internal competitive driver in the pivotal late 1940s, it is known that weeks after the Bardeen and Brattain point-contact transistor invention, Shockley experienced conflicting emotions. He recalled 'my elation with the group's success was tempered by not being one of the inventors…I experienced frustration that my personal efforts, started more than eight years before, had not resulted in a significant inventive contribution of my own'.[12]

---

[10] Ibid at 41.

[11] An important book on semiconductor innovation processes consistently orbits around the concept of iterative 'real innovation'. Rather than a linear discovery to product to market to profit model, semiconductor development to market follows a far more complex back-and-forth process as the inventors move from fuzzy initial ideas to many possibilities that are repeatedly put through the twin processes of learning and abstraction. See Fitzgerald, E. et al (2011) *Inside Real Innovation: How the Right Approach Can Move Ideas from R&D to Market and Get the Economy Moving*, World Scientific. Real innovation is covered in detail in Chapter 4 Strategic frameworks.

[12] Goldstein and Aspray (1997) at 14.

There had been an approximate two-year gap since Shockley went from intensively concentrating on semiconductor research to minimal attention. At the time of the Bardeen and Brattain invention, he was working on something completely different. Shockley is frank about the influence of the November 1947 discovery by Bardeen and Brattain. He recalled 'The breakthrough observation of 17th November that surface – states could be overcome… stimulated the will to think and act in minds conditioned to search for semiconductor amplifiers'.[13] Within one month of the point-contact transistor, Shockley had on his own pieced together research to invent a provable *p-n* junction transistor.

Externally, the stimulus to innovate before other organisations came from Purdue. During the Second World War, Purdue had significantly advanced understanding of germanium,[14] the semiconductor used in the point-contact transistor. Purdue had continued focus on germanium after the war. Rationally, Brattain and Bardeen were worried that the Purdue group might beat them to the discovery of the transistor. Yet while Purdue was researching germanium semiconductors, they were not close to an invention. As one of their key researchers recalled 'I guess we were on the verge of it in thinking about such [a possibility]…but it hadn't really formulated itself in our minds'.[15]

Overall, from the memories of Bardeen, Brattain, and Shockley it is clear they all:

> attributed the success of their research to the supportive atmosphere created by the Bell Labs in which management allowed those in research to spend many years, much money, and the talents of many people to explore solid-state physics. From the recollections, it appears that all three were motivated by an interest in surface physics and electron behaviour…[16]

As Chris Miller has put it:

---

[13] Ibid, at 14.

[14] There are important differences between germanium and silicon. See Dimitrijev, S. (2000) *Understanding Semiconductor Devices*, Oxford University Press USA, at 13.

[15] Ibid at 13.

[16] Goldstein and Aspray (1997), at 44.

> the chip industry only took off because graduates of these institutions [MIT and Stanford] spent years tweaking production processes to make mass manufacturing possible. It was engineering and intuition, as much as scientific theorising, that turned a Bell Lab's patent into a world changing industry.[17]

2.3 Dallas 1958 – the integrated circuit

Jack Kilby, an American engineer employed by Texas Instruments, provided the next competitive leap in advantage to the US semiconductor sector. His huge contribution was a hunch that, rather than using separate pieces of silicon or germanium to build each single transistor, many components could be assembled on the same piece of germanium semiconductor material. The patent documentation referred to his invention as an 'integrated circuit'.[18]

In common with other science-based sectors, the progress that led to the invention of the integrated circuit (IC) at this time can be categorised as based on cooperative teamwork. Jack Kilby has commented that 'progress in [ICs] is not the work of any single individual or small group of individuals. It has come about because of the contributions of thousands of Engineers and scientists in laboratories and production facilities all over the world'.[19]

2.4 California 1959 – the monolithic integrated circuit

In 1959, Robert Noyce, an American physicist and co-founder of Fairchild Semiconductor (Fairchild),[20] advanced the IC by applying the planar process that allowed capacitors, diodes, resistors, and transistors to all sit

[17] Miller (2022) at 28.

[18] See US patent US3138743 (A) – 'Miniaturized electronic circuits'.

[19] Kilby, J. (1976) 'Invention of the Integrated Circuit' *IEEE Transactions on Electron Devices*, 23(7), 648–54.

[20] Lécuyer, C. and D. Brock (2010) *Makers of the Microchip: A Documentary History of Fairchild Semiconductor*, The MIT Press; and Moore, G.E. (1998) 'The Role of Fairchild in Silicon Technology' *Proceedings of IEEE*, 86(1), 53–62.

on a single silicon chip with no freestanding wires.[21] The planar method of making ICs is used to this day. In current conversations an IC is most often referred to simply as a 'chip', because each IC is made from a piece of silicon chipped off a circular silicon wafer.[22]

2.5 The birth of Silicon Valley

From the 1960s increasing numbers of ICs were made in various locations in the US. However, there were a cluster of pioneers in the State of California. Subsequently, it was the monolithic IC which fuelled the personal computer revolution and gave Silicon Valley its name. As Chris Morris has observed, US semiconductor talent was also uniquely global, and many brilliant immigrants ended up in California:

> Amid Cold War chaos and the disruptions of decolonization that swept the world, the best and the brightest from many countries tried to make their way to the United States… At a time when most of the world had never heard of silicon chips, and still fewer understood anything about how they worked, America's centers of semiconductor production were drawing the world's most brilliant minds to Texas, Massachusetts, and above all to California.[23]

In particular, the growth of Fairchild can be attributed to its contracts with NASA to supply ICs for the Apollo guidance computers designed by MIT's Instrumentation Lab. Consequently, sales of Fairchild ICs generated profits of $21 million in 1961.[24] Chris Miller captures the significance of winning the confidence of such an exceptional client: 'NASA's trust in integrated circuits to guide astronauts to the moon was an important stamp of approval. Fairchild's micrologic chips were no longer an untested technology; they were used in the most unforgiving and rugged environment: outer space'.[25]

---

21 The planar concept was invented by Jean Hoerni, a Swiss physicist. See US patent number US3025589(A), Method of manufacturing semiconductor devices.

22 Miller (2022) at 15.

23 Ibid at 346.

24 Ibid at 21.

25 Miller (2022) at 21.

2.6 MOSFET

Earlier in this chapter reference was made to the fact that in the 1960s global semiconductor talent was arriving in America. Near the top of that list were an Egyptian and a Korean. In 1960, Mohamed Atalla and Dawon Kahng, researchers at Bell Labs, invented the MOSFET (metal–oxide–semiconductor field-effect transistor).[26] MOSFETs have become the fundamental building block of most electronic products.[27]

2.7 Moore's law

In 1965, Gordon Moore, then acting head of R&D at Fairchild, published an article in *Electronics* entitled 'Cramming More Components onto Integrated Circuits'. It included a graph indicating Fairchild was building double the number of transistors onto its ICs every two years.[28] A commercial way to look at his important observation is that the cost of electronic functionality halves every two years. Such an exponential reduction has meant that in recent years 'an inkjet printer has far more computing power than NASA had at its disposal getting to the moon.'[29]

The top graph line in Figure 2.1 shows how Moore's Law applies to date, and its expected plateau by 2030.[30] However, in the future the laws of physics mean it is likely to significantly slow down. By which is meant the current state of the art ICs are so small there is less scope for double the capability without advancing into sub-atomic levels of engineering.

---

[26] See US patent US3206670 Mohamed Atalla, Semiconductor devices having dielectric coatings, and US patent US3102230 Dawon Kahng, Electric field controlled semiconductor device. Both were filed in 1960 and describe the MOSFET.

[27] Dimitrijev (2000) at 211.

[28] Moore, G. (1965) 'Cramming more components onto integrated circuits' *Electronics*, 38(8), 11417.

[29] Nenni and McLellan (2013), at 14.

[30] Shalf, J. (2020) 'The future of computing beyond Moore's Law', *Philosophical Transactions of the Royal Society A*, 20 January 2020, graph adapted from original at 3, available at https://royalsocietypublishing.org/doi/10.1098/rsta.2019.0061.

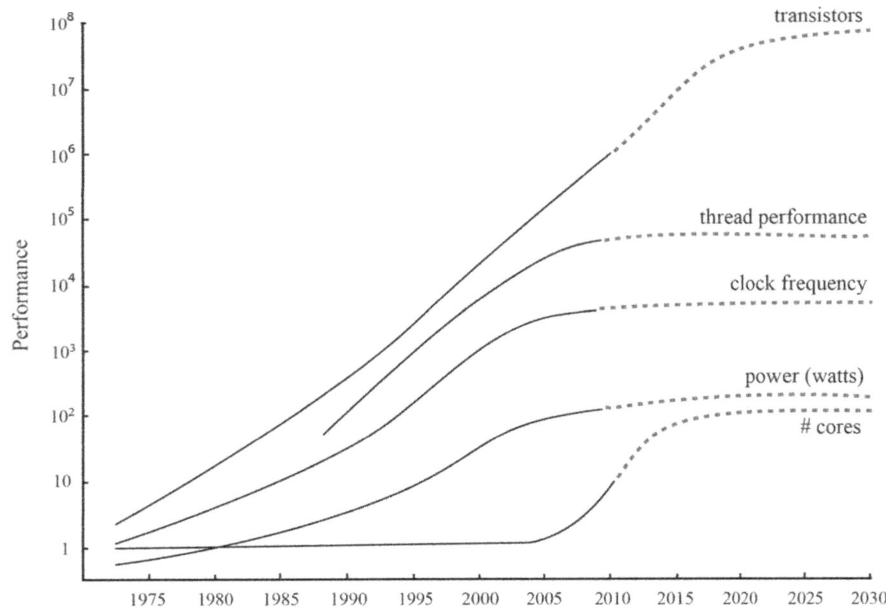

Source: Adapted from Shalf, J. (2020) 'The future of computing beyond Moore's Law', *Philosophical Transactions of the Royal Society A*, 20 January 2020, at 3, available at https://royalsocietypublishing.org/doi/10.1098/rsta.2019.0061

Figure 2.1 Computer performance to date and to 2030

2.8 Defence budgets

While history shows that the NASA contract established crucial large revenues for Fairchild to grow, US Government defence budgets facilitated the rise of Texas Instruments as well as other US firms. Texas Instruments had originally supplied test ICs to the MIT Instrumentation Lab for NASA. However, the Texas Instruments' leadership was within months of Kilby inventing the IC when presenting their offering to the Pentagon.

By 1962, at the height of the Cold War, the US Air Force awarded its Minuteman II contract for ICs to Texas Instruments, a seminal transformational moment for the firm. The significance of this military order cannot be understated. Within less than 12 months the firm was selling thousands of ICs driven by the perceived or real threat of Soviet Union ICBM superiority. Within 24 months, in 1964, Texas Instruments had supplied 100 000 ICs to the Minuteman programme. By 1965, 20 per cent of all ICs sold in that financial year were purchased by the US Air Force. The Pentagon was a unique customer.[31]

The impact of US military expenditure on US semiconductor firm growth continued for the duration of the Cold War. This included, in the early 1970s, laser-guidance systems for conventional bombs dropped by aircraft tested by the US Air Force during the Vietnam War.[32] Then, in the late 1970s, Pentagon procurement orders for ICs for ICBMS. The military calculations were not only about quantitative and qualitative military advantage, but also reflected Cold War economic tactics to bankrupt the USSR given that the Russians would be forced to pursue an anti-missile programme they could not afford.[33]

2.9 Japan

Akio Morita, the founder of Sony, has made many wise comments on the management of a successful company. Perhaps the comment that most sums up his and Sony's achievement is the blending of three types

---

[31] Miller (2022) at 21–2.

[32] Ibid at 60.

[33] Ibid at 75.

of innovation to achieve business success, namely (a) ideas, (b) planning and (c) marketing.

Morita justified that three-pronged analysis from the viewpoint that:

> it is possible to have a good idea, a fine invention, but still miss the boat, so product planning, which means deciding how to use technology in a given product, demands creativity. Only with these three kinds of creativity – technology, product planning, and marketing – can the public receive the benefit of a new technology. And without an organization that can work together, sometimes over a very long period, it is difficult to see new projects to fruition.[34]

In short, this is the essence of how, from the 1980s, Sony was successful at using principally Japanese semiconductors to contribute to vast sales of its consumer electronic products. Careful planning of technology, always with long-term perspectives, executed with effective teamwork and marketing.

What catapulted the success of Sony, and other Japanese dynamic random access memory (DRAM) semiconductor manufacturers such as NEC and Toshiba, was mastering quality control (QC).[35] Ishikawa promoted the concept of continuous improvement (kaizen) which over the long term in Japan produced DRAM semiconductors with reliability levels above US competitors.[36] For instance, tests performed in the 1980s by a Hewlett Packard executive tasked with benchmarking semiconductor options found that the three main Japanese providers all performed above US alternatives. None of the reported failure rates for these Japanese semiconductors were greater than 0.02 per cent in the first 1 000 hours of use, compared with 0.09 per cent for US firms.[37]

---

[34] Shimomura, M. (1987) *Made in Japan: Akio Morita and Sony*, Collins, at 188.

[35] Deming, W. (1982) *Quality, Productivity, and Competitive Position*, MIT Press; and Juran, J. (1962) *Quality Handbook: The Guide to Performance Excellence*, McGraw-Hill.

[36] Ishikawa, K. (1985) *What is Total Quality Control? The Japanese Way*, Prentice Hall.

[37] Miller (2022) at 81–2.

2.10 South Korea

In the early 1980s, the consensus in the global semiconductor industry was that Samsung would fail to compete. A Mitsubishi research division report entitled 'Five Reasons Why Samsung Cannot Succeed in the Semiconductor Industry', concluded that, among other things, South Korea had low-level technological capabilities. However, after some setbacks when attempting to collaborate with the American firm Micron Technology, Samsung eventually learnt the Very Large-Scale Integration (VSLI) process from Japan's Sharp Electronics.

From this point on Samsung has never looked back. It has been observed that:

> Samsung defied all odds and succeeded in building its first production plant in 1984. Since then, Samsung has managed to become a global leader in the semiconductor industry by continuing to excel in product development and innovation. Despite its humble beginnings, Samsung possess top market shares in the industry today.[38]

As the US semiconductor firms had benefited from government support in the form of military contracts, Samsung's entry into the sector was hugely influenced by South Korean governmental support. Hwy-Chang Moon, an eminent professor of strategy, and former dean of Seoul National University, has incisively commented that:

> for nearly three decades, the Korean government selectively intervened to promote targeted infant industries, by supporting the creation of large-scale establishments by *chaebol* that imitated the Japanese *zaibatsu*.[39] At their inception, targeted firms receive priority access to preferential credit as well as reductions or exemptions on tax and tariffs.[40]

A Japanese *zaibatsu* is the original term for a large conglomerate based around a bank and a trading company. In modern times the term *keiretsu* is used in Japan to refer to similar groups of autonomous firms. A current

---

[38] Moon, H-C (2016) *The Strategy for Korea's Economic Success*, Oxford University Press, at 55.

[39] For readers unfamiliar with the term *chaebol*, it refers to the South Korean large trading firms, which includes Samsung, Hyundai and Daewoo.

[40] Moon (2016) at 20–21.

example of a Japanese *keiretsu* is Mitsubishi. In June 2024 I had an opportunity to meet Moon in Seoul. He emphasised that an important distinction between Korean and Japanese groupings is that Korean regulation does not permit a bank to be a member. In short, the lack of an intra-group financing entity did not prevent South Korea semiconductor firms from succeeding.

2.11 Morris Chang

As mentioned earlier, from the 1950s the US inherited global talent emigrating to work at Bell Labs, Fairchild and Texas Instruments. Morris Chang was one of those exceptional talents. Born in Ningbo, he grew up mainly in Hong Kong. He then moved to the US to initially study at Harvard University, then transferred to MIT, subsequently graduating in mechanical engineering. After MIT, Chang joined Texas Instruments in 1958. During his early years of service Texas Instruments made a long-term investment in him and he was allowed to complete a PhD at Stanford University.

Chang's career included perfecting production efficiency to the degree that IBM executives would visit Texas Instruments to learn from him.[41] By the 1980s Chang was a senior director at Texas Instruments. What marks Chang out, even amongst the brilliant minds in the American semiconductor sector, is his vision for markets that did not yet exist. He had a unique blend of entrepreneurial ambition and technical intuition.

In 1976 he had proposed to Texas Instruments colleagues that there was a market for a company that would manufacture semiconductors designed by other semiconductor firms. He foresaw increasing numbers of design firms would provide semiconductors to meet the demands of myriad products, but that these design firms would not have the knowledge to make the actual semiconductors. Ultimately, Chang's Texas Instrument colleagues disagreed.[42]

---

[41] Miller (2022) at 27.

[42] Ibid at 166.

After 25 years' service, Chang left Texas Instruments. For one year he attempted to lead the US firm General Instrument Corporation, but without success. In 1985 he was hired by the Taiwanese Government to direct Taiwan's Industrial Technology Research Institute, which in turn led to the founding of TSMC with the promise of government financial support. In effect, Chang was being asked to lead Taiwan's next phase of semiconductor industrial policy. Like Chang, in the 1980s Taiwan had already been considering the concept of separating semiconductor design from manufacturing with the aim of creating a new market.

The Taiwanese Government provided 48 per cent of the capital for Chang's TSMC manufacturing start-up. However, despite this substantial government support, his former colleagues at Texas Instruments decided not to invest. Fortunately, the Dutch firm Philips took a 27.6 per cent share.[43] The remaining shares were purchased by some of the richest entrepreneurial families in Taiwan who had made their fortunes in many sectors.

Government taxation policy support also played an important role. As Chris Miller put it 'the government also provided generous tax benefits for TSMC, ensuring the company had plenty of money to invest. From day one, TSMC wasn't really a private business: it was a project of the Taiwanese state'.[44]

Chang envisioned demand at a time no one else did. A demand that 40 years later is met by TSMC. He created a unique win-win proposition – providing semiconductors for leading firms and growing smaller firms on the condition that he would not compete with them. Chris Miller captures his significance in this way:

> Chang's foundry model gave birth to dozens of 'new authors' – fabulous chip design firms – that transformed the tech sector lithography by putting computing power in all sorts of devices hardly anyone realised it at the time, but Chang, TSMC, and Taiwan were on a path towards dominating the production of the world's most advanced chips.[45]

---

[43] TSMC (1998) 'Philips, TSMC and EDB Investments Team to Develop New Chip Production Facility', 29 September 1998, TSMC Archives, available at https://pr.tsmc.com/english/news/2115.

[44] Ibid at 167.

[45] Ibid at 168.

The importance of Chan as an entrepreneurial individual cannot be underestimated in the success story of TSMC. As someone has commented on Chang he has:

> two traits which have helped to make TSMC a world-famous enterprise. The first is his ambition to make TSMC the number one in the world and to realise it successfully. Second is 'leadership charm', the capacity to draw together a bunch of outstanding talents to help fulfil the enterprises goals.[46]

2.12 Photolithography

2.12.1 The Process

The most common semiconductor production process relies on photoresist technology. Photoresists are photosensitive organic material.[47] Their practical significance in semiconductor production is that they are affected by exposure to light allowing patterns to be built up on a flat surface. As Figure 2.2 illustrates, the process starts with the chosen semiconductor wafer (1). A thin layer of oxide is formed on the surface of the semiconductor wafer (2). Then a thin layer of light-sensitive photoresist is then applied on top of the oxide (3). Thereafter, the photoresist is exposed through a mask or reticle which contains the detailed pattern to be printed (4). After development, the exposed areas are dissolved, revealing selected areas of the oxide layer (5). The oxide layer is removed, revealing selected areas of the semiconductor surface (6). Finally, dopants are diffused into the exposed areas (7).[48] These seven steps may be repeated, in some instances building up to 100 layers onto an IC.

2.12.2 Background

The origins of its use in semiconductor manufacturing can be traced to US military research labs.[49] Fairchild's first photoresist leader was one

---

[46] Tsai, T. and B. Cheng (2006) *The Silicon Dragon: High-tech Industry in Taiwan*, Cheltenham, UK and Northampton, MA, USA: Edward Elgar Publishing, at 96.

[47] Anslyn, E. and D. Dougherty (2005) *Modern Physical Organic Chemistry*, University Science Books, at 935.

[48] Goldstein and Aspray (1997) at 97–8.

[49] Nall, J. and J. Lathrop (1958) *The Use of Photolithographic Techniques in Transistor Fabrication*, DOFL Technical Report.

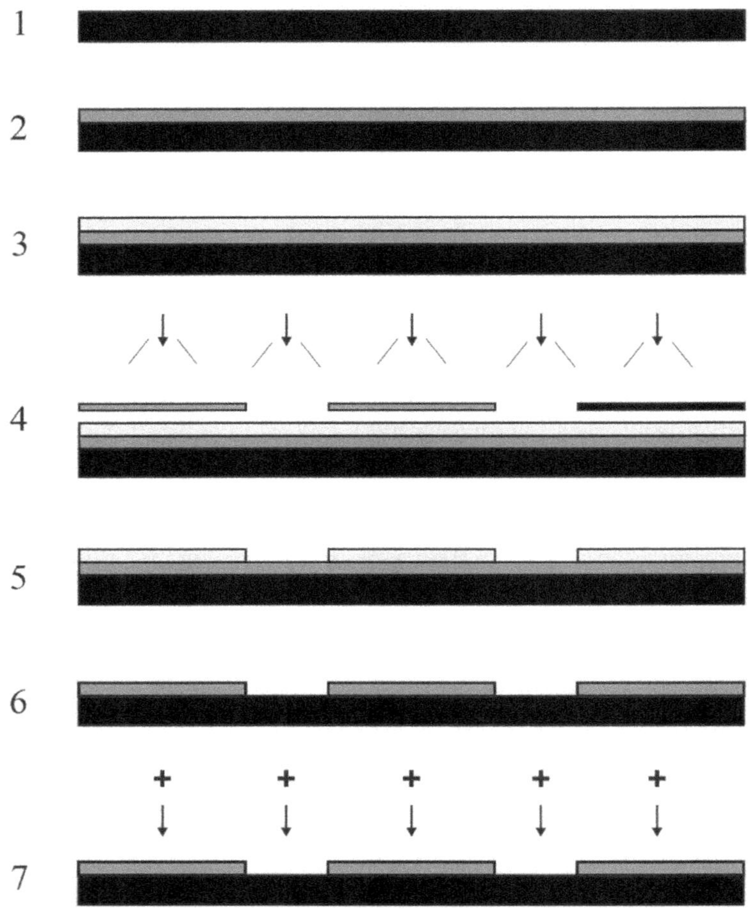

Source: Goldstein, A. and W. Aspray (1997) *Facets – New Perspectives on the History of Semiconductors*, IEEE Publishing, adaptation of figure at 97–98

Figure 2.2 Oxide masking and diffusion process

of the inventors of the technique.[50] While Canon and Nikon both supply advanced photolithographic machinery, the Dutch firm ASML has the

[50] Goldstein and Aspray (1997) at 99.

current global monopoly on the most advanced 'extreme ultraviolet light' (EUV) which achieves a wavelength of 13.5 nanometers.[51] Apple's iPhone 16 Pro was made with EUV technology.[52]

ASML is the world's exclusive maker of cutting-edge chip equipment known as extreme ultraviolet (EUV) lithography machines, enabling production of advanced semiconductors below the 7-nanometre level. In chipmaking, the smaller the nanometre size, the more advanced and powerful the chips. The mobile chip in the premium iPhone 16 Pro and Nvidia's graphic processors are built with 4nm tech, in which ASML's machines play an indispensable role.

ASML's latest EUV machines cost in the region of US $200 million to buy, but their commercial significance is that they operate below the 7nm level. Each EUV machine comprises of several modules with hundreds of thousands of components, relying on approximately 800 suppliers. Each module is built at one of ASML's 60 locations around the world and then shipped to Veldhoven for assembly. Once testing is complete, each machine is disassembled for delivery to the semiconductor manufacturer. ASML's five customers for the EUV machines are Intel, Micron, Samsung, SK Hynix, and TSMC.

Whether in the future ASML retains its monopoly is uncertain, partly because of geopolitics. Its chief business officer has commented:

> we do not believe in ASML that decoupling is possible. We believe this will be extremely difficult and extremely expensive… It's a matter of time until people realise that the only way to be successful in semiconductors is through co-operation… We prefer to use the very best suppliers [globally] … This is a lot more effective. It allows us to move a lot faster… The big difference [in strategy] is Canon and Nikon were trying to do a lot of things by themselves.[53]

---

[51] ASML provide a video briefing on their EUV photolithographic machine, entitled 'How do we generate EUV light/', Available at www.asml.com/en/technology/lithography-principles/light-and-lasers.

[52] To clarify, ASML's previous generation of machine with a wavelength of 193nm, known as deep ultraviolet (DUV), accounted for the vast majority of photolithographic machines it has sold in recent years. For instance, most advanced automotive semiconductors are made with DUV technology.

[53] *Financial Times* (2023) 'ASML says decoupling chip supply chain is practically impossible', 27 June 2023.

2.13 ARM Holdings

At the beginning of this chapter the sole mention of the UK was the fact ARM is still based in Cambridge, England. Its dominance in the intellectual property (IP) designs of semiconductors, especially logic ICs, mean that many cars, data centres, drones, laptops, industrial sensors and smartphones contain components which generate the firm licence fees.

At the heart of ARM's corporate strategy has been its simplified energy-efficient Instruction Set Architecture (ISA) for IC design. Its economic power consumption design has made and continues to make it an attractive choice for all portable devices. Through its highly talented workforce ARM has become prolifically successful. However, it has also experienced good fortune based on decisions made by other semiconductor competitors. For example, it is known that Intel had originally turned down the iPhone contract. Consequently, Apple had to look for another phone architecture and chose to contract with ARM.

In James Ashton's opus magnus on the history of ARM he concludes that for 'now ARM appears indispensable, powering the inexorable growth in computing and offering lessons about the importance of scale longevity continuous innovation…'[54] ARM continues to play a vital role for leading semiconductors such as Apple, Samsung, and Qualcomm. It also plays a highly valuable role in the growth of Amazon, Alibaba, Alphabet, Huawei, Meta, and Tesla. Given the collective diversity and power of these multinationals it is very likely that ARM will continue to be the lead provider of logic processor design for CPUs. Further, the fact leading artificial intelligence (AI)/machine learning firms such as Nvidia and Samsung combine their GPUs with ARM CPU designs suggests a bright long-term future.

2.14 Dependency on Taiwan

When we think of offshoring, even with technical products there is generally scope for all or some of the components to be made in multiple coun-

[54] Ashton, J. (2023) *The Everything Blueprint – The Microchip Design That Changed The World*, Hodder & Stoughton, at 391.

tries. In the automotive sector, BMW has been manufacturing in China for more than 15 years. However, in in the semiconductor sector, the scope to make cutting-edge processors, depending on the application, can be surprisingly narrow. In the mobile computing market, it is so narrow that even powerful multinationals can be solely dependent on TSMC in Taiwan. Apple is a good example.

The success of Apple has resulted in a capitalisation exceeding $3 trillion. That is has been achieved by a unique combination of exceptional leadership, design, marketing and R&D. However, Apple, despite all its capital and technical talents, has become solely reliant on TSMC. Chris Miller frankly encapsulates the situation as:

> today, no company besides TSMC has the skill or the production capacity to build the chips Apple needs. So the text etched onto the back of each iPhone - 'Designed by Apple in California. Assembled in China' – is highly misleading. The iPhone's most irreplaceable components are indeed designed in California and assembled in China. But they can only be made in Taiwan.[55]

Investment required for cutting-edge fabs explains the dependency that exists for a number of smartphone brands, exemplified by Apple. It is not as if these businesses have not adapted their strategies to maximise their profits. Consider, Apple's first-generation iPhone relied on Samsung to provide the logic processing unit, Intel the memory units, and Infineon the cell network modem.

By 2010, Apple was able to adapt and invest to design its own semiconductor processors, used in the Apple iPhone 4. This was partly achieved by acquiring a semiconductor design company in Silicon Valley which enabled in-house design of the A4 application processor.[56] Apple also made R&D investment in Germany and Israel. However, despite at one point having a huge share of the profits from the global smartphone market, it has not to date been able to diversify its manufacturing options

[55] Miller (2022) at 223–4.

[56] The acquired semiconductor design company was called PA Semi and excelled in energy-efficient processing. This reflects the importance of energy use as a practical commercial benefit to customers rather than Apple signalling green credentials in the noughties. There is a whole chapter of this book focused on sustainability issues, including detailed reference to energy efficiency. See Chapter 6 Sustainable innovation.

beyond TSMC.[57] The projected cost to build a cutting-edge fab equivalent to the ones run by TSMC is £30 billion. However, it is not just the capital barrier to entry, there is an immense amount of expertise required in running such a plant.

The example of Apple's dependency on TSMC could be easily misconstrued as specific to Apple. After all, South Korea produces more than 40 per cent of all memory chips, and Intel still provides the many cutting-edge logic processing units in cars, drones, and PCs. However, it is currently estimated that Taiwan produces more than 90 per cent of the most advanced semiconductor processing units.

2.15 Geopolitics

Since the end of the Cold War, geopolitical influences on the semiconductor have been secondary to commercial competition to supply businesses. However, from around 2015 the growth of Huawei and other Chinese firms, along with changes in China's foreign policy, have caused increased geopolitical tensions with a NATO-led West.

Arguably, such priorities are primarily centred on China–US relations. However, the nature of the politics means that each actor, both governmental and corporate, must factor in congruence with sanctions and supply chains depending on which side a government has communicated they support. Therefore, the situation is a complex one for semiconductor firms to navigate, especially those involved in the highest performance IC manufacture or supply of equipment that enables making the highest performing components.

2.16 Final points

Applying Moore's Law, the world has advanced exponentially its use of semiconductors. However, the competitive spirit and visionary motiva-

[57] Miller (2022) at 222–3. A whole chapter of this book is dedicated to strategic issues, of which dependence on Taiwan and especially TSMC is covered. See Chapter 5 Strategic issues.

tion of its participants cannot be understated as key contributing factors. Chris Miller's conclusion puts it this way:

> Technology only advances when it finds a market. The history of the semiconductor is also a story of sales, marketing, supply chain management, and cost reduction. Silicon Valley wouldn't exist without the entrepreneurs who built it… Fairchild Semiconductor's ability to cram more components onto its integrated circuits as Gordon Moore put it in his famous 1965 article - depended not only on the companies physicists and chemists but also on hard driving manufacturing bosses...[58]

Today, that same commercial acumen is evident in Hock Tan, CEO of Broadcom. At the annual Global Semiconductor Alliance (GSA) awards ceremony in December 2024, Tan won a lifetime achievement award. He chose the moment to include criticism of the sector for being naïve in accepting lower annual semiconductor prices even though car prices were rising annually.[59]

The competitive drive of the US participants, their business acumen, and technical knowhow, all blended to make the US a prolific first mover in semiconductors. However, the speed of technical advances, ambition, and industrial policy, have combined to enable Japan, South Korea, and now Taiwan to lead the way.

---

[58] Miller (2022) at 347.

[59] Global Semiconductor Alliance (2024) Annual awards ceremony, Santa Clara, 5 December 2024.

3. The UK semiconductor sector

An astute US travel writer, Bill Bryson, published a bestselling book entitled *Notes from a Small Island*.[1] From reading that book it is clear Bryson adores the United Kingdom (UK), and indeed, in 2014 he became a British citizen.

However, Bryson also spots British weaknesses. He imagines drawing a line between the River Severn at Bristol and The Wash. In so doing the UK is divided into two halves with almost equal numbers of people working on each side. Between 1980–85 the southern half lost about 100,000 jobs. Over the same period the northern half lost approximately one million jobs – ten times more. Many of the one million jobs were in manufacturing. Additional closures followed. Perhaps going forwards, semiconductor firms can play a modest role in redressing this imbalance. To contribute to increasing high-value manufacturing above that angled line.

3.1 Introduction

This chapter provides a summary of the UK semiconductor sector.[2] Most of the material has relevance to both UK-registered firms, and also international entrepreneurs seeking to grasp what activities happen where, as well as the likely future pattern of expansion.

---

1 Bryson, B. (1995) *Notes from a Small Island*, Doubleday, at 58.

2 I'm grateful to Dr Andy Sellars, previously a director at CSA Catapult, for providing an excellent geographical summary of the UK's clusters. He is a director at Silicon Catalyst, a venture capital (VC) firm that manages the flourishing UK Government-funded incubator UK Chip Start. See www.siliconcatalyst.uk/chipstart-uk.

While geographically fragmented in nature, the UK semiconductor sector has many clusters. This chapter summarises what these are to provide context to not only commercial readers that may not have had the time to fully appreciate what is being achieved elsewhere in the UK, but also for policy makers new to the sector. It also attempts to introduce the UK semiconductor landscape for foreign investors as future collaborative partners.

Legal, strategic and tax decisions are increasingly made against a background of geopolitics. For the UK, the driving forces have firstly been Brexit; secondly, the vacuum in UK Government semiconductor strategy; thirdly, turbulent relations with China; fourthly, the Covid-19 pandemic influenced global semiconductor supply chains as well because there has been a noticeable shifting in how multinationals function in global semiconductor supply chains; and fifthly, subsidies on offer first in the United States (US), and then the European Union (EU), also alter how the UK semiconductor sector can maximise its growth.

When conversing with any two semiconductor Chief Executive Officers (CEOs), each will give a biased view on where they think semiconductor activity occurs and where best at the governmental level efforts should be made to expand a region. Nobody is beyond bias and that includes lawyers.[3]

While UK-EU relations have taken a more constructive path since Brexit, the nadir can be found in a European Parliament report of a few years ago. Specifically, the EU Strategic Autonomy 360° report entitled *Strengthening EU Chip Capabilities – How Will the Chips Act Reinforce Europe's Semiconductor Sector by 2030?*[4] In that brief but authoritative

---

[3] To declare my origins at the outset, I'm originally from Stratford upon Avon, Warwickshire. Therefore, readers may seek to interpret what I say about the Midlands as biased. Guilty. But equally it cannot be overlooked that the Midlands is a huge centre of excellence for both educating engineering talent and advanced manufacturing. Aston University, Birmingham University, Warwick University...

[4] European Parliamentary Research Service (2022) EU Strategic Autonomy 360° report, *Strengthening EU Chip Capabilities – How Will the Chips Act Reinforce Europe's Semiconductor Sector by 2030?*

report there is not one reference to the UK. For a small island surrounded by EU countries that is the eclipsing concern.

A report entitled *The Semiconductor Industry in the UK* relied heavily on UK semiconductor expert opinion. It was produced for the House of Commons by its Business, Energy and Strategy Committee, and characterised the landscape in quite a bleak way. One passage observed the UK as having no 'no large-volume silicon semiconductor fabrication, no source of certain key base materials, limited capability in outsourced semiconductor assembly and testing (OSAT), and limited capacity in advanced packaging'.[5] There is also an incongruence between the niche products currently made with older technology and the vital semiconductor needs of UK manufacturing and technology firms.

Importantly, risking a photonics pun, where there is light there is hope. The same passage from the Business, Energy and Strategy Committee report made the point that one unknown reason for the incongruence between (a) what is produced and (b) the quantity needed, is that manufacturers may not fully be aware of what is currently available or can be ordered in the UK.[6]

3.2 National Semiconductor Strategy

At start of what will be a long journey, in May 2023 the UK Government produced a paper entitled 'National Semiconductor Strategy'. Most importantly it synchronised with the launch of the UK Semiconductor Infrastructure Initiative, a finance programme investing up to £200 million into the sector between 2023–25, with up to £1 billion up to 2032.[7] The main areas of research that should produce commercial gains include compound semiconductor material, power electronics, photonics, and RF/microwave.

---

5 UK House of Commons (2022) *The Semiconductor Industry in the UK*, Fifth Report of Session 2022–23, HC 291, at 48.

6 Ibid, at 48.

7 UK Government (2023) 'National semiconductor strategy', Policy Paper, 19 May 2023, available at www.gov.uk/government/publications/national-semiconductor-strategy/national-semiconductor-strategy.

Ongoing understanding of the UK's strategy can be found by reading updates from the Semiconductor Advisory Panel, a committee that was set up to maximise the chances of an objective growth plan relevant to all parts of the UK. Notably, its esteemed committee members include industry leaders from Wales and Scotland. The minutes of the Semiconductor Advisory Panel are also publicly accessible, although to date the minutes lack detail.[8] Given the UK Government changed from the Conservative Party to the Labour Party in July 2024, it is likely that more detailed minutes on the committee's progress will flow.

The main 'clusters' the UK Government has highlighted are shown in Figure 3.1. However, to these locations, in my view, it is also important to add other thriving centres of excellence. These include Manchester, the Midlands, Southampton, Surrey, and Torbay.[9]

3.3 South Wales

It is notable that in the last few years there has been increased investment into this regional cluster. If you are speaking with a CEO from any part of the global semiconductor industry they will have heard of or be interested in South Wales. For example, in the past Robert Rickman OBE, CEO of Rockley Group has chosen South Wales as Rockley's base for producing sensors. As part of his expert evidence to the UK House of Commons enquiry into the semiconductor sector, he commented that the 'compound semiconductor cluster in South Wales is a prime example of an effective collaboration to compete in a field on a global level and with additional support it would continue to see success on a global scale'.[10]

8 Available at www.gov.uk/government/groups/semiconductor-advisory-panel.

9 I am grateful to Dr Andy Sellars, former Strategic Development Director, Compound Semiconductor Applications Catapult, and current Operations Director of Silicon Catalyst, for his presentation Semiconductor Strategy, delivered to semiconductors leaders and MPs on 24 May 2023, hosted by the Foundation for Science and Technology at the Royal Society.

10 House of Commons (2022) *The semiconductor industry in the UK*, Fifth Report of Session 2022–23, HC 291, Rockley Photonics response to UK Select (SEM0032) Committee at para.3.

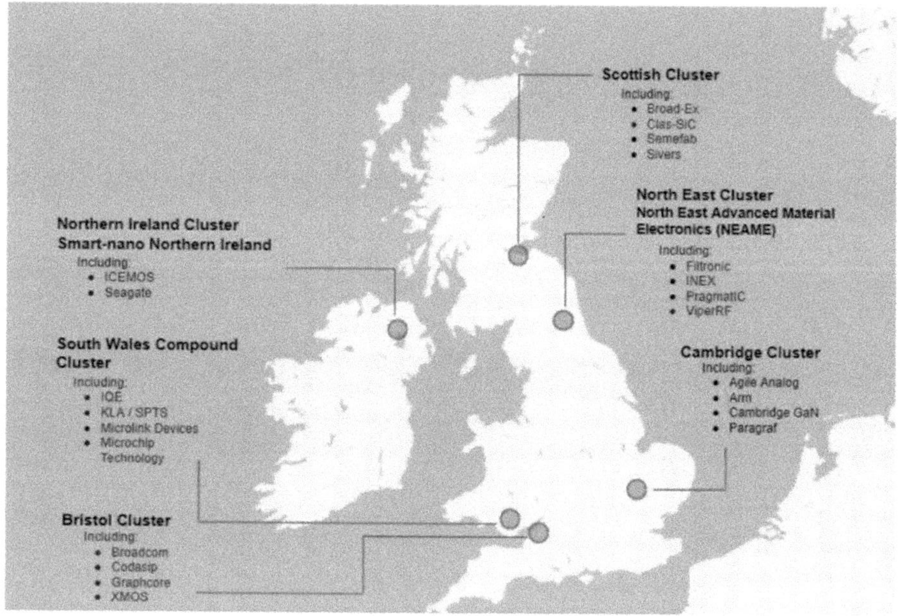

Source: UK Government (2023) Department for Science, Innovation and Technology (DSIT), 'National Semiconductor Strategy', at 21

Figure 3.1 *UK regional clusters*

The 'CSA Catapult' programme has been and remains the most important catalyst for promoting South Wales. It has made a valuable long-term contribution to positive change in the UK sector in the contexts of the Cardiff and Swansea area. Based in Newport, the Compound Semiconductor Applications Catapult (CSA Catapult) was formed to support the growth of the sector, especially compound semiconductor manufacturing.[11]

CSA Catapult functions to bridge the gap between research institutions and business. For example, collaborative opportunities with established compound semiconductor firms such as the Alternative Investment Market (AIM)-listed IQE[12] and SPTS Technologies.[13] Strategic partnerships include a signed commitment between CSA Catapult and the Industrial Technology Institute of Taiwan (ITRI) that aims to develop long-term supplier relationships between firms and researchers. Priority areas for CSA Catapult include electric vehicles (EVs), future 5G telecom networks, defence and quantum technologies.[14]

The Newport Wafer Fab (NWF) has also been an important centre for manufacturing excellence.[15] Historically, NWF has been a 200mm SMIF Wafer-fab, offering a wide range of semiconductor technologies, including metal–oxide–semiconductor field-effect transistors (MOSFETs) and trench insulated gate bipolar transistors (TIGBTs) using wafer-thinning methods to complementary metal-oxide semiconductors (CMOS), analog and compound semiconductors. On my visit to Boston, US firms were quick to compliment NWF.

---

[11] See https://csa.catapult.org.uk/csacatapult/.

[12] London Stock Exchange (2024), www.londonstockexchange.com/raise-finance/equity/aim.

[13] IQE (2024), www.iqep.com/; SPTS Technologies, www.spts.com/products. I was fortunate enough to learn more about IQE from one of its founders, Drew Nelson. An expert in fibre optics, Nelson pointed out there has always been the prerequisite engineering talent in South Wales, and throughout the UK. The recurring mistake has been omitting to consistently fully exploit UK research and development (R&D) over the long-term.

[14] UK Government (2023) 'National Semiconductor Strategy', Policy Paper, 19 May 2023, at 26, available at www.gov.uk/government/publications/national-semiconductor-strategy/national-semiconductor-strategy.

[15] The Newport Wafer Fab is considered in Chapter 10 National security law and Chapter 12 Conclusions on achieving growth.

The research infrastructure between Cardiff and Swansea is the collective catalyst for long-term commercial success. Cardiff University has the Institute for Compound Semiconductors (ICS). Swansea University has the Centre for Integrative Semiconductor Materials (CISM). The CISM facility offers R&D, prototyping and process development, collaborating with industry partners that include IQE, SPTS and NWF.[16]

3.4 Bristol

Less than 50 km from Newport South Wales is Bristol. This city is a thriving centre of semiconductor activity. A firm that deserves special mention is Graphcore. It has developed Intelligence Processing Unit (IPU) technology that has attracted many powerful financial backers, making it one of the UK's most valuable start-ups. It is possible that Graphcore will become the Nvidia of the future. That may sound premature, but its founders have incredible track records and an obvious ambition to succeed.[17]

Bristol University has completed many important semiconductor research contributions. Most recently, it has been selected as the base for a new £11 million Innovation and Knowledge Centre (IKC) REWIRE. The project leader is Professor Martin Kuball of Bristol University. His research team is supported by Ampaire, BMW, Bosch, Cambridge GaN Devices (CGD), Element-Six Technologies, General Electric, Hitachi Energy, IQE, Oxford Instruments, Siemens, ST Microelectronics and Toshiba.[18] The REWIRE IKC aims to focus on, among other things, EVs, wind energy power conversion and improving the efficiency of semiconductor device manufacture. It is very likely that some of this research will be responsible

---

16 Centre for Integrative Semiconductor Materials (2024), www.cism-swansea-semiconductors.co.uk/about-cism.

17 Graphcore has produced a three-minute video that captures the vision of its founders Simon Knowles and Nigel Toon. Available at www.graphcore.ai/about.

18 Bristol University (2024), *Cabot Institute for the Environment Newsletter*, www.bristol.ac.uk/cabot/news/2024/semiconductor-centre.html. University supporting partners include Cambridge University and Warwick University, mentioned elsewhere in this chapter.

for advances in semiconductor sustainability across diverse applications and devices.[19]

3.5 Southampton

There is a high concentration of photonics talent in Southampton. Southampton University has immense depth in the field of photonics. If policy makers are creating a mental image of a globally significant Cardiff-Compound Valley, so too should they create one of Southampton-Photonics Valley.

Two of the leaders at Southampton University, Sir David Payne, Professor of Photonics, and Head of School, Professor Graham Reed, are challenging questions about UK semiconductor strategy. Their ambitions and dedication to photonics amount to a national asset. Currently, Southampton University is also a world leading institution in Hollow Core Fibre (HCF).[20]

At the annual UK semiconductor conference hosted by Sheffield University, David provided an excellent presentation on the direction of photonics research.[21] His presentation focused on the National Hub in High Value Photonic Manufacturing, of which he is the lead researcher, funded by the Engineering and Physical Sciences Research Council (EPSRC). Sustainable electronic technologies and nanophotonic research groups are collaborating operating under this research umbrella.[22]

David is a highly accomplished fibre optics expert, whose research has led to 11 photonics spin-out firms in the Southampton cluster. Notably, he co-founded SPI Lasers, now owned by Trumpf Group. He has also pub-

---

[19] Sustainability is considered in Chapter 6 Sustainable innovation, and Chapter 12 Conclusions on achieving growth.

[20] Southampton University (2024) Hollow Core Fibre Research Group, www.southampton.ac.uk/research/institutes-centres/hollow-core-fibre.

[21] Sir David Payne (2023), 'National HCB in Future Photonics', UK Semiconductor Conference, 14 July 2023.

[22] Southampton University (2024) Research project National Hub in High Value Photonic Manufacturing, https://www.southampton.ac.uk/research/projects/national-hub-in-high-value-photonic-manufacturing.

lished over 650 conference and journal papers.[23] It is puzzling why he is not a member of the UK Government's Semiconductor Advisory Board, to mitigate the risk, if any exists, of compound or silicon group think.

From a regional strategic viewpoint, Southampton's local government, in coordination with county-level industry leaders, has put forward a bold vision for significant industrial expansion.[24] This includes expanded port facilities and better infrastructure, and new housing. With firms such as HiLight Semiconductors choosing to be based around Southampton,[25] the city has every chance of growing a far larger cluster, especially for photonics firms.

3.6 Surrey

Based in its Institute for Communications Systems, 5G/6G Innovation Centre, Surrey University collaborates on 5G/6G network research with an impressive range of firms. These include BT, McLaren Applied Technologies, Samsung, Telefonica, and Vodafone.[26]

There is also important, arguably under publicised, strategic leadership from the 5G/6G Innovation Centre. For instance, it has produced a thought-provoking white paper entitled 'From patchy to powerful: Creating a regulatory framework for high-quality universal mobile coverage that unlocks growth across the UK'.[27] This paper put forward the need for the UK to assess the merits of passing new laws to rebalance

[23] Southampton University (2024) Professor Sir David Payne KBE CBE FRS FREng, Professor of Photonics, www.southampton.ac.uk/people/5wydcg/professor-sir-david-payne#biography.

[24] Southampton produced a two-minute animation introducing its plans: Southampton City Council (2024), 'Southampton City Vision', available at www.southampton.gov.uk/planning/planning-policy/emerging-plans/cityvision/.

[25] HiLight Semiconductors, https://hilight-semi.com.

[26] Surrey University (2024) Institute for Communications Systems, 5G/6G Innovation Centre https://www.surrey.ac.uk/institute-communication-systems/5g-6g-innovation-centre.

[27] Surrey University (2023) 'From patchy to powerful: Creating a regulatory framework for high-quality universal mobile coverage that unlocks growth

the regulatory framework to require an upgrade in telecommunications infrastructure. In so doing, the full benefits of 5G/6G can be exploited.

Surrey University has a track record of collaborative innovation across its members – undergraduate to faculty. As a recent example, an undergraduate's final year project was advanced by a PhD candidate. In her final year project, Lea Motte researched the multimodal transistor, as a substitute for conventional thin-film transistors. Subsequently, Eva Bestelink, then a PhD student, looked at Lea's discovery, confirming measurements made and performing extensive simulations to grasp the physics underpinning its unique ability.

Dr Radu Sporea, Senior Lecturer in Semiconductor Devices and supervisor to both Lea and Eva's projects remarked that the discovery also showed the value of collaboration, including with other institutions. In this research, that also included Rennes University, France, Dr Sporea concluded it demonstrated that 'in our team, everyone's contribution can lead to important developments, even as undergraduates. That is why, at Surrey we encourage our students to explore widely and to challenge the boundaries of their assigned projects'.[28]

3.7 Northern Ireland

One example of an established firm in the Northern Ireland cluster is IceMOS Technology. Established over 20 years ago, its deep expertise is in wafer bonding, deep reactive ion etching (DRIE) and wafer shaping.[29] In 2024, with coordinated support from Invest Northern Ireland,[30] IceMos secured pre-initial product offering (IPO) funding valuing IceMOS at

across the UK', available at https://www.surrey.ac.uk/sites/default/files/2023-11/from-patchy-to-powerful-white-paper.pdf.

28 Surrey University (2021) 'Surrey student makes a discovery that could improve the reliability of future smart electronics', 21 August 2021, available at www.surrey.ac.uk/news/surrey-student-makes-discovery-could-improve-reliability-future-smart-electronics.

29 See www.icemostech.com/about-us.html.

30 See https://www.investni.com/media-centre/features/ni-investment-summit-unlocking-world-opportunities-investors; and www.investni.com/support-for-business/funding-for-innovation-and-research-and-development.

a market capitalisation of £80 million, enabling IceMOS the firm to expand its Belfast operations to more than 100 employees.

The Institute of Electronics, Communications and Information Technology, Queen's University Belfast, has deep experience in collaborative research. One of its leading members, Professor Maire O'Neil, has carried out collaborative research with South Korea's Electronics and Telecommunications Research Institute (ETRI), on a novel security architecture for EV charging systems which was licensed by LG-CNS.[31] An expert in hardware cryptography, Professor O'Neill has also led multimillion pound research carried out by the Research Institute in Secure Hardware and Embedded Systems (RISE).[32]

Northern Ireland as a whole, presents unique strategic advantages. First, it is close to Leixlip, Ireland, and Intel's growing manufacturing activity. Knowhow and talent are two constant benefits. Second, Northern Ireland has a land border with an EU member state.

3.8 South Devon

Torbay High Tech Cluster, which centres around the Electronics and Photonics Innovation Centre (EPIC), can trace its roots to the 1950s. It specialises in microelectronics and photonics.[33] Benefiting from close collaboration with both Exeter University and Plymouth University, examples of its successful firms include G&H and Lumentum.[34]

3.9 Cambridge

Silicon Fen is host to diverse cutting-edge research, world-class design, and connected spin-outs. It has been so for decades. Cambridge University conducts world-class research in areas such as perovskites and quantum

31 See https://www.lgcns.com/en/.

32 Queen's University Belfast (2024), Professor Maire O'Neil, www.qub.ac.uk/ecit/People/ProfessorMaireONeill/.

33 Torbay High-Tech Cluster (2024), https://epic-centre.co.uk/wp-content/uploads/EPIC-Torbay-Hi-Tech-Cluster-2022.pdf.

34 See https://gandh.com/ and https://www.lumentum.com/en.

computing. It also has the presence of ARM and Qualcomm. In sum, a dynamic combination of innovative research and commercial activity.

The Cambridge Centre for Gallium Nitride at Cambridge University conducts world-leading research into nitride based III-V semiconductors. Professor Rachel Oliver is carrying out research into LEDs and laser diodes using gallium nitride. The potential energy saving consequences could be widespread.[35] However, Cambridge University leaders such as Rachel Oliver are aware that to compete there is a need to be in tune with all promising areas. For instance, if you can forgive the pun, in an illuminating seminar hosted by the Royal Academy of Engineering she commented on the need to pivot with agility to new promising areas such as hybrid organic-inorganic perovskites.[36]

Fabless design is synonymous with Cambridge, because of ARM. Richard Gristenthwaite, ARM's Chief Architect, holds more than 100 patents, and is a current member of the UK Government's Semiconductor Advisory Board.[37] It has been observed that the success of ARM cannot be copied, it is a one-off.[38] Nevertheless, the pivotal role of ARM in the global semiconductor industry makes it a unique firm allowing all others to gain some marginal advantage, including the cluster of talent in and around Cambridge.

Additionally, ARM has evolved into a supportive champion of start-ups. Its Business Transformation Group offers the Arm Flexible Access for Start-ups service which enables entrepreneurs to access more than 80 of ARM's intellectual property (IP) cores, including many central processing units (CPUs) and also machine learning processors. In the Cloud, users can run simulations to compare different IP architectures. ARM makes no charge for these services at the prototype phase.[39]

---

35 Cambridge Centre for Gallium Nitride (2024), www.gan.msm.cam.ac.uk/.

36 Royal Academy of Engineering (2023) 'Semiconductors- a critical technology for a critical time?' Seminar, March 2023.

37 ARM Limited (2024), www.arm.com/company/leadership.

38 Ashton, J. (2023) *The Everything Blueprint – The Microchip Design That Changed the World*, Hodder & Stoughton, at 391.

39 ARM (2024) 'Flexible Access for Start-ups', available at https://www.arm.com/products/flexible-access/startup.

Members benefit from being able to evaluate and design with ARM IP ahead of paying any IP license fees. License fees are only payable when the design is ready for tape out. This helps start-ups with cash flow and gives them the flexibility to change IP during the design and evaluation phase. License fees are not made public and vary by product.

ARM also charges a royalty once commercial devices are shipped to end customers. This is charged as a percentage of the average selling price (ASP) for the semiconductor. ARM's royalty rates vary by the products used. All sizes of firm would be advised to instruct a lawyer practising English contract law to support the negotiation of terms and conditions.[40]

3.10 Scotland

Scotland is synonymous with engineers and technological innovation that traces back two centuries not decades.[41] Aliens might be puzzled why Taiwan and not Scotland is the semiconductor leader. The answer to that thought is partly because of inconsistent private investment and inadequate industrial policy. The first semiconductor investment in Scotland was made in 1960 by the microelectronics division of the Hughes Aircraft Corporation to make and test diodes. US investment in electronics firms dates back even earlier, with Honeywell and other firms in the late 1940s, then when IBM established a plant in Greenock in 1951.[42]

At a UK semiconductor strategy evening hosted by the Foundation for Science and Technology, the salient issues to make the UK semiconductor sector successful were discussed publicly in front of many of the industry's leaders. A key presentation was delivered by David Clark, Technical Manager for Clas-Sic Wafer Fab. Based near Dunfermline, the Clas-Sic Wafer Fab semiconductor is a case study on how a UK firm can evolve.

---

[40] I am grateful to Glenn Charter and Neil Parris both of ARM's Business Transformation Group for taking the time to direct me to details on this service.

[41] Current innovation includes research carried out at The James Watt nanofabrication Centre (JWNC) is a 1200m2 cleanroom at the University of Glasgow, www.gla.ac.uk/research/az/jwnc/aboutjwnc/.

[42] Henderson, J. (1989) *The Globalisation of High Technology Production*, Routledge, at 118–19.

At least in the past, the financial catalyst for growth was driven by US investors; but for the capital contributions of US investors UK firms can struggle to grow.

Clas-Sic Wafer Fab is a positive case study not only because it is proof that US capital is attracted to semiconductor investment in Scotland, but also as an example of how quickly a firm can grow. Clas-Sic Wafer Fab was established in 2017, a US venture capital investor provided the firm with its first £50 million. It is a 150mm pureplay foundry focused on MOSFETs and Schottky diodes. The firm has experienced 500% revenue growth, is now cash self-sufficient and is scaling up.[43]

Another successful example is Vector Photonics. This firm is a spin-out from Glasgow University. Its most significant innovative contribution has been the production of photonic-crystal surface-emitting laser (PCSEL)-based, III-V semiconductor lasers. It has several leaders with decades of semiconductor experience. For example, Adrian Meldrum, Executive Chair, has various insights on cutting-edge photonics products sold by Gooch & Housego, Oclaro Inc., IQE, and Bookham Inc.[44]

From a workforce viewpoint, the supply of science, technology, engineering and maths (STEM) talent extends beyond Edinburgh University, Glasgow University and Strathclyde University, to universities in Northeast England. Engineers and technicians training and working in the north of England, especially the Northeast, would typically view Scotland as part of their market.[45]

Encouragingly, firms such as Clas-Sic Wafer Fab and Vector Photonics have had the right blend of ambition and access patient capital to be able to grow. From Glasgow to Glenrothes, there are many other established semiconductor firms. With a high quality of life, renewable energy, and

43 https://clas-sic.com/capabilities/.

44 Vector Photonics (2024), www.vectorphotonics.co.uk/technology/.

45 In the context of photonics, a number of Scottish universities and collaborating organisations are involved in photonics research. See The Scottish Optoelectronics Association (2019) 'Photonics in Scotland A Vision For 2030', available at https://photonicsscotland.com/wp-content/uploads/2020/07/scottishphotonics-paper-final.pdf.

abundant water supplies, perhaps it is the cluster in the UK with the most potential.

3.11 Northeast England

In a cluster revolving around Newcastle and Durham there is growing semiconductor activity. Importantly, there is a local supply of STEM talent from not only the local Northeast universities, but also Scotland. Engineers and technicians training and working in Scotland treat the Northeast of England as part of their market and vice versa.

In Newcastle there is a highly innovative and well-established electronic design automation (EDA) firm called Pulsic.[46] It is the creator of Animate Preview, that enables analog circuit engineers to prototype using digital schematics rather than experience productivity gaps caused by waiting for physical layout.[47] This firm equally offers software for custom digital, mixed-signal, and memory designers.

Turning to manufacturing firms, Pragmatic Semiconductor has an established production site in Sedgefield. It has also secured investment for a 300mm fabrication plant encompassing a 59,000-square-metre (635,000-square-foot) site in Durham and collaborates closely with New College Durham (NCD), a leading further education college, and Durham University.

Pragmatic Semiconductor specialises in FlexICs, a substitute for silicon with low cost and fast production cycles.[48] It also provides Fab-as-a-Service (FaaS) based on renting a dedicated production line for a project. It offers a managed 'Fab-in-a-Box' service assisting other firms to build a self-contained production area. They claim Fab-in-a-Box requires 100 times less capital expenditure compared with a traditional silicon fabrication plant, and 100 times faster production cycle times.

---

[46] https://pulsic.com/.

[47] Pulsic produced a two-minute animation introducing Animate Preview, available at https://pulsic.com/video/introduction-to-animate-preview/.

[48] Pragmatic has produced a two-minute video introducing its FlexIC foundry that produces 200mm or 300mm wafers, available at www.pragmaticsemi.com/foundry.

The human entrepreneurial talent in the Northeast cannot be overlooked. Consider, one of its universities trained a leading Apple phone designer. In the context of semiconductors, Scott White, a founder of Pragmatic Semiconductor, has grown five previous ventures, and also sits on the UK's Semiconductor Advisory Panel. He has also lived and worked in Australia, Singapore and the USA.

3.12 The Midlands

There is an established cluster of STEM talent in the Midlands, with several universities offering engineering and science-based courses. Given the world-class STEM research produced by Oxford University, its spin-out incubator has had many successes. For decades Oxford Innovation has been assisting research teams to spin out.[49]

Perhaps the best example Oxford University research innovation is the evolution of its physics faculty research into Oxford Instruments plc (Oxford Instruments). Incorporated in 1958, its areas of expertise include designing and making. For example, Oxford Instruments has been using atomic layer deposition (ALD) to decrease the threshold voltage changes in gallium nitride (GaN) and aluminium gallium nitride (AlGaN) devices.[50]

Rockley Photonics for many years operated out of Oxford, so there has also been photonics talent in the area. Another example is the photonics design firm Salience Labs. Built on ten years of research from Oxford University it has designed a photonics processor that can be manufactured in 90nm and is suitable for machine learning applications.[51]

Turning to Warwick University, it has dedicated engineering faculties and a spin-out unit. For example, Professor Layi Alatise is a world leading expert in power electronics, with industrial experience at, among other firms, NXP Semiconductors. He gained his First Class honours degree in Electrical and Electronic Engineering from Newcastle University. Based on my direct research, Alatise is also an exceptional presenter. Warwick

[49] Oxford Innovation (2024), https://innovation.ox.ac.uk/about/.
[50] Oxford Instruments plc (2024), www.oxinst.com/applications/fabrication.
[51] See https://saliencelabs.ai/.

University has established links with the automotive sector: as Jaguar Land Rover and many other niche automotive manufacturers expand their EV volumes, there are likely to be more opportunities for local Midlands semiconductor firms to contribute to that growth.

For the benefit of readers thinking through the human resource factors for locating to or expanding in the UK, set out in Table 3.1, are the key semiconductor clusters based around a city. What is missing from this summary is the interplay between semiconductor hardware and software. In the UK there are dynamic software firms found throughout. That includes Southwest England and Northeast England and Scotland. Therefore, in the context of the levelling up policy supported by government subsidies, there is potential to grow semiconductor software clusters anywhere.

3.13 Hardware and software competitive advantages

A senior semiconductor industry analyst, Mario Morales, has commented on the pivotal interplay between high-quality hardware and the software that enables it. He analysed the interplay in this way: 'what we cannot forget is that when you look at a phone it is both hardware and software. What makes iPhone unique, what makes Samsung solutions unique, is that they not only put together the best hardware, but also the best software'.[52]

In the context of Manchester and its surrounding towns, it is possible to imagine that semiconductor software clusters could build around Siemens and other existing hardware providers. Siemens committed to collaborating in a partnership with the Compound Semiconductor Applications (CSA) Catapult in Newport focused on disruptive power electronics hardware.[53] There are also very experienced academics in the

---

[52] *Nikkei Asia* (2023) 'Chip War Part III, Beyond 2024: The next battlefields in global technology', Seminar, 21 November 2023.

[53] CSA Catapult (2024) 'Siemens Establishes Power Electronics Innovation Hub in the UK with the Compound Semiconductor Applications Catapult', available at https://csa.catapult.org.uk/news-insights/news/siemens-establishes-power-electronics-innovation-hub-in-the-uk-with-the-compound-semiconductor-applications-catapult/.

Table 3.1 *Monthly rent and air quality in semiconductor clusters*

Regional cluster	City	Monthly rent for one-bed flat outside city centre compared with London - £1,628	Air quality index (AQI) and PM2.5 air pollution[1] Bern = 8 London = 32
Northern Ireland	Belfast	£691; 57.2%	15
Southwest	Bristol	£1,007; 37.6%	35
Silicon Fen	Cambridge	£1,144; 29.1%	8
South Wales	Cardiff	£806; 50.0%	38
Midlands	Coventry	£756; 53.1%	37
Scotland	Stirling	£633; 60.7%	8
Northeast England	Newcastle	£658; 59.2%	22
Northwest England	Manchester	£918; 43.0%	17
Hampshire	Southampton	£868; 46.1%	33

Note: [1] www.numbeo.com/cost-of-living/comparison.jsp; and IQAir (2025), see www.iqair.com/gb/.
Source: © Iain Sheridan (2025)

cluster, such as Professor John Goodacre, a former ARM director able to maximise commercial output from research ideas and keep a broad sense of strategy.[54]

Another possible cluster could form around Stoke-on-Trent where cost of living and both commercial and residential rents are lower. For the ambitious foreign direct investment (FDI) project there could be scope to build a cost-effective state of the art software centre. Staffordshire University has been specialising in programming for more than 40 years,

[54] Manchester University (2024), https://research.manchester.ac.uk/en/persons/john.goodacre.

and in games development for more than 20 years. This institution has built a global reputation for talented games software graduates.[55]

3.14 Patient Capital

In 2018, the British Business Bank set up a subsidiary called British Patient Capital. The initial investment was £2.5 billion to invest over ten years in venture capital growth.[56] The government, in its Innovation Strategy, pinpoints electronics, photonics and quantum technologies as a 'family' in which the UK has globally competitive research and development capability and industrial strength. Their view is that these areas are the logical starting point for prioritisation. The government analyses it in this way:

> Attempting to lead in every technology within each family will likely prevent us attaining a world-leading edge in any one area. We will need to prioritise investments at a granular level, considering factors like UK comparative advantage, transformative potential, and security and societal need. Learning from the success of vaccine development we must be decisive in backing these priorities and be agile in reviewing those we back where circumstances change.[57]
>
> The Government is clear that semiconductors offer significant potential: The UK is already a leader in the design of semiconductors, and with sufficient support it has the potential to become a leading designer and manufacturer of compound semiconductor chips and technologies. This would allow the UK to capitalise on increased global demand for semiconductor chips and support domestic production in critical sectors like health, telecoms and automotive. By the mid-2030s UK companies, including those based at established clusters in Wales, Bristol and Cambridge, could play an increasingly central role in a supply chain of acute geopolitical importance.[58]

---

[55] Staffordshire University (2024) Games Development Department, www.staffs.ac.uk/about/schools/digital-technology-innovation-and-business/games-department.

[56] See www.britishpatientcapital.co.uk.

[57] UK Government (2021) UK Innovation Strategy, at 85.

[58] UK Innovation Strategy (2021) at 91.

3.15 Final points

There are many strategies for growing the UK semiconductor sector.[59] Here are just three to briefly mention, because they all have such clear economic and geographical elements.

3.15.1 Collaboration with the EU

At the beginning of this chapter reference was made to the fact that EU–UK relations have, in recent years, taken a more mutually beneficial path. In the first quarter of 2024, the UK Department for Science, Innovation and Technology announced that the UK had been permitted to join the EU's Chips Joint Undertaking.[60]

Sean Redmond, Managing Partner at SiliconCatalyst, said:

> UK Semiconductor startups have a rich history of collaboration with the European Union. Our semiconductor research base is the fourth largest in the world… Commercialising these inventions with the help of the EU Chips Joint Undertaking will significantly increase their probability of success, mitigating risks by local collaborations that provide a clear path from lab to fab.[61]

3.15.2 Informing STEM talent about the UK clusters

A challenge of relevance to all regional clusters is coordinating both domestic and foreign talent. To maximise the potential of each regional cluster to (a) be attractive to all STEM talent with options, and (b) maximise their technical experience and qualifications. For example, imagine a compound semiconductor engineer can only work in Cambridge, Massachusetts or Cambridge, England. One or the other. The factors they evaluate as important in that decision are quite different from

[59] Future strategic options are considered in chapter X Regional strategy and chapter Y Conclusions.

[60] Members of the Chips Joint Undertaking include all EU member states, Iceland, Norway, Turkey and the UK. See Chips for Europe Initiative (2025), available at www.chips-ju.europa.eu/.

[61] UK Government (2024) '£35 million boost for British semiconductor scientists and businesses on international chip research', Press Release, 13 March 2024, www.gov.uk/government/news/35-million-boost-for-british-semiconductor-scientists-and-businesses-on-international-chip-research.

attending leading STEM universities in either of those cities. The same decision-making process takes place when comparing any two cities to live in, including any two cities in the UK.

As part of early career decision making, the average semiconductor engineer may rationally want several potential future employers within 50 miles radius of their first employer. The collective UK semiconductor sector more effectively grows when it can communicate advantages and disadvantages of each regional cluster in an objective way, independent of local politics, and personal experiences.

The establishment of a UK national semiconductor advice body to act as a filter for technical information about what each semiconductor firm does and plans to do in each cluster would be helpful. Equally, such a centre could publish data on immigration law, especially visa options for STEM graduates, and how people can integrate from housing, schools and leisure facilities in each regional cluster.

3.15.3 The City of London

The City of London (the City) has a long history of supporting engineering, science and innovation. An often-heard misconception is that the City is a quintessentially English clubby place. Bowler hats, pageantry, pomp, the square mile... Perhaps in the past there were also elements of English cliques based on who you know not what you know. However, in the present consider the fact that Michael Mainelli, an American by birth, was the Lord Mayor of the City of London for 2023–24.[62] Additionally, at a London Stock Exchange event or at London legal conferences, the attendees are routinely from Brazil, India, China and South Africa. The City of London is a truly international culture.

The City, and Greater London have a potentially unique role to play in the interplay between hardware and software. For example, in the context of machine learning, Deep Mind established and retains its headquarters in the City. There is also a growing cluster of artificial intelligence (AI) firms in the City, levering machine learning talent in the Hoxton district and being close to a globally significant capital market where large budgets

[62] City of London Corporation (2024), https://democracy.cityoflondon.gov.uk/mgUserInfo.aspx?UID=1323.

are allocated for both hardware and software. For ambitious graphics processing unit (GPU) or equivalent designers London is a cluster with a bright future.

There may also be an important competitive advantage for small- and medium-sized enterprises (SMEs) seeking to grow and raise capital by a public listing. Too often in the past, UK semiconductor firms have chosen to raise capital from US stock exchanges. However, as the London Stock Exchange Group (LSEG) evolves to have more flexibility for firms seeking to list on the main London Stock Exchange or AIM, the greater the advantage will be for the LSEG and regulators to support semiconductor firms. There's also an educational element in the sense that the presence of semiconductor entrepreneurs will act as a trusted source of knowledge.

4. Strategy frameworks

Strategy is often erroneously associated with the planned choices of firms. In fact, strategy is never 'what to do', because describing any plan is not action, it is just words. Strategy is the how. The decisions, methods, and ways in which a firm chooses to compete. Sometimes the strategist in action is a Chief Executive Officer (CEO), Chief Strategy Officer (CSO), Chief Legal Officer (CLO) or general counsel. Whatever the title they hold, strategy frameworks support rational decision making based on ambition, caution, reflection, and speed.

4.1 Introduction

This chapter focuses on strategic thinking models for any semiconductor firm leadership team to apply. After assessing many established and new models, it presents the combined wisdom of three veteran strategic thinkers from Harvard, Massachusetts Institute of Technology (MIT), and Seoul National University (SNU).

Readers with established semiconductor firms will have that extra challenge of incorporating the proposed semiconductor strategic framework within existing, already successful ways of operating.[1] There is also the understandable reaction that your established methods have worked over countless product implementations, and new models of thinking

[1] There are other valuable corporate strategic frameworks that can be applied to the semiconductor sector. For instance, blue ocean strategy, as developed by two INSEAD professors: Kim, W.C., and R. Mauborgne (2004) *Blue Ocean Strategy: How to Create Uncontested Market Space and Make the Competition Irrelevant*, Harvard Business School Press. Their strategy concentrates on innovation and price as key determinants of a successful strategy. In 2015 the second edition of this insightful book was expanded to include, among other new chapters, how firms can incorporate a dynamic renewal process for sustaining performance.

are unnecessary. My respectful response is to propose you remain open-minded and invest a bit of time in what is a comprehensive, practical, and high-quality framework.

A practical, action-centred strategic framework can make marginal or even significant improvements to growth. Disruptive game changers make capitalism a dynamic, exciting environment for global trade. It means the market leadership of great products is not permanent, as shown in the past experiences of IBM, Nokia, and Blackberry.

The framework in Figure 4.1 combines three strategic models. Three frameworks presented as one mindset. Imagine these models are projected as dials within an augmented reality glass lens or contact lenses that support a leader monitoring the fundamental aspects of an effective strategy. The augmented strategy lens comprises of four dials forming a strategic framework for analysis and constant action-based decision making.

The central strategy is called 'real innovation'. It derives from Eugene Fitzgerald, currently MIT Professor of Materials Science and Engineering, and CEO of the Singapore-MIT Alliance for Research and Technology.[2] Fitzpatrick characterises real innovation as an iterative looping process rather than a linear one. A successful strategy is based on long-term patience, requiring mastery of Technology, the Market in which a product will be sold, and the basis of commercial Implementation.

On the left-hand side of the augmented reality lens is a value stick that determines profit margin based on willingness-to-pay and willingness-to-sell. The value stick was invented by Felix Oberholzer-Gee, Professor of Business Administration at Harvard University.[3] In short, willingness-to-pay is the most a customer would ever pay for a product or service. Whereas willingness-to-sell covers employees and suppliers representing the lowest price at which either of these groups are willing to sell products and services. Strategically, the value a firm creates is maximised by increasing willingness-to-pay and lowering willingness-to-sell.

---

[2] Fitzgerald, Y. et al (2011) *Inside Real Innovation – How the Right Approach Can Move Ideas from R&D to Market – And Get the Economy Moving*, World Scientific. Fitzgerald's co-authors were Andreas Wankerl and Carl Schramm.

[3] Oberholzer-Gee, F. (2021) *Better Simpler Strategy – A Value-Based Guide to Exceptional Performance*, Harvard Business Review Press, at 6–7.

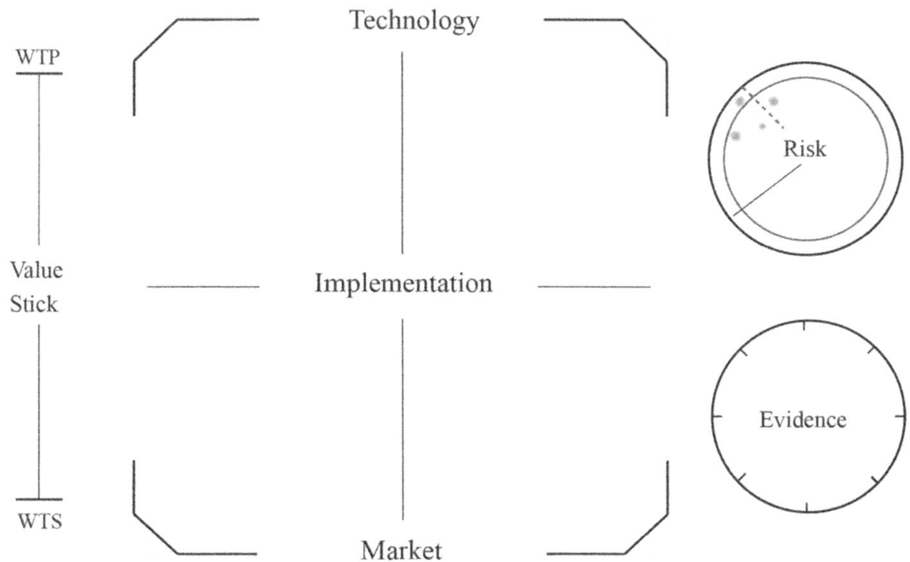

Source: © Iain Sheridan (2025)

Figure 4.1 *Augmented strategy lens*

The top right-hand dial of the augmented reality lens is dedicated to risk. Strategies focused on risk are relevant in the context of rivalry awareness: where competitors can improve on or offer alternative semiconductor devices or services to your customers. But the mini risk radar should equally, if not more so, concentrate more on customers. Drawing on the modern business interpretation of Sun Tzu, Professor Hwy-Chang Moon of SNU is an insightful counsel.[4] As a Korean he naturally has an in-depth understanding of all 13 chapters of *The Art of War* by Sun Tzu.

In his strategic treatise, Sun Tzu advises on the importance of knowing both the enemy and oneself. Yet as Moon sagely points out:

> in business many interpret knowing the enemy as knowing the competitors. However, in business, a comprehensive interpretation should include all the relevant stakeholders, particularly business customers. The customers make the final judgement for the products and services produced by companies... Knowing the enemy is a precondition for winning a war, knowing the consumers (or the market) is a key to success in business.[5]

The bottom right-hand dial is a constant reminder to focus on the importance of making strategic decisions that are supported by evidence. It represents the vital need for a general counsel to earn their keep by confidentially acting as an objective, dissenting voice. The eagle eyes that can scan the horizon for both opportunities and threats.

4.2 Real innovation

The central dial of the augmented lens set out in Figure 4.1 is the interaction between Technology, Market, and Implementation. Devised by Eugene Fitzgerald and his co-authors, the interaction of these three factors is collectively termed 'real innovation'. Background-wise, Fitzgerald invented high-mobility strained silicon and commercialised that technology with AmberWave System Corporation.[6] In 2007, Intel contracted to license AmberWave's strained silicon technology patents. In addition

---

[4] Moon, H-C. (2018) *The Art of Strategy – Sun Tzu, Michael Porter, and Beyond*, Cambridge University Press.

[5] Ibid at 25–6.

[6] For further detail on Eugene Fitzgerald see https://dmse.mit.edu/faculty/eugene-a-fitzgerald/.

to starting other semiconductor firms and performing leadership roles at MIT, Fitzgerald also found time to collaborate with two colleagues to produce a book entitled *Inside Real Innovation.*[7]

The central concept of Fitzgerald's strategic analysis is that innovation is not a linear process. Traditional innovation flows from a source of discovery and ends with profit-making from commercialisation. The linear innovation view comprises of:

discovery→invention→development→product→market→profit

Rather than linear, Fitzgerald and his colleagues characterise real innovation as running across time as iterative loops. A fundamental innovation taking 10 to 15 years to enter a market as a product. He concludes that real innovation begins in the minds of innovators as a confluence of factors. The innovators are:

> aware of certain technologies that exist or could exist… the emerging innovation is liable to be pushed and pulled in all sorts of directions by events that range from unexpected problems to new ideas. Every twist adds to the multiplicity of choices and trade-offs that one must consider...to iterate repeatedly until the innovation rounds into shape.[8]

The dynamics of real innovation revolve around three interconnecting elements, iteratively adjusting for the practical realities of (a) the Technology, (b) the Market that will buy the semiconductors, and (c) the chosen best Implementation methods. Technology includes all objective, scientifically verifiable components. Market includes all human factors, including the envisaged consumers of the innovation, the benefits of using the innovation, and how much people are prepared to pay for it. All measurable uncertain factors. Implementation includes all factors relevant to connecting technology to market, covering everything from manufacturing methods to ways of delivery.[9]

---

7 Fitzgerald et al (2011).

8 Ibid at 17.

9 Of course, this strategy raises the issue of the best thinking strategies to continuously employ to maximise the effectiveness of implementable business decisions. John Boyd's OODA is an established structure and certainly one familiar to many semiconductor leaders. In summary, strategies require obser-

To elaborate, all semiconductor firms can organise their strategies for growth based on continuously applying (a) Technology factors, (b) Market factors, and (c) experienced, thoughtful Implementation. At first instance, real innovation might seem most appropriate for small- and medium-sized enterprises (SMEs) that have more than one idea and limited time and money to break even.

Yet the 'technology + market + implementation' model may have equal validity to the largest semiconductor multinationals. This is because patent research, the metrics of filing and granting match the flow of traditional linear innovation. In the future, the largest R&D budgets could be partly redirected towards fewer patents. Instead, researchers could be tasked with simultaneously taking one of several ideas to market as part of a multi-disciplinary team. The practical everyday functioning of such real innovators would look quite different from the siloed and structured processes often associated with linear innovation.

The mindset of real innovation in the context of Implementation is vital, because any successful semiconductor product must be made in (a) cost-effective quantities, at (b) consistent quality levels, and (c) factoring in the complexities of actual commercial use. The daily, practical implications of real innovation require not only greater flexibility from employees, but also a higher investment in training. For instance, a research and development (R&D) researcher would need to know the costs of using x semiconductor material, the time to complete y manufacturing processes, and z consumer price sensitivities of the consumer product. Consequently, better functioning products are the long-term benefits.

At start-up and scale-up levels, the process of real innovation must ensure teams are able to achieve Implementation without duplicating effort, avoiding flawed decision making or wasting product development costs and time. Implementation is a synonym of execution or action-centred behaviour. Implementation is the opposite of performance goals or budgetary planning.

A memorable example of Implementation is Nvidia's strategic decisions that contributed to its early pre-artificial intelligence (AI) success in

vation (O), orientation (O), decision (D), and action (A). See Osinga, F. (2018) *Science, Strategy and War: The Strategic Theory of John Boyd*, Routledge.

selling graphics processing units (GPUs). Originally, Nvidia GPUs were inserted into different boards, with each board maker providing their own software driver program. Consequently, different software drivers were contributing to performance flaws, including game-playing malfunctions, because of the challenge of old drivers managing new GPUs without appropriate updates.

In 2006, Nvidia's leaders sought to optimise GPU performance, including improving frame rates, and reducing crashing or freezing during game play. Nvidia achieved this by introducing a unified driver architecture (UDA). To this day, customers can download the Nvidia UDA from the Internet based on GPU type, version, and computer operating system.[10]

Fitzgerald encapsulates the practical reality of a highly continuously iterative process in this way:

> All three elements – the nature of the product, the implementation into reality, the market to be addressed – are continuously being balanced against each other, and thought of in relation to one another. And typically all elements, or at least the details of them, change as innovation progresses. The process is one of iterating through the elements again and again until they converge in optimum form into a product implemented in a market.[11]
> Researchers used to the linear way of thinking about innovation, moving neatly from discovery to market, may initially be alarmed by the amorphous process of repeated iterations across Technology, Market, and Implementation. Real innovation is messy in form. Yet its substance is one of effectiveness. As Fitzgerald explains 'it can maximise the chances for success at every step, reduce the risk of waste or loss at every step, and give early indication of when a significant change of the innovation course would be advisable.[12]

In the context of semiconductor teams, it is well-established wisdom that clearly defined goals are more likely to achieve Implementation. Stan Boland, a British semiconductor entrepreneur and semiconductor venture capital (VC) investor, has successfully built and sold four scale-ups. These were Element 14 to Broadcom; Icera to Nvidia; Neul

[10] The UDA has since expanded to be a platform that includes a compiler, libraries, and an application programming interface (API). It has been renamed the Compute Unified Device Architecture (CUDA).

[11] Fitzgerald et al (2011) at 14.

[12] Ibid at 15.

to Huawei; and Five to Bosch.[13] His track record spans more than four decades of successfully executed product development strategy. He has truly mastered real innovation.

Boland has confidence in the thought leadership of Marty Cagan, owner of Silicon Valley Product Group. Cagan advocates that product development teams need three clearly defined roles. First, product managers – experts in customers from both qualitative and quantitative angles. They have an encyclopaedic knowledge of the market sector. Second, product designers – experts in every aspect of the users' senses relating to the product. Third, engineers – experts in how to create the product.[14] Put another way, real innovation is a team game, and everyone has their own defined responsibilities.

4.3 Value stick

Oberholzer-Gee (Oberholzer) juggles consulting, entrepreneurship, and teaching strategy at Harvard Business School. His latest strategy book is entitled *Better Simpler Strategy – A Value-Based Guide to Exceptional Performance*.[15] As positioned in Figure 4.1 on the left-hand side, the central strategic concept he contributes is the 'value stick' that determines profit margin based on willingness-to-pay (WTP) and willingness-to-sell (WTS). Strategically, the value a firm creates is maximised by increasing WTP or lowering WTS, or both.

My initial caution over accepting Oberholzer's value-based strategy is that his experience spans every sector. However, it is evident from reading the book that he has applied his analysis to many semiconductor firms, including Intel, Nvidia, and Sony. Further, his analysis allows the semiconductor CEO to also think about how demanding customers create

---

13 Boland, S. (2024) 'Building a successful scale-up', Presentation at ChipStart UK conference, 13 June 2024. Launched in October 2023, the ChipStart UK incubator programme is managed by Silicon Catalyst. Both ChipStart UK and Silicon Catalyst have been phenomenal successes under the leadership of sector veteran Sean Redmond. See www.siliconcatalyst.uk/.

14 Cagan, M. (2018) *Inspired: How to Create Tech Products Customers Love*, John Wiley & Sons.

15 Oberholzer-Gee (2021) at 6–7.

their own WTP which will impliedly or explicitly influence semiconductor procurement decisions. That list includes Apple, AT&T, Dell, IBM, Telsa, and Toyota.

As briefly explained in the introduction to this chapter, WTP is the most a customer would ever pay for a product or service. Multiple factors can determine the price at which a customer is not prepared to contract. In the context of semiconductor components that is clearly going to centre on energy use, performance, production capacity, and reliability. For services, the level of customer support, efficiency, functionality, reliability, and user-friendliness would be key factors. For both products and services, sustainability credentials that are trackable or traceable are also increasingly relevant.

For example, a current WTP strategy in action is Wise-Integration, a French start-up. This firm supplies customers with gallium nitride power integrated circuits (GaN ICs). Additionally, it provides a silicon-based microcontroller with embedded software. Consequently, application engineers can drive GaN with digital signals rather than with analog signals. Wise-Integration is applying a value-added strategy that will significantly increase the WTP of its customers.

A key target market for Wise-Integration are original equipment manufacturers (OEMs) of TVs. Its CEO has explained: 'You have a very small, very thin display, and all the OEMs are looking to introduce power supplies inside the panel, so they need to have a very thin power supply. Our technology allows this requirement, thanks to digital'.[16] The strategy is to sell a digital controller with up to four of its GaN ICs.

Another memorable WTP example is provided by Oberholzer. He summarises the major operational changes made to Intel's technology transfer strategy. Called 'Copy EXACTLY!', Intel transformed its transfer processes from R&D to manufacturing, up to world-class levels by requiring 100 per cent detail on any changes, precisely applied across all fabrication plants. A four-level matching process is based on physical inputs, process

---

[16] Satevenson, R. (2024) 'A wise investment in the GaN IC', *Compound Semiconductor*, 18 March 2024, available at https://compoundsemiconductor.net/article/118949/newsletter.

or equipment, module, and product.[17] The strategic consequence of Copy EXACTLY! was that Intel increased production volumes anywhere in the world, in less time, simultaneously ensuring product quality was uncompromised. Widening its WTP based on improved operational effectiveness.[18]

A third example of WTP strategies is Ampere Computing.[19] Known as 'Ampere', this firm uniquely sells ARM-based server processors in the open market.[20] While, Amazon's Graviton series, Google's Axion, Microsoft's Cobalt, and Nvidia's Grace are all dedicated semiconductors for their own cloud services, Ampere sells its central processing units (CPUs) to any cloud computing provider.

Ampere's strategies are based on sustainable CPUs dedicated to, among other applications, cloud computing. Compared with legacy x-86 architecture, its CPUs benefit from lower power usage, resulting in better performance per rack. Therefore, WTP is increased by the efficiencies of decreasing energy use and physical space required for racks.[21]

Additionally, Ampere's approach is solving societal problems, because economies seek more cloud computing resource but need to avoid stress on local electricity grids and mitigate climate change. Cloud data centre

---

[17] McDonald, C. (1998) 'The Evolution of Intel's Copy Exactly Technology Transfer Method' *Intel Technology Journal*, Q4 1998.

[18] Oberholzer-Gee (2021) at 6–7.

[19] Still a start-up, it has some powerful financial backers, including The Carlyle Group.

[20] See https://amperecomputing.com/solutions.

[21] Ampere Computing (2024) 'How to Triple Efficiency, Double Performance and Save in on Your Data Center', Seminar, 16 March 2023. In this seminar the firm gives the example of its Ampere Altra Max requiring 36 CPUs to manage 1.3 million web service requests per second, compared with 54 AMD EPYC (3rd generation) and 82 Intel Xeon (3rd generation) CPUs to complete the same task. Therefore, up to a 2.5x performance improvement per rack. The practical effect is that Ampere is using a third of the rack space compared with Intel's Xeon CPUs. Further, to execute 1.3 million web service requests per second, a single rack of Ampere Altra Max uses 12.7kW of power, compared with 22.7 kW for the AMD EPYC and 34.9kW for the Intel Xeon. Available at https://amperecomputing.com/webinars. Also see https://amperecomputing.com/home/efficiency-footnotes.

power consumption is predicted to increase fourfold between 2020 and 2030, which will inevitably result in the need for more regulation to manage usage, which makes Ampere's strategies even more attractive.

4.3.1 Lowering WTS with employee strategies

WTS includes the lowest price at which employees are willing to sell their services. Oberholzer points out that by increasing salaries there will be greater employee satisfaction, but with the negative effect of lowering a firm's margins. In contrast, the strategy of providing more attractive working conditions creates value by reducing WTS.[22] Another example of lowered WTS is increasing employee satisfaction by providing education on finance and pension management.

The strategy of providing quality training was witnessed first-hand by me at a small fabrication plant in Shenyang, Northeast China. The winter mean daily minimum temperature in Shenyang is −10°C. However, the fabrication plant technicians were highly motivated and interested in their work. Some stages of their training took place in Germany. Their employer was providing them with first-class training opportunities. If you have a choice between a firm paying market rate salaries and no guaranteed training, or a firm providing globally respected training, which employer would you choose? The Shenyang firm was successfully lowering its WTS.

In the UK there is an opportunity for semiconductor firms to lower their WTS by supporting employee living options. In most UK semiconductor clusters rental prices are high, and for first-time buyers it is a challenge to get onto the property ladder. Strategies to lower WTS could include offering loans for house deposits. Alternatively, employers could pay a percentage of employee rent thereby giving the recipient an opportunity to save a deposit for their own property. Who would not want to work for such an employer? Implementing such policies would lower WTS and create more long-term value for any semiconductor firm.

---

22 Oberholzer-Gee (2021) at 116.

4.3.2 Lowering WTS with supplier strategies

Based on Oberholzer's considerable experience with leading firms, he has spotted a pattern of variables that successfully lower suppliers' WTS period. His three criteria for selecting partner-suppliers, as set out in Figure 4.2, are (a) value potential, (b) specificity, and (c) completeness. First, value potential refers to the likelihood of a close collaboration that is instrumental in lowering WTS, lowering costs, and increasing WTP.

Second, specificity concerns the degree of specific exchanges between a buyer firm and the supplier firm. The more closely the partners collaborate, the greater the trust, and the more effective the buyer-supplier relationship.

Third, more uncertainty as a criterion makes the point that the more successful buyer-supplier relationships are based on incomplete contractual detail, because at the initial point of contract formation it is too challenging to describe and measure buyer expectations of the supplier. By which is meant, the relationship should evolve so that the initial contractual details are quickly out of date.

Arguably, completeness is the least intuitive of the three criteria, at least from a legal viewpoint! Contractual risk is mitigated by the long-term lowering of WTS, because a positive buyer-supplier relationship continuously evolves.[23] My view would be that the contract should allow for an annual renegotiation of the main commercial terms so that there is not too wide a gap between the ongoing course of dealings and recorded expectations.

4.4 Risk

Logically, risk is assessed in the context of any differences, no matter how marginal, between the cultural mindsets of different competitors, customers, and suppliers. This is especially true in the semiconductor sector that has many successful Chinese, Dutch, French, German, Japanese, Korean, Taiwanese and US firms.

---

[23] Ibid at 150–51.

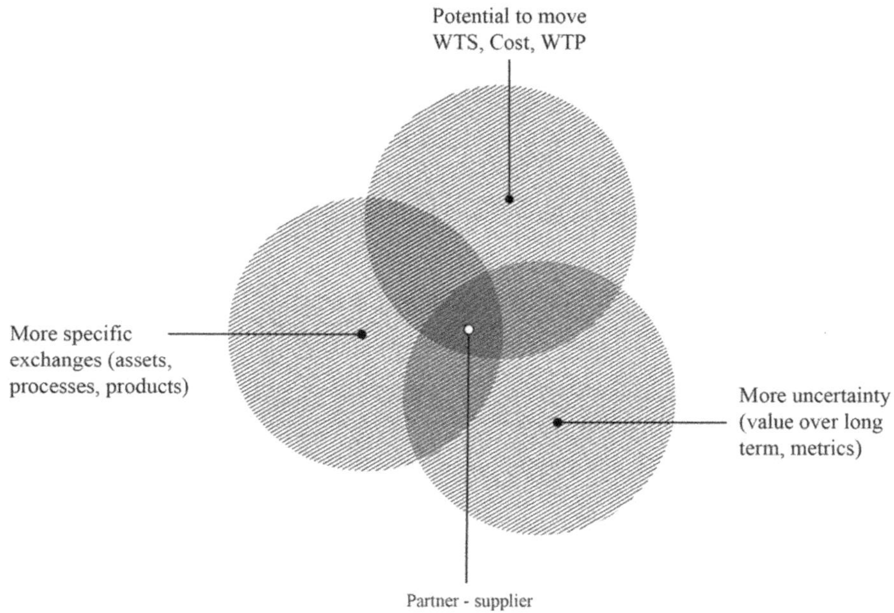

Source: Oberholzer-Gee, F. (2021) *Better Simpler Strategy – A Value-Based Guide to Exceptional Performance*, Harvard Business Review Press, at 150

Figure 4.2 *Supplier selection criteria*

Both Eastern and Western corporate strategy are influenced by Harvard's Michael Porter, because for over four decades Porter's five forces model has provided a robust tool for analysing the attractiveness of entering a specific market and the level of competitive intensity within it.[24]

However, it is evident that Asian corporate strategic risk approaches can also be influenced by some principles found in modern corporate interpretations of Sun Tzu.[25] Indeed, most semiconductor industry veterans will have at some point already consumed *The Art of War*. For example, Jim Keller, CEO of Tenstorrent and architect of AMD, Apple, Intel and Tesla, has mentioned Sun Tzu.

Professor Hwy-Chang Moon of SNU has written a thought provoking analysis that blends key elements of Sun Tzu's strategies with Porter's well-known corporate strategy models. Table 4.1 illustrates that the risks in each professional discipline have marked contrasts and aspects in common.

In sum, the semiconductor leader faces the threats of no demand and potential insolvency. There are many other significant risks, including high barriers to enter certain markets, fierce competition within markets, key supply chain vulnerabilities given the sources of many key components are concentrated in Asia. For instance, from a geoscience viewpoint both Japan and Taiwan are located on fault lines. In the event of a high-level earthquake in this region, especially one on Taiwan, the global supply of processing semiconductors would experience a severe reduction. During the Covid-19 pandemic the global economy experienced the consequences of supply chain disruption.

---

[24] Porter, M. (1980) *Competitive Strategy – Techniques for Analysing Industries and Competitors*, Simon & Schuster. As a reminder the five forces are competitor rivalry, threat of new entrants, ease of substitution, customer power and supplier power.

[25] Moon (2018). Sun Tzu's famous work The Art of War, first published in the fifth century BC, is a seminal treatise on military strategy. A recent insightful translation has been produced by Professor Michael Nylan of UC Berkeley. Her book has received many favourable reviews from leading journals and newspapers. See Nylan, M. (2020) *The Art of War Sun Tzu, A New Translation*, W Norton & Company.

Table 4.1 Comparing military leadership with CEO leadership

Military Leadership	Commercial Leadership
Strategic competence derives from ongoing training and first-hand operational experience. Both training and experience are applied within a framework of Army Doctrine.[1]	Strategic competence derives from ongoing training and first-hand business experience. Specific MBA and executive education modules provide many strategic frameworks.
Military law and the laws of armed conflict apply. Generals rely heavily on legal counsel to form accurate opinions, often with limited or no notice.	Commercial law and international tax treaties apply. CEOs rely heavily on legal counsel to form accurate opinions, often with limited or no notice.
The existential threat is the enemy. It is vital to fully understand, and then outsmart the enemy.	The existential threat is no demand for the goods or services of the firm. It is vital to fully understand, and then satisfy customers.
Military strategy can be 100% defensive involving limited territorial gain.	Corporate strategy must always include offensive plans for growth.
Competitive advantage includes minimising disclosure of tactics and techniques.	Competitive advantage includes minimising disclosure of IP and trade secrets.
Deception and concealment are important preconditions for success.	Deception is unlawful, and concealment is often not possible. Firms rely on strategic fit.
Costs are government-backed. Consequently, insolvency is highly unlikely.	Ordinarily, costs have no government backing. Insolvency is an existential threat.

Military Leadership	Commercial Leadership
Reliable supply chains are vital for operational continuity and are typically restricted in their scope.	Reliable supply chains are vital for operational continuity. They are likely to be regional if not global in complexity and scale.
Allies often form part of a successful strategy.	Joint ventures and other collaborative arrangements can form part of a successful strategy.[2]

Notes: [1] My gratitude goes to Major General John Mead OBE, NATO Allied Joint Force Command, for introducing me to the British Army's impressive range of Army Doctrine. [2] See Chapter 5 Strategic issues, and Chapter 8 Contract law. There are limits, especially in the long term, to how successful joint ventures can be. By which it is meant that sustaining a mutually beneficial joint venture relationship requires 100 per cent trust backed up by robust contractual arrangements.
Source: © Iain Sheridan (2025)

From a strategic viewpoint, the most crucial variable to monitor on a risk radar are customers rather than competitors. As Moon succinctly puts it 'while knowing the enemy is a precondition for winning a war, knowing the consumers (or the market) is a key to success in business'.[26] In the semiconductor sector there are many extraordinarily successful firms that have fatally ignored consumer demand.

Nevertheless, a semiconductor risk leader will also monitor competitors. Moon mentions that in 1983 Mitsubishi Research Centre produced an internal report entitled 'Five Reasons Why Samsung Cannot Succeed in the Semiconductor Industry'. One of the decisive factors in Samsung's survival in the semiconductor sector was its decision to learn from Japanese firms, in particular Sharp Electronics.[27] Therefore, assessing but not obsessing over competitors, will be valuable when analysing iterative processes in the Fitzpatrick framework of Technology, Market, and Implementation.

For example, a competitor may provide excellent power efficiency and performance in its components, but present weaknesses in the sustainabil-

[26] Moon (2018), at 26.

[27] Moon, H-C. (2016) *The Strategy for Korea's Economic Success*, Oxford University Press, at 55.

ity of both the materials used or production processes or both. Knowing the weaknesses of a comparable competitor device must rationally form part of strategic implementation.

4.5 Evidence

CEOs often miss opportunities to involve legal counsel early in specific technology initiatives, market analysis, and implementation activities. General counsels (GCs) with experience advising boards are value-added strategic contributors, because they are professionally trained to be evidence-led. CEO awareness and implementation of legal strategy is supported by the relevance and weight of evidence.

The application of law can be a source of competitive advantage on diverse, subtle levels. Contract law, export regulations, innovation protection, joint venture structures, and tax decisions all have significant consequences. Further, less obvious points of strategic value include the benefits of individually negotiated contracts.[28]

To counter some of the prejudices and stereotypes of lawyers as the department that says no, CEOs would gain immediate strategic value by making one assumption and posing one question. First, assume your GC believes your strategy is a clever idea. Second, ask what evidence can the legal function provide to support its opinion? After this short conversation, the GC now represents the CEO. Of course, all oral arguments need to be supported with evidence.

The proposed Figure 4.1 strategic framework incorporates an Evidence dial, as a visual reminder to manage evidence and assess proof. Potential benefits include the following:

- challenging how each key decision is compatible with Fitzgerald's strategic framework based on Technology, Market, and Implementation;
- justifying why a key decision is going to be made. In this sense, justification includes reference to independent proof;

[28] Bird, R. (2011) 'Law, Strategy, and Competitive Advantage' *SSRN Electronic Journal*, at 7.

- reducing the chance a decision that seems initially the right path for the firm, but after assessing evidence is judged unsuitable is carried through regardless;
- proving that human resources decisions, costs, complexity, and time-frames are based on evidence;
- engaging all board members by highlighting evidence countering potential ego or politically motivated decision making;
- expanding the limits of boardroom-bounded rationality because leaders can cultivate the bad habit of choosing not to factor in evidentially-supported independent advice.

Of all the above benefits the chance to expand bounded rationality with independent evidence is extremely valuable. As the brilliant Harvard cognitive scientist, Steve Pinker, put it 'none of us, thinking alone, is rational enough to consistently come to sound conclusions: rationality emerges from a community of reasoners who spot each other's fallacies'.[29] The alternative is to risk replicating the fatal group-think paths already travelled by BlackBerry, Fairchild, IBM, Motorola, Nokia, and Texas Instruments.

To illustrate with a specific example, only a few years ago boards within many listed firms took the view that, subject to compliance with lawfulness, maximising profits for shareholders presents no obligation for other stakeholders. Yet climate change and general sustainability issues, especially the use of plastic, are currently influencing decision making in semiconductor firms.

Under English law, there is a statutory duty to 'promote the success of the company for the benefit of its members' and have 'regard to', among other factors, employees, business relationships with suppliers, the long-term consequences of decisions, and the environmental impact of the firm's business operations.[30] Evidencing how a board makes decisions that have regard to other stakeholders is becoming increasingly important. The English High Court has already dealt with a derivative application

---

[29] Pinker, S. (2021) *Rationality: What It Is, Why It Seems Scarce, Why It Matters*, Penguin, at 16.

[30] Section 172 Companies Act 2006, see www.legislation.gov.uk/ukpga/2006/46/section/172.

brought by ClientEarth,[31] a non-profit environmental law organisation and UK charity.

As an owner of 27 shares in Shell, ClientEarth was qualified to make a derivative claim against Shell and its directors.[32] In the High Court, ClientEarth argued, among other things, because Shell's strategy set out in the firm's annual report focused on hydrocarbons, its directors failed to act in good faith in ways that would most likely promote the long-term success of the company for the benefit of its members as a whole.[33]

On this occasion, ClientEarth's application was unsuccessful. The High Court concluded it was satisfied that a person acting in accordance with section 172 of the Companies Act 2006 would not seek to continue the claim. Notably the lack of specific expert evidence from ClientEarth significantly influenced the judge in reaching his decision. ClientEarth failed to provide scientific and quantitative expertise from climate change experts, instead relying on an environmental policy expert.

No semiconductor firm's emission will remotely compare with those of any oil or gas multinational. However, given the complexity of supply chains and Scope 3 absolute emissions from end of use electronic components, there is a need for evidence to be available in the event of any legal claims or media assertions that may pose reputational risks. Both are tasks that sit in a GC's areas of competence. Further, a legal counsel is the appropriate supporting professional to assess proposed scientific and quantitative expert evidence from suitably qualified experts that the British judiciary are likely to place the most applicability and weight on.

The bottom right-hand dial of Figure 4.1 represents the vital need to test and welcome dissent that is supported by authoritative, reliable information. Every CEO, and board member, can factor in evidence. Each CEO

[31] Under English law, a derivative claim first requires a preliminary High Court hearing before a substantive hearing. The applicant has an obligation to establish a prima facie case. The evidential burden to do so rests with the applicant. For more detail on shareholder rights see Hollington, R. (2022) *Hollington on Shareholder Rights*, 9th edn, London: Sweet & Maxwell, at paras 6-03 and 6-14.

[32] *ClientEarth v Shell Plc & Ors (Re Prima Facie Case)* [2023] EWHC 1137 (Ch).

[33] Section 172 Companies Act 2006 is a subjective test. See *Regentcrest Plc v Cohen* [2001] 2 BCLC 80, per Jonathan Parker J at [120].

can simultaneously improve their succinct presentations by developing what has been termed 'legal astuteness'. To manage lawyers, especially the GC, as strategic partners in decision making.[34]

4.6 Concluding remarks

For semiconductor firms, Figure 4.1 is a practical combination of three strategic frameworks for continuous use. Crucially, the interaction between iterative real innovation revolving around the elements of Technology, Market, and Implementation. Second, value-based strategy based on adjusting for WTP and WTS. Third, monitoring for strategic risks by blending Eastern and Western approaches. Finally, it is rational that all important strategic decisions are supported by evidence to reduce the occurrence of group-think, and board-level decisions that amount to vague goals, and evasive compromises that signal an unwillingness to change plans.

[34] Bird (2011) at 7.

5. Strategic issues

Practical strategic advantages depend on each firm's unique technical innovation, target customers, and growth plans. However, whether thinking about compound, photonics, or silicon solutions, there are patterns in common. Concentric circles of decision making radiating out from a primary location to potentially across the world. The most pressing strategic issues include critical material supplies, geographic risks such as earthquakes, geopolitical uncertainties, human talent pools, legal risks on innovation protection, legal risks in contract decisions, types of subsidies, sustainability, and taxation.

5.1 Introduction

It would be a mistake to think this chapter is United Kingdom (UK)-centric. My analysis covers diverse cities in which I have first-hand, ground truth experience. The due diligence includes American, Austrian, Belgian, British, Canadian, Chinese, Czech, Dutch, Finnish, French, German, Irish, Italian, Japanese, Korean, Norwegian, and Swedish cities. An assessment of the opportunities and risks. Further, I have been able to access relevant foreign direct investment (FDI) and semiconductor-focused government policy documents in each country to assess if cooperation or independent expansion is viable.[1]

5.2 Strategic tasks that deserve time investment

Box 5.1 lists some of the key areas for CEO decision making, factoring in that many or some of these activities can be delegated to a Chief Strategy

1 Of course, the detailed issues of applying for export licences is a moving object and something that always requires consultation with trusted legal advisers to determine special or unique circumstances.

Officer (CSO) or equivalent strategy director. In the context of semiconductors, mergers and acquisitions activity requires in-depth understanding of the global supply chain, geopolitical dynamics across the relevant product or service chain, and state aid regulation. Further, general counsels (GCs) are well placed to contribute to all these areas. To not involve legal counsel early to input their evidence-based analysis and independent contributions is a lost commercial opportunity or potentially negligent behaviour or both.

Box 5.1 Strategic tasks

Competitive analysis
Divestitures
Geopolitical knowhow
Innovation protection knowhow and intellectual property law
Investor relations and communication with other stakeholders
Market research
Mergers and acquisitions
State aid and foreign subsidies regulation
Strategic alliances
Strategic initiatives
Strategic tax scenario analysis
Supply chain knowhow
Sustainability knowhow and regulation
Technology knowhow beyond the firm's current specialism

Source: © Iain Sheridan (2025)

5.3 Clusters

Long-term government investment is most effectively targeted at an existing semiconductor cluster. The concept of an industrial cluster has been analysed as a strategic advantage for more than 130 years.[2] An established definition is 'a geographical proximate group of interconnected compa-

[2] Marshall, A. (1890) *Principles of Economics*, Macmillan.

nies and associated institutions in a particular field, linked by commonalities and complementarities'.[3]

Based on Porter's well-respected analysis, clusters increase firm competitiveness in three main ways. First, by increasing the productivity of firms within a geographic area. Second, by driving the direction and pace of innovation. Third, by encouraging the development of new firms.[4] In short, clusters are catalysts for increasing productivity, innovation, and new market participants.

In the twenty-first century, the advanced nature of the commercial Internet, cloud computing, and global supply chains, enables a cluster to form across several domestic cities in one region. Chapter 3 provided an overview of the clusters found across the UK. The most established being the South Wales cluster of Cardiff, Newport, and Swansea, that has been strengthened in recent years by CS Connected.[5] The marketing strategy implemented by CS Connected revolves around branding the South Wales cluster, with the support of all the key regional stakeholders.[6] Under the leadership of Chris Meadows, CS Connected has established worldwide recognition for the South Wales cluster.[7]

Figure 5.1 highlights how UK policy makers need to factor in distinct cluster strategies that may be relevant to growing one innovation cluster.[8]

---

3 Porter, M. (1998) *On Competition*, Harvard Business School Press, at 199.

4 Porter, M. (1998) 'Clusters and the New Economics of Competition', *Harvard Business Review*, 76(6), 77–90.

5 CS Connected (2024), *Annual Report: Compound Semiconductor Cluster in South Wales*, at 6. Also see https://csconnected.com/about/who-we-are/.

6 The consortium consists of Cardiff University (lead), Swansea University, IQE, SPTS, Vishay Intertechnology (previously Newport Wafer Fab), Microchip, Microlink Devices, the Compound Semiconductor Centre, the Compound Semiconductor Applications Catapult, the Cardiff Capital Region (CCR) City Deal and the Welsh Government.

7 Based on my meetings in Cardiff, Newport and Swansea, Chris Meadows is credited with playing a pivotal role. Other clusters would be shrewd to seek his counsel as a consultant or non-executive director (NED).

8 Organization for Economic Cooperation and Development (OECD) (2022) 'An Industrial Policy Framework for OECD Countries – Old Debates, New Perspectives', OECD Science, Technology, and Industry Policy Papers, No.127, at 25.

A firm may label their strategy as one type, but in fact their strategic choices are borrowing from several types of strategies. Policy-maker funding needs to factor in that a successful semiconductor sectoral strategy may not have a place-based approach in the sense of it being anchored to just one location. In turn, Chief Executive Officers (CEOs) need to determine which projects can be supported within each area.

To illustrate, a semiconductor innovation cluster serving the UK automotive sector may maximise its success by adopting a place-based strategy. For compound semiconductor firms serving automotive sector customers, being close to clients in more than one location is a wise long-term decision. In this context, in the future, compound semiconductors developed in South Wales may have the greatest growth potential by committing additional manufacturing activity in Northeast England. Policy makers could direct funding to the Northeast to support this strategy. In short, the UK's innovation cluster strategy needs to balance place-based geographical depth with proximity to sectoral clients.

Interestingly, the UK Government has already established funding provisions for many sectors with the aim of supporting small- and medium-sized enterprise (SME) clusters. Called a Launchpad, each cluster benefits from various forms of support such as funding for research and development (R&D), opportunities for networking and facilitating collaboration.[9] For example, South Wales has been designated a net-zero cluster, offering funding for, among other projects, floating wind technologies, green hydrogen, and modular solar power.[10] One or more of these projects could intersect with the long-established semiconductor cluster in South Wales.

[9] See https://iuk.ktn-uk.org/programme/launchpads/.

[10] It is notable that one of the leaders at Swansea University's Centre for Integrative Semiconductor Materials, Professor Paul Meredith OBE, is a world authority on solar power. He is the recipient of multiple sustainable energy innovation awards by the Queensland Government. It would be wrong to presume that world-class solar expertise is monopolised in sunnier climates.

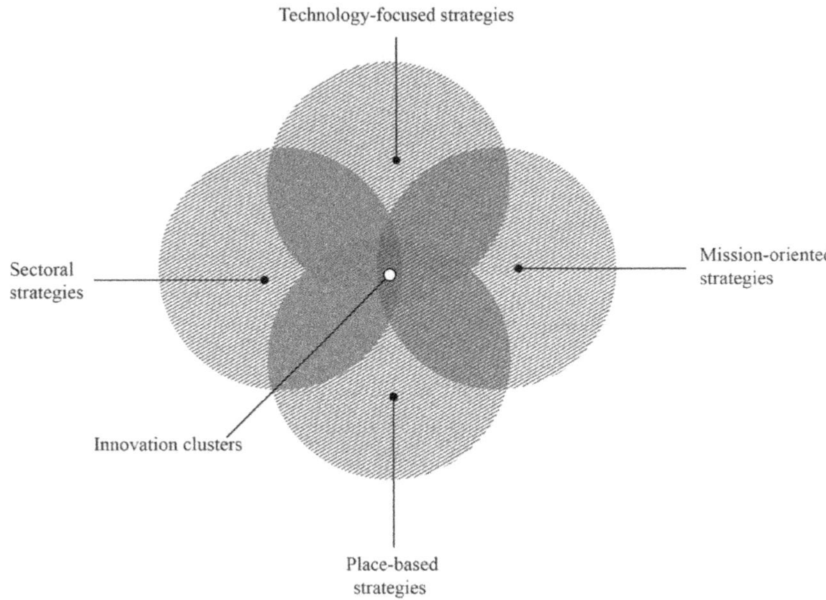

Source: OECD (2022) 'An Industrial Policy Framework for OECD Countries – Old Debates, New Perspectives', OECD Science, Technology, and Industry Policy Papers, No.127, at 25

Figure 5.1 Aspects of innovation clusters

5.4 Regional partnership towns

A potentially effective semiconductor strategy for implementation at a regional level is that of partnership towns. By which is meant two or more cities or large towns committed to collaborating, cost sharing, cost information sharing, risk information sharing, supply chain opportunities, and coordinated international expansion. Notably, the flight time between each partner node location does not exceed four hours. Distribution of equipment and goods between each node location does not exceed 72 hours travel by land or sea or both.[11]

Figure 5.2 illustrates, with the example of Leuven and Swansea. Between each town there could be regular bilateral communication about hiring, manufacturing, R&D, and a host of other activities. They are a form of town twinning or 'Partnerstadt' focused on the business of semiconductor growth. Within each twinned city and surrounding county, there are two areas to strategically concentrate, with the benefits of ongoing understanding of costs, logistics, talent pools, and other variables.

Equally, a regional partnership between Swansea and Einhoven could be a personal identification number (PIN) code for growth. The Netherlands is often overlooked. An entrepreneurial and innovative culture that has produced ASML, NXP, and many other brilliant firms. Readers that can relate to that thought of overlooking Dutch towns are invited to reflect on TSMC's birth. The Taiwanese Government provided 48 per cent of the capital for Chang's TSMC manufacturing start-up. Texas Instruments decided not to invest, despite having the full measure of Chang's abilities.

---

[11] I am grateful for meeting Martin McHugh, CEO of Catapult Compound Semiconductor. He pointed out to me that the national challenge is to create clusters across UK regions. My concept of regional partnership towns was originally conceived as most relevant across borders, for example between Ireland and the UK. But regional efficiencies and opportunities equally happen within borders as well. McKinsey has often included clusters in emerging market analysis, so their work may support future analysis on strategic cluster planning that seeks to maximise growth. Whilst attempting to build a China legal practice in Beijing and Northeast China (2009–12), I benefited tremendously from McKinsey's cluster analysis of Chinese cities. Tunde Olanrewaju, their current managing partner for the UK, Ireland, and Israel, holds an MEng in electrical and electronic engineering from Imperial College.

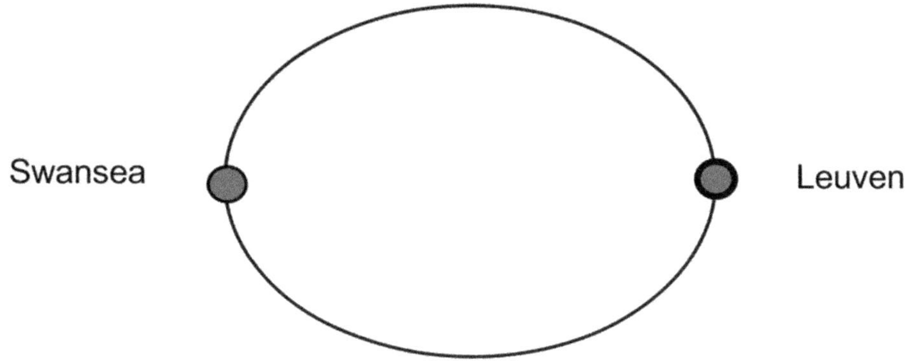

Source: © Iain Sheridan (2025)

Figure 5.2 *Regional partnership towns*

The Dutch firm Philips took a 27.5 per cent share.[12] Looking back from the second quarter of the twenty-first century any rational thinker would conclude that the Dutch are visionary businesspeople.

As pointed out in my introduction, this chapter is not UK-centric. These are not just UK-only or European Union (EU)-only strategies. Table 5.1 sets out numerous examples of options for regional partnership towns in Asia, Europe, and North America. There are potentially scores of viable permutations. The partnership towns share valuable features and variables in common. They have high productivity factor, zero or low seismic activity, and each twinned city has access to high-quality electrical engineering or science graduates or both.

5.4.1 Swansea-Leuven regional partnership

Swansea University has recently completed a new £54 million Centre for Integrative Semiconductor Materials (CISM).[13] The main partners financing the facility are Swansea University, IQE, SPTS and Newport Wafer Fab. There are also an additional nine partners.

The CISM provides state of the art manufacturing grade, ISO-qualified clean rooms for process development, an epitaxial growth facility, backend materials integration, packaging capability, and SME incubation areas. In sum, CISM will play a pivotal role in bringing high-value jobs to South Wales.

As part of my South Wales research for this book, I had the opportunity to visit Swansea University on two occasions, including a tour of the CISM. Four eminent professors are dedicated to the CISM's growth, namely Owen Guy,[14] Mike Jennings, Paul Meredith, and David Ritchie. Their vast collective expertise includes the chemistry, electrical engineering,

---

12 TSMC (1998) 'Philips, TSMC and EDB Investments Team to Develop New Chip Production Facility', 29 September 1998, TSMC Archives, available at https://pr.tsmc.com/english/news/2115.

13 The CISM has produced an illuminating two-minute video introducing its facility, some of its key people, and areas of expertise. See www.swansea.ac.uk/science-and-engineering/research/semiconductors/.

14 Professor Guy kindly made time to give me a two-hour tour of the CISM facility. I am grateful for those insights.

Table 5.1 Asian, European and North American regional partnership towns

Region	Sphere boundaries	Capital raising	University spin-out centres
Western Europe	Swansea + Eindhoven	LSEG[1]	Swansea Centre for Integrative Semiconductor Materials (CISM), TU Eindhoven
Western Europe	Swansea + Leuven	LSEG	Swansea Centre for Integrative Semiconductor Materials (CISM), IMEC
Western Europe	Leuven + Newcastle	LSEG	IMEC, Newcastle University
Western Europe	Cardiff + Leixlip	LSEG	Cardiff ICS
Western Europe	Brighton + Grenoble	LSEG	Sussex University, CEA-Leti
Eastern Europe	Dresden + Wroclaw	Warsaw Stock Exchange[2]	Dresden University, Wroclaw University of Science and Technology
CEE	Dresden + Graz	Deutsche Boerse, Wiener Boerse	Dresden University, TU Graz
CEE	Brno + Graz	Wiener Boerse[3]	Brno University, TU Graz
West and Eastern Europe	Leuven + Dresden	Deutsche Boerse[4]	Dresden University, KU Leuven
Nordic Europe	Malmo + Oslo	Euronext (Oslo), NASDAQ Stockholm[5]	Swedish Chips Competence Center (SCCC)
Nordic Europe	Helsinki + Tallinn	NASDAQ Baltic, NASDAQ Helsinki	Finnish Chips Competence Center (FCCC)
North America	Detroit USA + London, Ontario, Canada	NASDAQ, Toronto Stock Exchange	Michigan University, Waterloo University

Region	Sphere boundaries	Capital raising	University spin-out centres
North America	Bethlehem USA + London, Ontario, Canada	NASDAQ, Toronto Stock Exchange	Lehigh Valley University, Waterloo University
East Asia	Daegu South Korea +Shenyang China	Seoul Stock Exchange, Shanghai Stock Exchange	Kyungpook National University
East Asia	Daegu South Korea + Fukuoka Japan	Seoul Stock Exchange, Tokyo Stock Exchange	Kyungpook National University, Kyushu University

Notes: [1] See www.londonstockexchange.com/ for public capital raising and hybrid capital raising. For venture capital and private equity see https://www.bvca.co.uk/. [2] See https://www.gpw.pl/en-home. [3] See https://www.wienerborse.at/. [4] See https://deutsche-boerse.com/dbg-en/. [5] See https://www.euronext.com/en/markets/oslo.
Source: © Iain Sheridan (2025)

and physics aspects of next generation electronics. In short, Swansea and the CISM can compete at the cutting-edge meeting current and future demand.

The CISM presents a unique opportunity to advance commercial semiconductor activity in the UK, and for its international customers. My research in South Korea included understanding from equivalent level professors of electrical engineering, that it is precisely the combination of chemistry, electrical engineering, and physics expertise that is required for next generation electronics.

A plan for the CISM to collaborate with IMEC merits consideration.[15] IMEC's start-up influence is impressive. Based on a biennial ranking by UBI Global, in the category World Top University Business Accelerator, out of 109 start-up programmes from 56 countries, IMEC ranked number

[15] IMEC's resources include a 300mm semiconductor cleanroom with a total area of 8000m2, and extreme ultraviolet (EUV) equipment. IMEC also owns numerous state-of-the-art laboratories, including ones dedicated to RF and high power, Silicon PV, Organic PV, gallium nitride (GaN) and Photonics.

one. This survey applies 50 parameters mainly classified around (a) impact on the ecosystem, (b) performance of the programme, and (c) performance of the portfolio start-ups.[16]

The entrepreneurial and innovation advantages of IMEC would benefit Swansea University and its local semiconductor start-ups, and any other future UK semiconductor centre of excellence. In 2024, IMEC established its first UK presence in Cambridge, so that is a positive addition to the Silicon Fen cluster.[17] However, unique compound semiconductor strengths also reside in the South Wales cluster, so the logical development of IMEC collaboration in the UK includes South Wales.[18] The CISM presents no threat to IMEC, given the latter organisation has grown over decades. IMEC would benefit from the range of experts based at the CISM. Additionally, the CISM's cutting-edge facilities would provide IMEC and its customers with unique technical innovation as well as market access.

5.4.2 Dresden-Leuven regional partnership

Currently, based on scale of manufacturing, potentially the most dynamic growth sphere is a combination of everything IMEC has achieved to date, combined with the current ambition of Dresden and the wider Saxony region. Firms deciding to build new or expanding existing operations in that region include Infineon, with a €5 billion fab, and Robert Bosch expanding its existing plant.

Adjacent to Bosch's fab, TSMC has committed to building its first European fab investing in a €10 billion chip facility, with co-investing from Infineon and NXP. Additionally, this manufacturing investment will, in the long term, benefit from the fact that Fraunhofer is increasing its R&D activities in the Dresden area focused on advanced chip pack-

16 See www.ubi-global.com/incubator-accelerator-rankings.

17 IMEC, Cambridge, UK (2024), https://www.imec-int.com/en/uk.

18 In an era of UK Government commitments to build new residential housing, we can imagine novel partnerships beyond established clusters. For instance, the twinning of an entirely new town in commuting distance of an established cluster. For example, a new town in Somerset that allows semiconductor workers to enjoy a career working in any semiconductor fab in the Southwest England and South Wales.

aging.[19] The German Government has also committed €5 billion in aid for the Dresden fab, which has already been approved by the European Parliament.[20]

5.4.3 UK regional partnership towns

Within the UK, as set out in Table 5.2, there are many possibilities for regional partnership towns based on all areas of expertise. A challenge for government funding is to factor in the tendency for some semiconductor research leaders to engage in what the Germans term '*der Narzissmus der kleinen Differenzen*' – the narcissism of small differences.

It is healthy that universities in every city, county, or region compete against each other. However, when that technical competition turns into non-cooperative behaviour or political feuding, that affects long-term growth across a whole cluster. Often the most effective government funding allocations may be based on collaborative university research and testing facilities.

In the past, a brilliant Stanford professor of electrical engineering rhetorically observed to me that in the UK semiconductor space there is a need to bang heads together. Surely, semiconductor leaders can work out the win-win scenarios for themselves. For a better future, perhaps the UK minister with responsibility for the semiconductor sector should annually meet the heads of electrical engineering university departments. Each professor should be asked which of the other present leaders have they not cooperated with and why? All stakeholders need to keep the bigger picture in mind.

All the above points provoke the following question. How can the advantages of a local cluster apply to two regional partnership towns? Inevitably the process of collaboration and the pace of efficiencies will be slower. However, consistent with frugal innovation strategies entrepreneurs and policy makers may be interested by the fact that regional partnership towns require minimal infrastructure investment. Each town is borrow-

---

[19] Ting-Fang, C. (2024) 'Can investment from TSMC, Infineon and others revive Europe's chip dreams?', *Nikkei Asia*, 3 May 2024.

[20] Ryugen, H. (2024) 'TSMC breaks ground on first Europe chip fab with eye on auto sector', *Nikkei Asia*, 21 August 2024.

Table 5.2 *UK regional partnership towns*

Sphere boundaries	Capital raising	University spin-out centres and research facilities	Competitive advantages
Bristol + Swansea[1]	LSE AIM or Main Market[2], local VC	Bath, Bristol, Cardiff ICS, Newport, Swansea CISM	Compound and MEMS
Glasgow + Edinburgh (Central belt of Scotland) + Southampton	LSE AIM or Main Market, local VC	Glasgow, Fraunhofer CAP, Strathclyde, Southampton	Photonics
Manchester + Newcastle	LSE AIM or Main Market, local VC	Durham, Manchester, UMIST, Newcastle	Compound and MEMS
Cambridge + London	LSE AIM or Main Market, local VC	Cambridge, Imperial	Design
Brighton + Exeter	LSE AIM or Main Market, local VC	Exeter, Surrey	Photonics/5G/6G

Notes: [1] The Bristol and South Wales cluster presents a potential super cluster, because Bristol is less than 50km away from Newport. The most significant advantage would be the collective talent pool. [2] The London Stock Exchange Group (LSEG) provides a useful online capital raising evaluation tool, available at www.londonstockexchange.com/raise-finance/equity/assess-your-funding-options. For venture capital and private equity see https://www.bvca.co.uk/.
Source: © Iain Sheridan (2025)

ing from, sharing with or supporting the other on a commercial equitable basis.[21]

[21] This is not to ignore that each firm or institute is competing with the other as well. For example, the poaching of semiconductor talent, something that can sour cooperative relations, could be managed by allowing employees of one place to be contracted out 'on loan' to the other.

The following aspects may assist, in a marginal way, to maximise the dynamics of regional partnership growth:

- Twinning of towns based on formal mayor level ceremonies with nationally supported media coverage.
- Local government councillors from each twinned town appointed as liaison officers.
- Taxation schemes of equivalent net pay for semiconductor workers moving between semiconductor firms based in the twinned towns.[22]
- Local government R&D funding concentrated on semiconductor activity in each twinned town.
- Subsidised housing rents in both twinned towns for semiconductor workers.
- Branding, for example a science, technology, engineering and maths (STEM)-inspired coat of arms or logo to reinforce the sense of commitment between the twinned towns.
- University faculty rotations between the twinned towns.

5.5 Subsidies

The World Trade Organization (WTO) has implemented the WTO Agreement on Subsidies and Countervailing Measures (Subsidies Agreement). Under the Subsidies Agreement, a subsidy is defined to include: (i) a government transfer of grants, loans, as well as loan guarantees; (ii) fiscal incentives such as tax credits; (iii) government provision of goods or services or purchases goods[23]; (iv) a government making payments to a funding mechanism, or entrusting or directing a private body to carry out one or more of the type of functions illustrated in (i) to (iii).[24] The WTO definition is broad, but clear. The challenge is to accurately know the quantity of subsidies, especially when WTO signatories provide incomplete information.

[22] At first glance, this may seem an unconventional proposal, but the concept of net-pay equalisation is an established system within the United Nations for permanent employees moving from one station to another.

[23] As an exception, infrastructure is not classified as a subsidy.

[24] Article 1.1(a)1. See https://www.wto.org/english/docs_e/legal_e/24-scm.pdf.

5.5.1 Industrial policy approaches in the EU

The proximity of the UK to other European countries makes EU subsidies in the semiconductor sector important in the context of (a) congruence with the EU to increase trade, and (b) congruence with EU policies as industrial policies develop globally. By which is meant any UK policy on semiconductor subsidies should rationally seek to match proportionate, rational subsidies made by key trading partners.[25]

The UK has created an additional challenge of having to establish how its industrial policies can efficiently interweave with the EU. Positively, the UK's ongoing desire to cooperate with the EU can make UK clusters part of some EU-resourced emerging growth.

The EU Chips Act offers similar opportunities to the US CHIPS Act. Only entities established in the European Economic Area (EEA) are eligible for funds. The EU is contributing €4.175 billion from the Horizon Europe and Digital Europe programmes. The European Commission states that the EU Chips Act 'is to be supported with an estimated overall level of policy-driven investment in excess of €43 billion up to 2030'.[26] Promisingly, because the UK is now back in the Horizon Europe Programme, that is one route to collaborate in EU semiconductor research albeit on a self-funded basis.

A significant point of difference exists between the US CHIPS Act and the EU Chips Act in that the EU law seeks to promote sustainability. Additionally, the EU has broader industrial policy commitments to a green transition over the period 2021–26 that dovetail with its intention to support energy-efficient semiconductor policies. From a commercial strategic viewpoint the EU green agenda is starting to be implemented. For instance, at the end of 2024 in Silicon Valley, I had an opportunity to

---

[25] A group of lawyers have provided subsidy rules that seek to manage not only trade imbalances but also sustainability issues. Entitled the Villars Framework, this detailed plan represents a promising collection of future solutions to achieve global consensus on subsidies. From a current practical viewpoint, its contents include many action points that could valuably enhance UK policy makers negotiating with trade blocs on sustainability aspects. See Villars Framework for a Sustainable Global Trade System (2024) Version 2.0, January 2024, available at https://remakingtradeproject.org/villars-framework.

[26] European Commission (2022) A Chips Act for Europe, SWD 147 final, at 96.

speak with and hear a presentation from Jean-Marc Chery, the President and CEO of STMicroelectronics. It was clear that his firm is making sustainability a strategic priority.

In terms of existing examples of EU state aid, in April 2023 the European Commission approved a French Government subsidy supporting STMicroelectronics and GlobalFoundries to build a new semiconductor manufacturing facility in Crolles, France. The French subsidy will take the form of direct grants to both firms to support their investments in a project estimated to have a total value of €7.4 billion. Scheduled to be fully operational in 2027, the project focuses on the manufacturing of FD-SOI technology.[27] The factory will produce semiconductors for European markets in the automotive, 5G/6G, defence, security, and space sectors. The facility is projected to produce 620,000 wafers of 300mm diameter per annum.[28]

A search of the EC State Aid Transparency Public Search indicates a range of similar level investments being made in other EU member state provinces and states.[29] For example, just six months before the STMicroelectronics and GlobalFoundries facility decision in France, the EC approved state aid provision of €292.5 million, through the EU Recovery and Resilience Facility (RRF), to support STMicroelectronics building a silicon carbide (SiC) wafer plant in Catania, Sicily.[30]

The future STMicroelectronics and GlobalFoundries facility in Crolles, and the STMicroelectronics facility in Catania both indicate a renewed appetite within the EU for industrial policy. The EU's support for the

[27] Fully Depleted Silicon On Insulator (FD-SOI) technology has the technological advantage of significantly reduced power consumption.

[28] European Commission (2023) 'State aid: Commission Approves French measure to support STMicroeconomics and GlobalFoundries to set up a new microchips plant', Press Release, 28 April 2023.

[29] The EC's State Aid Transparency Public Search database is available at https://webgate.ec.europa.eu/competition/transparency/public?lang=en.

[30] European Commission (2022) 'State aid: Commission approves €292.5 million Italian measure under Recovery and Resilience Facility to support STMicroelectronics in construction of a plant in the semiconductor value chain', Press Release, 5 October 2022, available at https://ec.europa.eu/commission/presscorner/detail/en/ip_22_5970.

new French STMicroelectronics and GlobalFoundries facility has broader significance for all global semiconductor firms because EU law has not traditionally supported state aid. There will be more opportunities or joint ventures and individual entity fabs. We can imagine that, at the right time, there will be an emerging demand for new plants across Europe. Likely locations will include Dresden, Leixlip, and Leuven.

It is significant that the EU has already committed to semiconductor subsidy information sharing with Japan and the US. A coordinated effort by Brussels, Tokyo, and Washington to exchange information on the criteria for subsidies, the amount of grants, the logic behind specific grants, as well as projected supply and demand from the incentives.[31]

The international subsidies dedicated to the semiconductor sector are evolving rapidly because of multiple factors. These include geopolitics affecting supply chains, and realisation that the UK semiconductor sector has collectively underachieved despite several champion firms. There has also been competitive stimulation from (a) EU industrial policy (b) US industrial policy, and (c) East Asian industrial policies. Included in the third category are Japan, South Korea, and Taiwan. It is not meaningful to analyse the UK's subsidy offerings and plans without acknowledging recent subsidy activity exists in many other jurisdictions. Table 5.3 captures just a selection.

An essential element of the STMicroelectronics and GlobalFoundries initiative in France is the aim of broadening and deepening the EU semiconductor sector by increasing the R&D activities of some SMEs and third parties. To allow these other firms to evaluate and develop their products in a real industrial production environment.

The UK subsidies available in 2024 are modest.[32] Yet there is a strong collective will across the UK semiconductor community to expand the

[31] Nagao, R. (2023) 'Japan and EU to share chip subsidy information to disperse production – Three-way exchange with U.S. aims for better supply chain distribution', *Nikkei Asia*, 15 July 2023.

[32] Note that under the Northern Ireland Protocol, EU law covering EU state aid rules continues to apply in Northern Ireland. Government policies that seek to support Northern Ireland semiconductor firms, for example to grow a cluster, would need to seek advice on both the UK and EU law implications.

Table 5.3 Subsidies confirmed in 2024

Location	Planned expansion	High tech jobs created	National domestic government contribution in GBP £
Agrate Brianza and Catania, Italy	A loan to finance research and development (R&D) and new innovative production lines.[1]	N/A	£504 million
Chitose, Hokkaido, Japan	Rapidus consortia, in collaboration with IBM, plans to build a plant to make 2nm node technology.[2]	>1,000	£1.73 billion
Magdeburg, Saxony-Anhalt, Germany	Planned Intel plant	3,000	£8.32 billion
Crolles, Crolles, Isère department, France	Joint construction and operation by Switzerland incorporated STMicroelectronics (ST) and US incorporated GlobalFoundries (GF) of a new microchips manufacturing plant. The highest aim is to develop FD-SOI technology.[3]	1,000	£6.22 billion

Notes: [1] Italian Finance Ministry (2022) 'Italy and France: EIB supports strengthening of Europe's semiconductor industry with €600 million loan to STMicroelectronics', 3 March 2022, available at www.mef.gov.it/en/ufficio-stampa/comunicati/2022/Italy-and-France-EIB-supports-strengthening-of-Europes-semiconductor-industry-with-600-million-loan-to-STMicroelectronics-00001/. [2] Johnston, E. (2023) 'Rapidus breaks ground on key Hokkaido chip factory', *Japan Times*,1 September 2023. [3] Re STMicroelectronics, France and Italy are the largest shareholders, each owning a 13.75 per cent.
Source: © Iain Sheridan (2025)

sector. One possibility is for the UK Government to learn from Japan. The Japanese Government has agreed to subsidise up to one-third of the capital costs of any domestic or foreign manufacturing of specified types of semiconductor devices. Additional conditions include a minimum ten-year production commitment and a requirement to prioritise Japanese supplies in the event of any global shortage.[33]

To date, the most ambitious Japanese Government initiative is Rapidus. See the entry in Table 5.3. This start-up semiconductor firm has been established by eight multinationals, namely Denso, Kioxia, MUFG Bank, NEC, NTT, SoftBank, Sony and Toyota. The three core policies of Rapidus are:

(a) creating new industries together with customers;
(b) developing world leading reduced cycle time for design, wafer processing and 3D packaging;
(c) collaborating with globally best in class design teams, equipment manufacturers, and material manufacturers.[34]

The initial primary aim of Rapidus is to collaborate with IBM designers to manufacture at the 2nm level or less.[35] The ambition of the Japanese Government with its Rapidus start-up is unprecedented. Rapidus has already joined a consortium with IBM and IMEC, with the goal of taking IBM's 2nm chip design and manufacturing it by 2030. The question being asked is, is it too ambitious? One team of analysts from a Washington DC think tank, the Center for Strategic and International Studies, observed:

> The Rapidus-IBM-IMEC collaboration is arguably one of the most ambitious in the history of the global semiconductor industry. As noted, Japan is currently 10 years behind world leaders TSMC and Samsung in chip manufacturing technology, operating at the 40 nm node. The consortium proposes to leapfrog multiple intervening nodes in two to three years, to begin production at 2 nm. This would constitute an unparalleled technological feat. Skipping even one node places major demands on a company…[36]

A more modestly ambitious lower-subsidised UK version of Rapidus could realistically expect SoftBank to provide not only funding but insights on how to improve on Rapidus decision making. If MUFG Bank

---

[33] CSIS (2023) *Japan Seeks to Revitalize Its Semiconductor Industry*, Report, 25 August 2023.

[34] www.rapidus.inc.

[35] IBM's technology is based on Gate-all-round (GAA) transistors or nanosheet Field-effect transistors (FETs). A type of 3D transistor.

[36] CSIS (2023) *Japan Seeks to Revitalize Its Semiconductor Industry*, Report, 25 August 2023, at 4.

has committed to the opportunity, perhaps there is also an equivalent for Barclays or HSBC. If NTT has seen the vision, perhaps Vodafone also does if such an opportunity arises. If Toyota in Japan wants to invest in such a venture, perhaps Nissan in Sunderland does as well. Given IBM's history and success in the UK, scaled imitation, a UK-IBM-IMEC collaboration could be effective with obvious global efficiencies to link with Rapidus-IBM-IMEC.

No doubt the Rapidus decision to invest in Hokkaido is partly cost driven. However, it is still uncertain that this project can, from 2027, manufacture at a competitive unit level. Additionally, Hokkaido does not to date have a supply of the prerequisite talent and it has a limited ecosystem of suppliers.[37]

Turning back to the UK, there may also be regional governmental funding for which to apply. For example, funding that forms part of devolution packages for Northeast England or South Wales. Whatever the mix of subsidy support, the probability of success must be raised by the involvement of established multinationals that invest in R&D for the long term.

5.5.2 Industrial policy approaches in the US

Brought into force in August 2022, the US CHIPS and Science Act (the CHIPS Act) provides $52.7 billion for semiconductor research, development, manufacturing, and workforce development. This total sum is divided into $39 billion allocated for manufacturing incentives, including $2 billion for the legacy components used in automobiles and defence systems. Additionally, $13.2 billion is set aside for R&D and workforce development. There is also $500 million allocated for international information communications technology security and semiconductor supply chain activities.

The CHIPS Act provides a 25 per cent investment tax credit for capital expenses for manufacturing of semiconductors and supporting equipment.[38] For further thoughts on taxation see Chapter 11.

---

[37] *Financial Times* (2024) 'Japan's audacious bid to become a semiconductor superpower', 4 December 2024.

[38] US Government CHIPS Act 2022, available at www.congress.gov/117/plaws/publ167/PLAW-117publ167.pdf.

My own on the ground research into the potential impact of the CHIPS Act, included visiting Detroit, Michigan and Professor of Electrical Engineering, Alex Yasha Yi of Michigan University. My meeting with Yi underlined to me that there is a realistic opportunity for Michigan State to grow its semiconductor sector.[39] Firms such as Calumet Electronics, KLA, and SK Siltron CSS are creating hundreds of new jobs in Michigan. IMEC has also signed a memorandum of understanding (MOU) with Michigan University, which infers international cooperation is part of its strategy.[40]

My enduring impression of Michigan is its collective self-belief and rational choice to become a globally competitive sweet spot in the electric vehicle (EV) semiconductor market. A $10 million investment in Michigan Semiconductor Talent and Technology for Automotive Research (MSTAR), a public-private project, aims to support Michigan to become the world's leader in automotive semiconductor technology. Opportunities exist in the UK to create similar automotive-focused initiatives.[41]

For UK policy makers, and all other governments analysing the potential importance of the CHIPS Act, an often-raised point is that it is a substantial amount of financial industrial policy intervention. In my view, the irony is that it takes competition with China to restimulate US dedication to semiconductors, when, even if international relations between these superpowers was amicable, it is rational to invest heavily in domestic semiconductor industry.

A second thought provoking geopolitical risk aspect linked to the CHIPS Act has been raised by Chris Miller, author of *Chip Wars*.[42] In a *Financial*

[39] My meeting with Alex Yasha Yi took place in Detroit, 8 June 2023.

[40] Michigan Economic Development Corporation (2024) 'Gov. Whitmer Announces $10 Million Investment to Help Michigan Lead Future of Semiconductor Manufacturing and Talent', Press Release, 6 June 2024, available at www.michiganbusiness.org/press-releases/2024/06/mstar/. Members of MSTAR include semiconductor firm KLA, Belgium-based IMEC, Michigan University, Washtenaw Community College, and General Motors.

[41] Ibid.

[42] Miller, C. (2022) *Chip Wars – The Fight for the World's Most Critical Technology*, Simon & Schuster.

Times podcast entitled 'Who is winning the chip wars?' Miller was asked about the financial scale of the CHIPS Act subsidies. He observed that any future disruption in the Taiwan Straits would result in trillion dollar losses to world manufacturing. The right mindset was to view the CHIPS Act as an insurance policy rather than an industrial policy. In this context, the scale of CHIPS Act investment, rather than looking too large, may potentially be too small relative to the size of a disruption to Taiwanese manufacturing and supply chains.[43]

5.5.3 Industrial policy approaches in South Korea

South Korea has organised their semiconductor sector based around clusters of firms. Semiconductor firms are concentrated in Gyeonggi-do province, with some in the neighbouring provinces of Chungcheongbuk and Chungcheongnam. In coordination with the South Korean Government, Samsung and SK Hynix plan to create what has been termed a 'mega cluster' surrounding the capital, in Gyeonggi-do province. The final production area may extend to 21 million square meters, approximately the size of 30,000 football pitches.[44] The ambition is to join several clusters together and move from its dynamic random access memory (DRAM) dominance to become an all-round semiconductor powerhouse.

5.5.4 Potential industrial policy approaches in the UK

There are three questions that require answers to maximise semiconductor activity in the UK. First, how can UK regulation facilitate start-ups to continue to grow in the UK under British ownership? Second, how can UK regulation support established British firms to conduct high-value manufacturing in the UK? Third, how can UK regulation encourage closer human relations between academic, entrepreneur, investor, and policy maker units in the semiconductor sector?

More broadly, UK semiconductor activity has expanded less than expected based on the experience and talent rooted in Cambridge, Scotland, Wales,

---

43 (2024) 'Who is winning the chip wars?' *Financial Times* podcast, 25 August 2024.

44 KOTRA (2024) 'Semiconductor Clusters Led by Samsung Electronics and SK Hynix', available at www.investkorea.org/ik-en/cntnts/i-312/web.do?clickArea=enmain00023.

and elsewhere across the UK. Notably, a UK Select Committee highlighted three areas to effect significant growth improvement:

- more government-led incentives to encourage later stage funding for mature semiconductor firms;
- facilitating greater efforts to build closer relationships between venture capital investors, and universities to increase the effectiveness and quantity of spin-out firms;
- increased government funding in collaboration with private funding, dedicated to the construction of new facilities.[45]

If the UK Government decides to offer subsidies, it should do so without affecting the frugal innovation policies of firms.[46] Frugal innovation in the context of semiconductors is especially important for R&D expenditure. The observation is that the quality of innovation needs to be rewarded not the quantity of innovation. By which is meant limited subsidies are provided in terms of money, but in the broader context that too much funding may be counterproductive.[47]

However, given the costs of rent and land purchases, policies concerning land use should be generous and multifarious in nature. For example, large areas of land could be provided free for the building of factories in cluster areas in or around regional partnership towns. Long commercial leases based on heavily subsidised rent could be offered to start-ups. Local governments could waive property and general local council taxes. For individual semiconductor talent, house deposits and mortgage support could be provided based on a seven-year commitment to a semiconductor cluster area.

In my view, what matters is that funding is diversified to maximise its impact. That is a complex process given the range of firms that cover silicon, compound, and photonics-based products. Further, ARM's success in Cambridge means the UK has a deep design talent pool in that

---

45 Business, Energy and Industrial Strategy Committee (2022), *The Semiconductor Industry in the UK*, Fifth Report of Session 2022–23, HC 291 (2022), at 33.

46 Radjou, N. and J. Prabhu (2015) 'Frugal Innovation – How to Do More With Less', *The Economist* and Profile Books, at 23.

47 See Zhang, W. (2024) *Re-Understanding Entrepreneurship – What It Is and Why is Matters*, Cambridge University Press, at 222–4.

cluster, so fabless design clusters elsewhere in the UK are logical beneficiaries of funding.

But what do technical veterans in the sector think? An influential trade association with expert insights to guide UK strategy is TechWorks. Originally formed as the National Microelectronics Institute in 1996, its membership consists of UK-based semiconductor manufacturing, design and systems companies. The current CEO is Charles Sturman; other board members include entrepreneurs Hermann Hauser, Stan Boland, and Luke Ibbetson of Vodafone Group Strategy.[48] TechWorks coordinates 300 member firms across four communities.[49] Through grassroots collaboration, thought leadership, and government advocacy,[50] it aims to maintain the UK as an important location to start, build and scale deep tech firms.[51]

In late 2024, I met Charles Sturman. He observed that a good use of government funding would be an innovation and pilot facility enabling future materials and process development and supporting early-stage companies with prototyping and low-volume piloting. There are several options here outside of advanced complementary metal-oxide-semiconductors (CMOS), such as silicon photonics, microelectromechanical systems (MEMS), and 3D interconnect (interposers), as well as compound semiconductor and 3D packaging.

Sturman estimated that a modest pilot fab around the 28nm level could be built for less than £500 million. While there are new materials that provide immense promise, there are also many future innovation opportunities based on silicon and the UK has little capability in this area today. A facility providing access to domestic manufacturing, but also providing

[48] See www.techworks.org.uk.

[49] The four communities are DESN (Semiconductor and Embedded Systems Design), NMI (Semiconductor Manufacturing and Supply Chain), AESIN (Automotive Electronic Systems Innovation) and IoTSF (IoT Cybersecurity).

[50] www.techworks.org.uk/semiconductor-leadership-group.

[51] Deep Tech is defined as 'an area of business or research that involves using advanced science and technology, such as artificial intelligence, blockchain, or advances in biotechnology, to provide solutions to complicated problems'. Source: https://dictionary.cambridge.org/dictionary/english/deep-tech.

an environment for new firms to advance innovation on a smaller scale could unlock these.

5.6 Software opportunities

Further, there is a strong British software development sector that could play an increasing role in some forms of electronic design automation (EDA). As Moore's Law slows further, greater performance is being sought by leading multinationals to co-optimise hardware and software.

The decision to base manufacturing in any jurisdiction is a complex risk analysis. However, costs are important to the extent that many entrepreneurs are quick to mention these when asked impromptu questions about their choice of manufacturing base. Therefore, regulation must facilitate attractive industrial rent rates and loans for high-value manufacturing equipment in the context of semiconductor business. Tax policies must also be attractive.[52]

5.7 Funding start-ups

Real innovation requires following the technology, market and implementation dynamics as set out in Chapter 4 Strategic frameworks. It can be imagined as a version of Newton's cradle made up of three balls where rational decision making replaces kinetic energy – moving forwards and backwards. Technology ↔ Market ↔ Implementation. Most R&D follows this pattern of real innovation, improving on existing technology, and meeting demand at the right time.

However, industrial policy must be receptive to making these long-term investments. At a Future of Britain event, former UK Prime Minister Tony Blair observed that in the context of artificial intelligence (AI) 'the biggest risk is not being too bold but being too timid'.[53] Brave ambition equally applies to the hardware that allows AI to function. For example,

52 See Chapter 11 Taxation law.

53 Tony Blair Institute (2024), 'Governing in an age of AI', Future of Britain Conference, Executive Chairman Tony Blair, 9 July 2024.

the Tokyo start-up Edgecortix has designed a processor with comparable performance to a graphics processing unit (GPU) made by Nvidia, but the Edgecortix design uses one-tenth of the power. This power efficiency is achieved by reducing the number of times the processor needs to access memory.[54]

The growth of start-up firms dedicated to machine learning logic and memory components can also significantly benefit from commercial investment. It is notable that before Graphcore was purchased by SoftBank, substantial funding was provided by several international firms, including Robert Bosch and Samsung. Nigel Toon, co-founder of Graphcore, wrote in a 2023 letter to then Prime Minister Rishi Sunak:

> Too often we have seen British-made innovation leading the world, only to be edged-out or bought-out by overseas rivals. By directing at least some of the UK taxpayer's investment towards world class UK businesses, the Government has the power to grow our knowledge economy... It would mean that graduates in these fields can consider roles in Bristol, Cambridge, London and other parts of the country, instead of San Francisco and Santa Clara.[55]

5.8 Scale-up challenges

Legislative solutions need to incorporate the challenge illustrated in Figure 5.3. It is inspired by a thought-provoking contribution by Andrew Chen, a partner at Andressen Horowitz. This venture capital (VC) firm invests in start-ups. This firm has provided capital to allow, among others, Github and Reddit to grow. Additionally, Chen was the former head of growth for Uber. He has first-hand experience of disruptive success, which is some of the secret sauce needed in any semiconductor firm seeking to do more.[56] Chen's main point is that networks of customers or stakeholders are the catalyst for growth. However, he highlights that the

---

[54] Satoh, R. (2024) 'Nvidia vs. the startups: AI chip challengers chase efficiency', *Nikkei Asia*, 16 August 2024.

[55] Toon, N. (2023) 'Open letter to the UK prime minister on investment in exascale compute', 31 March 2023, available at www.graphcore.ai/posts/open-letter-to-the-uk-prime-minister-on-investment-in-exascale-compute.

[56] Chen, A. (2021) *The Cold Start Problem – How to Start and Scale Network Effects*, Penguin, at 44.

scale-up challenges for the firms he has assisted revolve around building these networks.

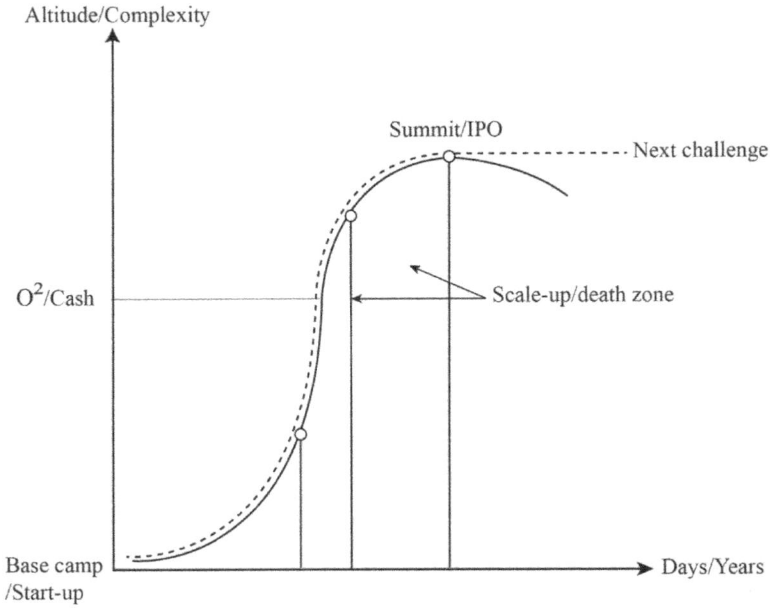

Source: © Iain Sheridan (2025)

Figure 5.3 *Scale-up challenges*

The scale-up challenge for semiconductor firms contrasts with high-altitude climbing on a Himalayan scale. High-altitude climbing is logistically, and in timescale, the opposite of semiconductor entrepreneurship. A start-up might typically begin with three people. But the commercial summit, by which is meant an initial public offering (IPO) or high-value private sale, can only be reached with the support of many team members, including professional advisers. Such a climb typically takes 7–10 years.

Figure 5.3 illustrates that, after leaving base camp, start-up entrepreneurs must survive the 'death zone',[57] by which is meant a period when firms have a working prototype but are not yet generating revenues, or are experiencing slow revenue growth. Across this time period the cost of capital requires significantly more funding.[58]

Under such conditions, VCs are less willing to provide late-stage funding rounds. There is increasing complexity and risk in the scale-up to the death zone. The period here can vary, but for semiconductor firms this can easily be more than five years. Many firms perish before reaching the summit. Successful firms overcome many challenges to reach an IPO or high-value private sale.

5.9 Non-monetary ways the UK Government can support scale-up

UK legislation can provide for both financial and tax support to ease the challenges of scaling-up through the death zone. However, there are also non-financial governance and management aspects to consider as well. We are in an era of increasing innovation in terms of how capital can be raised from stock exchanges.

There might be productive reasons to change legislation governing regulated markets, especially those managed by the London Stock Exchange

[57] In fundraising circles the term 'Valley of Death' has the same meaning. In my view, the metaphor of climbing more accurately captures that entrepreneurship is an energetic challenge based on teamwork and is perennially a challenging process from base camp to summit. However, even high-altitude mountaineering does not completely convey the long-term semiconductor challenge. It is not uncommon to see successful semiconductor technologies taking 7–10 years to be commercially implemented. Sometimes even longer.

[58] The firm's position might typically equate to Technical Readiness Level (TRL) 9 as applied by the UK Government and across the semiconductor sector. However, some aspect that would increase demand, for instance a revised sub-system or a procurement communicated request for a change, requires further R&D at TRL 6, 7 or 8. Applying real innovation as set out in Chapter 4, firms have to strategically adapt to the changing dynamics of Technology ↔ Market ↔ Implementation.

Group (LSEG). For example, a new regulatory requirement could be imposed on LSEG to brief all semiconductor SMEs registered with Companies House from their second year of trading. In this way, SME owners can better understand the different ways of raising capital.

LSEG executives would also achieve more impact by travelling roadshow-style across the regions, briefing in towns around the UK with local government involvement. Busy engineers in each semiconductor cluster would benefit from the knowledge and leadership shown by LSEG. To draw a lateral parallel example, it is memorable that the current UK Prime Minister, Sir Keir Starmer, was respected within the Crown Prosecution Service, partly because he would make the effort and time commitment to tour the country.

5.10 Public listing options

James Ashton, a former City editor of the *Sunday Times*, has contributed an engrossing tome about the Cambridge-based technology company ARM Holdings plc (ARM). In his concluding chapter Ashton observed that ARM uniquely went against the tide of multi-billion-dollar factories and government support. Instead, it relied on adequate finance, depth of experience, and energetic youthful leadership.[59]

ARM is an incredible past achievement and ongoing global success. However, from a UK viewpoint it is disappointing that it did not re-list on the LSE, but instead chose to list on the NASDAQ.[60] Consequently, policy makers need to have detailed analysis on the main areas of resistance to London listings, and then implement nuanced capital-raising policies.

In the context of any start-up that has received the benefit of UK Government funding, the trade association UK Finance, a financial services trade association, has proposed that it is reasonable to expect long-term commitment to list in the UK. It proposed that if a government-funded start-up seeks to list outside the UK, it must pay

[59] Ashton, J. (2023) *The Everything Blueprint – The Microchip Design That Changed the World*, Hodder & Stoughton, at 390–91.

[60] Trading under the NASDAQ ticker symbol ARM, available at www.nasdaq.com/market-activity/stocks/arm.

back all the public funding, including clawing back tax breaks.[61] In effect, a deterrent stick.

Waving a stick in front of start-ups is going to irk some young entrepreneurs, even though such a policy may seem to be a reasonable mechanism. In my view, a better solution to reduce instances where the UK acts as an incubator for New York listings, is to offer carrots. When a UK start-up proceeds to plan a London listing, the UK Government should provide free advice on the regulatory requirements and detailed costs connected with the following two established methods of accessing international capital and simultaneously raise brand awareness.

First, make entrepreneurs aware that a London-listed firm has the option to cross-list.[62] By which is meant, that an LSE listing still allows an incorporated firm to list elsewhere. For example, the electronics group Sony first listed on the Tokyo Stock Exchange, and then cross-listed on the New York Stock Exchange (NYSE).

Second, the option to create depositary receipts that can be traded on multiple exchanges. For instance, imagine if in the future Raspberry Pi chose to trade depository receipts. This option provides not only the prospect of more capital markets, but also powerful marketing that revolves around globally influential banks, such as Barclays and HSBC. An investment bank's depository receipt marketing communication would be along the lines of:

> Raspberry Pi develops and manufactures small single-board computers. It has an established global customer base across diverse applications, including consumer electronics, microcontrollers, and satellites. The company is listed

---

[61] *Financial Times* (2024) 'UK should penalise start-ups that take state aid but list abroad, says lobby group – UK Finance, a banking body argues for clawback of tax breaks to halt flow of business overseas', 4 July 2024.

[62] For readers less familiar with capital market options, cross listing needs to be differentiated from dual listing. The arrangement of dual listing is completely different, because it is allowing two separate legal entities to list on two exchanges. Under one brand name two legal entities will operate as a single business. An example is the global robotics behemoth ABB. On the Swedish NASDAQ Stockholm it trades under the symbol ABB. Whereas on the Swiss SIX Zurich exchange it trades under the symbol ABBN. See https://global.abb/group/en/investors/investor-and-shareholder-resources/share-listing.

on several exchanges, including the London Stock Exchange, the Frankfurt Stock Exchange and NASDAQ, under the symbol 'RPI'.[63]

Encouragingly, effective from 29 July 2024, the UK Financial Conduct Authority (FCA) approved revisions to the LSE's main market listing rules.[64] This included abolishing the requirement of prior approval of shareholders for related-party transactions. This rule was part of the reason SoftBank chose not to list ARM on the LSE. Additionally, the new rules allow for dual class share structures favoured by founders that provide them with better voting rights compared with other investors.

Other legislative changes could include accelerating government vetting and timelines, especially for defence-related devices. Consequently, semiconductor firms would have a steadier flow of revenue earlier on. There could also be effective governance changes linked to government-supported loans and finance. For example, a loan condition that a non-executive director (NED) comes onto the board with prerequisite experience of working not only with start-ups, but also managing at scale.

Additionally, there could be a loan obligation clause for all start-ups to have a legal counsel assigned after the first 24 months of operation to contribute on the same typical quarterly basis as NEDs often function. That individual legal counsel would need experience of working with start-ups and at scale. They would provide independent advice at critical points potentially mitigating leadership group-think, assisting boards to articulate the logic of changing direction, and to avoid rigidity in decision making.

---

63 Raspberry Pi is well known for its experimental kits. However, across industry its applications are diverse, including machine learning, as well as ambitions to build satellites. See www.raspberrypi.com/for-industry/; and www.raspberrypi.com/for-industry/powered-by/product-catalogue/?.

64 FCA (2024), 'FCA overhauls listing rules to boost growth and innovation on UK stock markets'. See https://www.fca.org.uk/publications/policy-statements/ps24-6-primary-markets-effectiveness-review-feedback-cp23-31-final-uk-listing-rules.

In sum, legislative changes, to reduce the risks for semiconductor firms in the scale-up death zone, are an eclectic mix of capital-raising rules, and corporate governance rules, industrial policy and taxation.

5.11 Collaboration and cooperation

Another important question is how can UK regulation encourage closer human relations between academic, entrepreneur, investor, and policy maker communities with the aim of increasing semiconductor growth?

What is entirely different in hardware manufacturing, especially semiconductors, is the exceptionally long pilot, scaling and commercial lead times. This makes long-term appreciation of which firm specialises in what area especially important. The establishment, in May 2024, of a UK Semiconductor Institute to support the UK Government's semiconductor sector is encouraging.

On the day of its formation, Martin McHugh, CEO at CSA Catapult said: 'The UK Semiconductor Institute will ensure the UK has a strategic and coordinated approach to developing new technologies, improving skills and exploiting areas in which the UK has existing strengths'.[65] The UK Semiconductor Institute would maximise its influence by commissioning a building whose architecture encourages meetings from firms across the UK.[66]

5.11.1 Future collaboration with US firms and institutions

The US has also planned a National Semiconductor Technology Center (NSTC) based on an initial $5 billion and a maximum investment of $11

[65] UK Government (2024) 'New independent Institute to steer UK semiconductor innovation and support semiconductor strategy – UK Semiconductor Institute announced to support key components of the government's Semiconductor Strategy', Press Release, 20 May 2024.

[66] Perhaps the most strategically effective choice of location for the UK Semiconductor Institute is Birmingham or Coventry. A convenient Midlands base for all firms to access. Bristol or Newport are another two logical options.

billion.[67] The NSTC will play a similar coordinating role compared with the UK Semiconductor Institute. The aim of the NSTC is to be the collaborative platform for semiconductor firms, entrepreneurs, government agencies, investors, national laboratories, customers, suppliers, educational institutions, and workforce representatives.[68]

Chris Miller, author of *Chip War*,[69] and two other dedicated US semiconductor pundits, have underlined that the key goal for the NSTC is to facilitate collaborations as an independent body focused on long-term research. Further, that the NSTC presents opportunities for researchers from all specialisms to produce prototypes in cutting-edge semiconductor fabs. That approach would ensure such opportunities are not dominated by the incumbent largest firms.[70]

UK collaboration with the NSTC, as well as Asia and EU equivalents, would maximise efficiencies such as international standards, for instance concerning heterogenous integration. That is a logical use of the UK's smaller budget, location in Europe and increasing willingness to cooperate with Asian countries. In effect what the UK can achieve is its own smaller, nimbler version of Belgium's IMEC with British characteristics and strengths – mighty oaks from little acorns grow.

5.11.2 Future alliances with Korean firms and institutions

As mentioned in the preceding chapter, the eminent strategist, Hwy-Chang Moon, has dedicated a significant amount of his career to analysing South

---

[67] NIST (2024) 'Biden-Harris Administration Announces Over $5 Billion from the CHIPS and Science Act for Research, Development, and Workforce', 9 February 2024.

[68] NSTC (2024) 'The National Semiconductor Technology Center – The vision for 2024', 24 May 2024.

[69] Miller, C. (2022) *Chip War: The Fight for the World's Most Critical Technology*, Simon & Schuster.

[70] Miller, C., J. Schneider and A. Ebrahimi, (2024) 'To win the chip war, the U.S. must prioritize revolutionary research – success against China requires that America maintain a technological edge', *Washington Post*, 30 May 2024. Jordan Schneider is the founder of ChinaTalk, a podcast and newsletter on technology and US–China relations; Arrian Ebrahimi is editor of the Chip Capitols newsletter on Substack.

Korea's economic success in the context of corporate strategies.[71] The UK-Republic of Korea Semiconductor Framework, signed in 2023, provides UK firms with an opportunity to share technical expertise, and learn from a culture that has imagined leading in semiconductors, then planned it, and is succeeding in it.[72]

When meeting Moon in Seoul, he made many insightful comments about why South Korea is so successful. One of the major factors is benchmarking the best features of competing firms. South Korea learnt from both Japanese and US semiconductors leaders. It seems clear that for UK firms to maximise their potential, benchmarking against Korean firms would be a valuable long-term investment. The most cost-effective way to achieve that is via strategic alliances.

There are also opportunities to position UK firms in South Korea near to local firms that are benefiting from Korean Government support packages.[73] Further, there are opportunities for UK firms planning joint ventures with Korean start-up firms, supported by UK Government funding. In 2024, British firms were invited to apply for grant funding of up to £900,000 per project. UK firm applications are assessed by Innovate UK, and South Korean partners apply via KIAT.[74]

One specific area for potential cooperation is co-packaged optics (CPO). However, delay will close this opportunity. Already US firms, such as Lightmatter, are offering important advances in integrated photonics.[75] Lightmatter's programmable photonic device, called Passage, removes the need for fibre optic cables acting as the connection between arrays of heterogenous semiconductors. South Korea has global leading strengths

---

71 Moon, H-C. (2016) *The Strategy for Korea's Economic Success*, Oxford University Press.

72 UK Government (2023) UK–Republic of Korea framework for semiconductor cooperation: joint statement, November 2023. See www.gov.uk/government/publications/uk-republic-of-korea-framework-for-semiconductor-cooperation-joint-statement/uk-republic-of-korea-framework-for-semiconductor-cooperation-joint-statement.

73 *Nikkei Asia* (2024) 'South Korea announces $19 billion aid package for chip industry', 23 May 2024.

74 UK Government (2024) UK-South Korea Collaborative R&D 2024.

75 See https://lightmatter.co/story/.

in DRAM and NAND, and solid-state drives (SSD). However, Samsung is a relatively newcomer in photonics. UK firms with photonics expertise are potential joint venture partners.

5.11.3 Consortia

It is notable that one of the strategies deployed by the Japanese Government to reinvigorate its semiconductor sector is the establishment of a new semiconductor consortium.[76] Successive Japanese governments have implemented sophisticated industrial policy, including covering semiconductors.

In 2022, METI coordinated the establishment of Rapidus.[77] This new semiconductor venture has been established by eight firms, namely Denso, Kioxia, MUFG Bank, NEC, NTT, SoftBank, Sony and Toyota. Rapidus exists with the aim of manufacturing at the 2nm level or less.[78] Within a very short space of time, Rapidus has strengthened its international position by cooperating with not only IBM[79] but also IMEC.[80]

Any future UK semiconductor consortium is unlikely to closely match the capital and technical expertise of these eight great Japanese firms. However, there is no reason for an equally dynamic, albeit proportionally smaller, British equivalent of Rapidus. For instance, a consortium that includes BAE Systems, Barclays, British Telecom, HSBC, McLaren, Rolls-Royce, and Vodafone.

---

[76] Sposato, W. (2023) 'Japan bets big on bringing semiconductor manufacturing home', *Foreign Policy*, 9 January 2023, available at https://foreignpolicy.com/2023/01/09/japan-semiconductor-chip-manufacturing-china/.

[77] www.rapidus.inc.

[78] *EE Times* (2022) 'Toward domestic production of the 2nm generation, Rapidus, a manufacturing company funded by eight domestic companies, started', available at https://eetimes.itmedia.co.jp/ee/articles/2211/11/news155.html.

[79] IBM Research (2022) 'Rapidus has partnered with IBM Research to propel Japan's push for leadership in semiconductor research and manufacturing', 13 December 2022, available at https://research.ibm.com/blog/rapidus-ibm-2nm-chips.

[80] IMEC (2023) 'Rapidus, Japan's newly founded chip manufacturer, joins Imec's Core Partner Program', 4 April 2023, available at www.imec-int.com/en/press/rapidus-japans-newly-founded-chip-manufacturer-joins-imecs-core-partner-program.

5.11.4 A British industrial group

In Chapter 2 covering the global semiconductor sector, mention was made of Japanese *keiretsu* and Korean *chaebol* business groupings. As mentioned earlier in this chapter, my own research in Seoul included interviewing Hwy-Chang Moon, South Korea's leading strategy professor.[81] Towards the end of our meeting, we were floating ideas, thinking about how a future UK-based semiconductor venture could grow to a global scale.

Moon imaginatively put forward the idea of the London-headquartered Deep Mind working with Samsung. His idea then made me think that a future UK firm could be the centre of a business grouping that included established designers and manufactures of semiconductors. UK Government money would be the financial catalyst for its formation. In essence, an established British engineering brand working with a range of semiconductor subsidiaries, both UK and international, applying the best qualities of existing Japanese *keiretsu* and Korean *chaebol*. Possible corporate parent entity candidates include BAE Systems, Rolls-Royce, and Vodafone.

5.12 Anticipating future customers

An anticipatory strategy can be applied to manoeuvring for semiconductor customers. The automotive sector is just one example. S&P Mobility analysts have calculated that the average cost of semiconductors per car is forecast to rise from $700 in 2020 to $1 138 by 2028.[82]

Although manufacturing plants are dispersed across the UK amongst more than 20 producers, data indicates production volumes above 200,000 units per annum exist for three firms – Jaguar Land Rover, Mini,

---

81 Professor Moon is the author of Moon, H-C. (2018) *The Art of Strategy- Sun Tzu, Michael Porter, and Beyond*, Cambridge University Press; and Moon, H-C. (2016) *The Strategy for Korea's Economic Success*, Oxford University Press.

82 *Financial Times* (2023) 'Chip designer Arm targets car market for growth', 4 January 2023.

and Nissan.[83] There is commercial sense in a semiconductor firm with an existing automotive focus or investment plans being located near one of these three mass manufacturing sites. Alternatively, for a firm to locate units in the Midlands and the Northeast. Acknowledging that Jaguar Land Rover is owned by an Indian parent, Mini by a German parent, and Nissan by a Japanese parent, proximity to these giants may accelerate integration into global supply chains.

Hybrid cars, for the foreseeable future, will remain a significant part of both second-hand and new automotive markets. That is partly because an EV is not an affordable item for a large percentage of the UK population. Another important reason is the grey energy associated with EVs. Any EV leaves the production line with a 'carbon debt'.[84] By which is meant the energy expended to manufacture an EV battery is significantly higher compared with fossil fuel engine manufacturing.[85]

Automotive manufacturers realise EV sales will not be at the levels originally projected, making hybrids a greater strategic priority. Therefore, existing semiconductor products and new innovative products used to manage the function of internal combustion engines alongside batteries have ongoing, increasing demand. Mazda, Subaru, and Toyota have all committed to fuel-based technology. Most notably, in Q2 of 2024, Toyota announced a new generation of combustion engines that are planned to be up to 20 per cent smaller.[86]

---

83 Society of Motor Manufacturing and Traders (SMMT) (2024), SMMT Vehicle Data. Notably, in 2024 out of the total 713 870 cars made in the UK, 8 out of 10 were exported and of those exported 60.3 per cent were purchased in the EU. See www.smmt.co.uk/vehicle-data/manufacturing/.

84 The carbon debt of an EV battery is approximately 60 per cent more compared with fossil fuel engine manufacturing.

85 *The Guardian* (2023), 'Do electric cars really produce fewer carbon emissions than petrol or diesel vehicles?', 23 December 2023. It is important to also mention that the campaign group Transport and Environment has calculated that life cycle emissions for EU electric cars are three times lower compared with petrol cars.

86 *Financial Times* (2024) 'Toyota bets on new line of combustion engines in challenge to Tesla – Japanese carmaker unveils latest fuel-based technology to be used alongside batteries in hybrid cars', 28 May 2024.

From a forward-looking viewpoint, there may also be success in building a start-up, or moving an established SME, close to EV and plug-in hybrid automotive producers. Further, EVs and high-end vehicles are not mutually exclusive. Examples include Bentley Motors' production of its plug-in hybrid offerings in Cheshire[87] and Aston Martin's manufacturing of its planned EV/plug-in cars in Warwickshire.[88]

5.13 Heterogeneous integration research

There is sense in UK semiconductor firms setting aside some R&D budget to share with universities researching heterogenous integration challenges using the most sustainable materials. Cutting-edge R&D facilities already exist in Cardiff, Cambridge, Southampton and Swansea. Published progress and knowhow would develop quickly. The UK has the same opportunity to advance innovation in heterogeneous integration as any other market. To be architects of implementation of a known technology into markets that demand it.

This is a formidable real innovation challenge, but one that can be overcome with substantial cooperation across multiple UK firms. Charles Townes, a Nobel prize-winning laser physicist, was known for quoting from a cartoon that shows a beaver and a rabbit admiringly peering up at the Hoover Dam. The beaver remarks 'No I didn't build it myself, but it is based on an idea of mine'. The task of commercially implementing the sustainable 3D semiconductors of the future requires collective effort to advance a known invention. Nvidia's huge market capitalisation reflects strategic foresight to meet the demand for GPUs. Jason Huang did not invent parallel computing. But he is its strategic architect.[89]

---

[87] Bentley (2024) Press Information, 19 March 2024.

[88] *Financial Times* (2024) 'Aston Martin losses shrink but launch of first electric model delayed', 28 February 2024.

[89] Ridley, M. (2020) *How Innovation Works*, 4th ESTATE, at 245.

5.14 Future alliances led by a telecommunications firm

An issue I raised with leading engineers attending a Turing Institute AI workshop is that a successful smartphone firm, such as Apple, poses a potential threat to any automotive brand in the context of EVs. Therefore, smartphone providers and other leading telecommunications firms may be excellent collaborative partners or future new clients. The Turing Institute event included directors from a UK-based world-leading automotive firm, so no doubt automotive incumbents are aware of the threat.

An existing new entrant is Xiaomi. Incorporated in 2009, Xiaomi is the world's third largest smartphone maker. In April 2024 it started to sell its debut EV, the Speed Ultra 7 sports sedan for just under USD $30,000.[90] At this level in China it closely compares with the price of Tesla's Model 3 standard version.

Xiaomi is not alone in this type of ambitious diversification. For example, the fourth-bestselling EV in China in 2024, the Aito M7, is made by Huawei. An automotive analyst commenting on the competitive advantages available to such firms put it this way: 'A company that has a smartphone product and a self-developed operating system indisputably enjoys an edge over traditional automakers in terms of car connectivity'.[91]

There is also logic in investing time in seeking to collaborate with new Chinese entrants. Such an opportunity would require significantly more stable and reciprocal trading relations, but, in the long term, it is a possibility. See the Chapter 8 section on joint venture essentials, especially equal equity shareholding and rotating leadership.

UK semiconductor firms need to horizon scan and reposition themselves to be providers of components that are valued by dynamic new entrants

---

[90] *Financial Times* (2024) 'China's smartphone maker Xiaomi bets on EVs even as Apple pivots. Weeks after the tech giant abandons car project, Chinese tech company debuts model that out-accelerates Tesla and Porsche', 29 March 2024.

[91] Ibid, Yale Zhang, founder of Shanghai-based consultancy Automotive Foresight.

to the automotive sector. Accomplished telecommunication firms, such as Vodafone, could decide to reassess how they can diversify and cooperate. Any such diversification plan would need to factor in access to domestic R&D facilities, how to accelerate reaching high semiconductor performance levels, security, and supply chain procurement decisions.

5.15 Diversifying semiconductor supply chains in Asia

Semiconductor activity is often characterised as operating as a global business. That is most evident when looking at supply chains. Unfortunately, the Covid-19 pandemic, climate change, earthquakes, the return of inflation, and less stable bilateral international relations have all contributed to a reassessment of the global supply chain.

Clearly China-US relations have been the cause of supply chain changes for the most advanced semiconductors at the 3nm level. The rational decision is to include all commercially viable countries in the global supply chain, based on the well-established logic of complex interdependence. Therefore, in my view, every investment in diplomatic effort must be focused on keeping China in the global supply chain, subject to any necessary detailed negotiated agreements on semiconductors and adherence to WTO rules. I had the opportunity to speak with the preeminent Harvard international relations professor, Joseph Nye. My question concerned China and cooperation. Specifically, I asked Nye how the US was able to balance trade relations and security concerns in the Indo Pacific region?

Nye explained that he had recently returned from a dialogue that took place at the Beijing Central Party School. The constructive, open way to manage all technology-related trade was based on three baskets. First, cutting-edge ≤3nm semiconductors. Second, harder, grey area cases covering a wide range of dual-use semiconductors. Third, commoditised products.[92]

[92] Oxford University event 'Joseph Nye, A life in an American Century', held at Exeter College, Oxford, 22 May 2024.

The three-basket approach makes sense. The first basket, covering ≤3nm semiconductors, represents a security advantage relevant to missiles. The second basket is wide and deep for maximising continuing potential trade but requires negotiated detail so that all actors are clear on what is permissible. The third basket is straightforward because commoditised products can easily apply existing WTO rules.

When thinking about diversifying UK supply chains in Asia, beyond the established markets of China, Japan, South Korea, and Taiwan, the first two obvious names are Malaysia and Singapore. Both these Southeast Asian countries seek to move up the semiconductor value chain from their traditional back-end roles in the production process to more front-end production, and even design.

Further, given Malaysia's land mass, it may also increase its back-end global market share. For instance, in 2023 Intel announced that it intended to quadruple its advanced 3D chip packaging services in Malaysia, with a new plant in Penang.[93]

However, it is the relative newcomers of India, Thailand, the Philippines and Vietnam that present new possibilities for the global leading semiconductor firms. First, in India, at the opening of SemiconIndia 2023, Indian Prime Minister Narendra Modi posed the question 'Who can be a more trusted partner than the world's largest democracy?' Modi's presence and words at SemiconIndia encapsulate Indian ambitions to become an increasing part of the global semiconductor supply chain. Given its quantity of engineers it has a realistic chance. However, bureaucracy, and limited electricity and water are great national hindrances.[94]

Thailand also has ambitions to expand semiconductor business. Thai corporate tax policy provides exemptions for upstream semiconductor firms entering the supply chain in Thailand for up to 13 years. The Thai Government also seeks to build up an EV sector. Given EVs require significant semiconductor quantities it hopes that growing an EV sub-sector will increase the attractiveness of Thailand for semiconductor investment.

---

[93] Ting-Fang, C. (2023) 'Intel to quadruple cutting-edge chip packaging capacity by 2025', Nikkei Asia, 23 August 2023.

[94] Farhat, L. (2023) 'Can India Emerge a Global Chip Powerhouse?', *Diplomat*, Issue 100, at 118–121.

Additionally, while details are unavailable, Thai media has recorded that talks have taken place with TSMC with the aim of attracting that firm to build a presence in Thailand.[95]

Turning to the Philippines, it offers a mix of lower costs, innovative culture and hard work ethic as a long-term strategic partner. Geopolitics in the region also plays a significant role in the Philippines semiconductor industry potential. For instance, following an April 2024 trilateral summit, Japan, the Philippines and the US intend to collaborate in semiconductors. There is a tentative plan for US firms to develop semiconductor facilities in the Philippines, and for Japan to provide training to Filipino engineers.[96]

Vietnam is an established location for R&D centre investment. The Vietnamese Government is ambitious to increase its semiconductor talent pool. The US firms Marvell and Synopsis have been present in several Vietnamese cities for nearly ten years. German, Korean and Taiwanese firms are also increasing investment. Alchip Technologies (Alchip), Taiwan's leading provider of AI chip design services, plans to have an R&D team in Hanoi or Ho Chi Minh. Alchip's CEO remarked 'Vietnam's promising pool of engineering talent and their strong work ethic make it a highly attractive option for us. We've been impressed by the dedication and commitment of Vietnamese engineers, who are eager to learn and contribute'.[97]

5.16 Conclusions

All established semiconductor firms have a detailed understanding of strategies to increase growth at local, national regional, continental regional, and global levels. However, there is always the risk that opportunities are overlooked. Regional partnership towns, government funding

[95] Akama, K., R. Hanada and Y. Nitta (2023) 'India and Thailand jockey for spot on Asia's chipmaking map', *Nikkei Asia*, 15 August 2023.

[96] Nikkei staff writers (2024) 'Japan, U.S., Philippines to cooperate in clean energy, chips. Interview with Prime minister Kishida', *Nikkei Asia*, 4 April 2024.

[97] Hoang, L., C. Ting-Fang, K. Jaewon and L. Li (2024) 'Vietnam turns chip sector magnet with affordable, quality talent pool', *Nikkei Asia*, 14 August 2024.

and facilitation of growth, and global supply chain management are all prominent opportunities or risks. Further, listed below are a variety of issues that may mean adjustment, no matter how marginal, to each unique firm's strategic issues list.

- Committing to specific alliance forms through firm-wide cooperation in the nature, form and membership of a chosen alliance.
- Grasping global geopolitical realities based on evidence and risk simulations.
- Managing sustainability to world-class levels.
- Managing global supply chains in a proportionate and risk-simulated way.
- Taking advantage of local-focused expertise.
- Taking advantage of regional talent and infrastructure.
- Partnering areas of expertise nationally based on regional partnership towns.
- Partnering areas of expertise across Europe based on regional partnership towns.
- Partnering areas of expertise across Asia based on regional partnership towns.
- Partnering areas of expertise across North America based on regional partnership towns.
- Rare earth and other essential material risk-management analysis.
- Thorough ongoing research into the subsidies available in each semiconductor cluster and region of excellence.

For many of the strategic issues raised in this chapter, geopolitics has direct or indirect relevance. Uncertain international relations, especially in Asia and the Middle East, have created a momentous change in corporate leaders' mindsets. Consequently, in recent years my own legal advice has included presentations on how political risks can be efficiently managed. For industrial policy makers there is the complex remit of supporting domestic firms and simultaneously encouraging foreign investment across the rolling fulcrum of geopolitics.

A semiconductor firm may operate locally within one country and receive a large share of total revenues from that same jurisdiction. Nevertheless, often China–US relations and China–Taiwan relations must be factored into medium- and long-term decisions. Chapter 4, Strategy frameworks, included emphasis on monitoring both risk and obtaining sufficient evidence. Three useful questions to pose in the specific context of political risk analysis are:

1. How can we get good information about the political risks we face?
2. How can we ensure rigorous analysis?
3. How can we integrate political risk analysis into business decisions?[98]

Rigorous analysis needs to challenge assumptions about the future. As the brilliant Caltech theoretical physicist, Richard Feynman put it, analysis is how we avoid fooling ourselves.[99] There also needs to be sensitivity to group dynamics that so often include a propensity for group-think. All of which requires frameworks, procedures and documented decision making, but without bureaucracy.

A recent co-authored book by a Stanford law professor, a behavioural scientist, and a physicist, argues that part of human evolution in the twenty-first century should include applying scientific thinking to decision making.[100] Co-author Saul Pearlmutter, a Nobel prize-winner in physics for the accelerating expansion of the universe, reasons it is critical to have discussions with people who have different opinions.

Pearlmutter has remarked that our first reason for meeting people with different opinions is 'not to convince them that you are right, but to get them to help you figure out where you might be wrong so that you can sharpen your understanding of the world and become much more effective in pursuing any important goal'.[101] In my experience and view, lawyers are, more often than not, that invaluable analytical, dissenting filter.

A sense of national pride in semiconductor growth is also part of a UK strategy. Generally, US, Chinese, Japanese, and Korean citizens are patri-

---

98 Rice, C. and A. Zegart (2018) *Political Risk – Facing the Threat of Global Insecurity in the Twenty-first Century*, Weidenfeld & Nicolson, at 158.

99 Feynman, R. (1974) 'Cargo Cult Science', commencement address, California Institute of Technology, 14 June 1974, available at http://calteches.library.caltech.edu/51/2/CargoCult.htm.

100 Perlmutter, S., J. Campbell and R. MacCoun (2024) *Third Millennium Thinking – Creating Sense in a World of Nonsense*, Little, Brown Spark.

101 Schreiber, M. (2024) 'Thinking Our Way Through the Third Millennium', *Stanford Lawyer*, Spring/Summer 2024, at 27.

otic people. What about Britons? British patriotism is a constructive way of thinking that will allow local investment not just from friends and family, but also through regional and national involvement. After the Covid-19 pandemic, Gordon Brown, former UK Prime Minister, agreed to speak at the London School of Economics. My question to Brown was along the lines of 'Does part of the solution for stronger UK employment figures and financial markets include valuing being British more?'

Brown agreed that patriotism was positive but cautioned that the opposite of patriotism is nationalism which is not conducive to signalling that the UK welcomes FDI.[102] Positive forms of British patriotism include ensuring incoming engineering students feel welcome and are financially supported to achieve long-term success in British semiconductor firms. Too often foreign engineering graduates of UK universities do not professionally flourish in the UK, but in another country.

Finally, for CEOs the issues in this chapter require daily scrutiny to determine what is missing. To ask what is the overlooked risk or opportunity? Corporate strategy requires models that enable leaders to alloy courage, evidence, political awareness and risk analysis for success. In my view, the strategic framework in the previous chapter, based on Technology ↔ Market ↔ Implementation, supports business leaders in their individual missions, applying the frameworks of Fitzpatrick, Oberholzer and Moon to assess all strategic issues.[103]

---

[102] London School of Economics (2001) 'Seven Ways to Change the World – How To Fix The Most Pressing Problems We Face', Seminar, Gordon Brown, HonFRSE, 6 July 2021.

[103] Fitzgerald, E. et al (2011) *Inside Real Innovation – How the Right Approach Can Move Ideas from R&D to Market – And Get the Economy Moving*, World Scientific; Oberholzer-Gee, F. (2021) *Better Simpler Strategy – A Value-Based Guide to Exceptional Performance*, Harvard Business Review Press; Moon (2018).

6. Sustainable innovation

But I am now about no waste; I am about thrift.[1]

Before moving down to the nanometre scale, let us reflect on the contrasting perspective of space exploration. The NASA Apollo 8 mission of 1968. Perhaps apocryphal, but some people say that when those pioneering astronauts first caught a sight of Earth, they looked at each other and humorously asked 'Is it inhabited?'

Curiosity got the better of me. The official NASA mission transcripts provide a reflective record, although I did not find this specific existential banter. However, I did verify the following recording: 'Sunrise coming up... We see the earth now, almost as a disk. We have a beautiful view of Florida now... And at the same time we can see Africa. West Africa is beautiful...'[2]

While it is alarmist to argue the Earth could become uninhabitable,[3] leading scientists certainly support a more cautious approach to how we choose to manage human-induced climate change. Our choices extend to chemicals and materials used to make semiconductors. How we design and make components. Thereafter, what we do when we do not need devices anymore.[4]

---

1 Shakespeare, W. (1602) *The Merry Wives of Windsor*, Act 1, Scene 3, https://shakespeare.mit.edu/merry_wives/merry_wives.1.3.html.

2 NASA (1969) Apollo Onboard Voice Transcription (NASA), at 00012106 to 00033800.

3 Wallace-Wells, D. (2019) *The Uninhabitable Earth – A Story of the Future*, Penguin, at 222.

4 Note that the Wallace-Wells book, which is an expansion of his original articles in the *New York Times*, has received countless favourable reviews by scientists. However, many scientists, including professors from the universities of Berkeley, Bonn, Exeter, and PennState, conclude that some of his suggestions

6.1 Introduction

Sustainability has become a top priority for many CEOs.[5] For instance, in December 2024, at an event held in Silicon Valley, I had an opportunity to speak with and hear a presentation from Jean-Marc Chery of STMicroelectronics.[6] It was evident that a strategic priority of this European firm is sustainable production.

The challenge to solve is how to create competitive advantage in a cost-efficient and legal way. Sustainability issues, often encompassing an Environmental, Social and Governance (ESG) framework, have been elevated to near the top of boardroom agendas. In what measurable ways do semiconductors contribute directly or indirectly to climate change? How can a semiconductor firm measure and monitor carbon emissions?

When thinking about sustainability and semiconductor manufacturing, even well-informed industry professionals would understandably answer 'I don't know the precise detail, let me check'. It is easy to perceive that semiconductor firms, as advanced manufacturers, are at the cleaner end of the spectrum. Manufacturers using gallium nitride and silicon are not appearing in the courts. No part of the sector is a source of dispute for environmental activists seeking justice for major contamination or carbon emission or both. However, the use of multiple hazardous chemicals and non-recyclable water add to the challenge. For citizens affected by emissions stemming from their jurisdiction as well as those affected by pollutants travelling across borders, the stakes could not be higher. The complex task ahead for all semiconductor firms is to balance sustainable solutions with making a profit.

---

are not scientifically supported or are incorrect. See https://climatefeedback.org/evaluation/scientists-explain-what-new-york-magazine-article-on-the-uninhabitable-earth-gets-wrong-david-wallace-wells/.

5 McKinsey (2024) 'Eight Top Priorities for CEOs', Seminar, 13 March 2024.

6 Global Semiconductor Alliance (2024) Annual awards ceremony, Santa Clara, 5 December 2024.

6.2 The underlying science of climate change

Before delving into the issues most pertinent to semiconductor firms it is necessary to first anchor the mind on the extent of climate change from an evidence-based scientific viewpoint. My practitioner contributions on climate change and ESG litigation publications, have required understanding not just what is universally respected but also determining what the British judiciary rely on.[7] Currently, the most respected expert authority is that of the Intergovernmental Panel on Climate Change (IPCC).[8]

The contents of IPCC reports have evolved tremendously over its life. However, there are two qualities of the IPCC to highlight, namely the scientific rigour of its 2018 report on global warming, and its success at coherently summarising the diversity of climate change impacts.[9]

The IPCC's 2018 report is a universally respected key reference source for the Paris Agreement, because it crystalised years of research by many experts. Further, the IPCC 2018 report highlighted the priority of reducing greenhouse gas (GHG) emissions if global warming is to be limited to 1.5°C. Its conclusions included the following guidance:

> Pathways limiting global warming to 1.5°C with no or limited overshoot would require rapid and far-reaching transitions in energy, land, urban and infrastructure (including transport and buildings), and industrial systems (*high confidence*). These systems transitions are unprecedented in terms of scale, but not necessarily in terms of speed, and imply deep emissions reductions in all sectors, a wide portfolio of mitigation options and a significant upscaling of investments in those options (*medium confidence*).[10]

IPCC reports are technical given the substance is science-based. Fortunately, the material is presented with brevity, clarity, and memorability in mind. Each IPCC report provides objective statistics to communicate its collective hypotheses. For instance, as illustrated in Figure

---

7 Mitsi, M. (2025) *ESG Dispute Resolution*, Kluwer. See chapter on Climate Change and Sustainability Litigation in the English High Courts.

8 Established in 1988, the IPCC is a scientific and governmental body of the United Nations, whose reports draw on current scientific information from around the world. See www.ipcc.ch/.

9 IPCC (2018), *Global Warming of 1.5°C, Special Report.*

10 Ibid, Chapter 2, at 15.

6.1, the 2023 report captures the impact of human activity on climate change.[11]

Turning back to the specifics of the semiconductor sector, all these spheres of adverse impacts have some connection to manufacturing activity. For example, if we consider Taiwan. As the main base of TSMC and numerous other important semiconductor firms, climate change is an ongoing challenge. Semiconductor facilities in Taiwan must consider the availability of their physical water supply.

Extreme weather events will play apart in damage to factory and road infrastructure. Increasing average temperatures will also affect the productivity of fabrication workers. In sum, climate change affects ongoing costs and strategic decision making in the operation of Taiwanese semiconductor firms. The same variables apply to many other jurisdictions reliant on semiconductor jobs, shareholder revenues and corporate taxes.

6.3 Task Force on Climate Related Financial Disclosures

The Task Force on Climate Related Financial Disclosures (TCFD) provides important detail to follow.[12] Given the breadth and depth of climate change professional literature and regulation, anyone at the outset can be forgiven for being overwhelmed. However, if there is an exception to that sense of 'too much data' the four pillars for climate-related financial

[11] IPCC (2023), *Climate Change Synthesis Report*, Summary for Policymakers, at 7.

[12] In the UK, climate-related disclosures build on the TCFD pillars through International Sustainability Standards Board (ISSB) standards forming part of the broader International Financial Reporting Standards (IFRS) accounting standards. To distinguish climate-related disclosures, they are known as IFRS-S – the 'S' for sustainability. See www.ifrs.org/groups/international-sustainability-standards-board/.

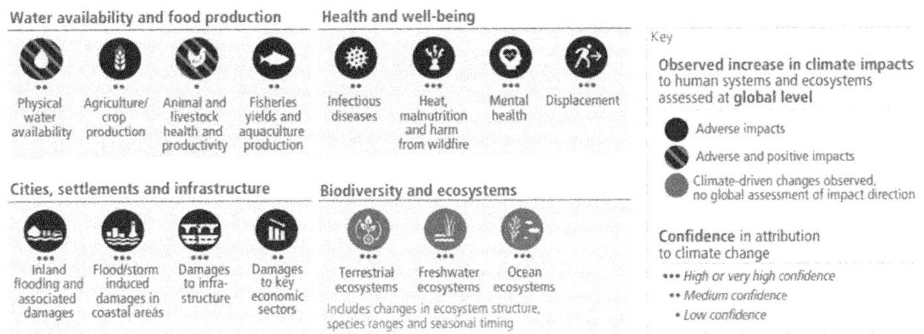

Source: IPCC (2023), *Climate Change Synthesis Report*, Summary for Policymakers, at 7

Figure 6.1 *Observed widespread and substantial impacts and related losses and damages attributed to climate change*

disclosure provided by TCFD are essential.[13] Each pillar requires detail to be provided on:

- Governance
  - The board's oversight of climate-related opportunities and risks.
  - The management's role in assessing and managing climate-related opportunities and risks.
- Strategy
  - The climate-related risks and opportunities the organisation has identified over the short, medium, and long term.
  - The impact of climate-related risks and opportunities on the organisation's businesses, strategy, and financial planning.
  - The resilience of the organisation's strategy, taking into consideration different climate-related scenarios, including a 2°C or lower scenario.
- Risk management
  - The organisation's processes for identifying and assessing climate-related risks.
  - The organisation's processes for managing climate-related risks.
  - How processes for identifying, assessing, and managing climate-related risks are integrated into the organisation's overall risk management.
- Metrics and targets
  - The metrics used by the organisation to assess climate-related risks and opportunities in line with its strategy and risk management processes.
  - Scope 1, Scope 2, and, if appropriate, Scope 3 GHG emissions, and the related risks.
  - The targets used by the organisation to manage climate-related risks and opportunities and performance against targets.[14]

[13] Note that firms applying IFRS S1 General Requirements for Disclosure of Sustainability-related Financial Information and IFRS S2 Climate-related Disclosures, are considered as satisfying the TCFD recommendations, because these recommendations are fully incorporated into the ISSB Standards. For firms moving over to ISSB compliance, the TCFD recommendations are a comprehensive starting point. See www.ifrs.org/sustainability/tcfd/.

[14] TCFD (2021) *Task Force on Climate-related Financial Disclosures Implementing the Recommendations of the Task Force on Climate-related Financial Disclosures*, at 17–22. Note that this document is an update of the original 2017 version.

6.4 Semiconductor-specific TCFD climate-related financial disclosures

The general requirements outlined under governance strategy risk management and metrics applies to all sectors. As importantly, are the sector-specific recommended disclosures. The relevant sub-category for semiconductors is Electrical and Electronics.

Differentiation is made between device firms and assembly firms. First, device firms are defined as 'those that primarily manufacture semiconductors and other electronic components that are built into electronic devices but not used on their own. Therefore, it is important for device companies to reduce GHG emissions in the manufacturing phase'. Assembly firms cover businesses that 'manufacture final products from various parts'.[15]

Sustainability includes supply chain risks. Manufacturing activity factors in supply chain risks and sustainability at every stage. Figure 6.2 visualises that challenge for product manufacturers that increasingly, to some degree, design their own semiconductors. The pivotal strategic interplay is between (a) resilient supply chains, (b) research and development (R&D) competitive advantage (c) and sustainability. To clarify, resilient supply chains encompass not only materials for all semiconductor firms, but also delivery of packaged goods.

An example of a firm implicitly applying these dynamics is Nokia. A senior corporate partnerships executive from the Finnish firm encapsulated Nokia's strategy this way:

> We are aware that from 4G moving to 5G and now to 6G, the capabilities and understanding of what the requirements are very much linked to how we can actually deliver a greater performance with lower power consumption…we could continue to go out and buy [semiconductors], but when it comes to how we want to have the performance and how we want to have the stability, that means the design needs to be in-house.[16]

---

[15] TCFD (2022) *Guidance on Climate-related Financial Disclosures 3.0*, Section 2(4) Electrical and electronics, at 16.

[16] Li, L. (2024) 'Telecom chips move in-house and the U.S. takes aim at TikTok', *Nikkei Asia*, 14 March 2023.

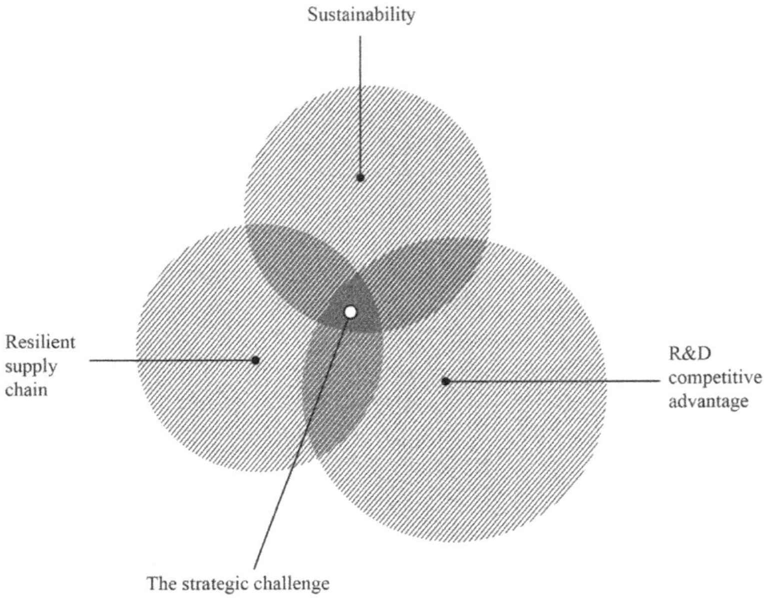

Source: © Iain Sheridan (2025)

Figure 6.2 *The sustainability challenge*

Nokia's mindset could equally apply to Apple, Ericsson, Huawei, or Samsung. For lawyers there will be the added task of checking the known carbon emissions, and costs associated with sustainability compliance, in partnership jurisdictions. Going forwards manufacturers will be required to apply TCFD disclosures and comply with other national regulations to remain legally sustainable. Simultaneously, to remain competitive, these same firms must solve the challenge of key component procurement and investing in R&D that includes semiconductor design.

6.5 Sustainable manufacturing equipment

The United States (US) conglomerate 3M was a pioneer in waste minimisation and has conceptually presented the challenge in four stages:

(a) reformulation – can the product be made with fewer toxic materials?
(b) equipment redesign – can energy from one process drive another?
(c) process modification – can changes be made to reduce quality control problems?
(d) resource recovery – can a waste product be reused as a material in a process, as a product or as source of energy?[17]

This established four-question framework provides an ongoing and long-term compass with which semiconductor firms can navigate towards greater innovative sustainability.

The process of making semiconductors has, to date, been associated with huge energy and water use. Grundfos, a Danish firm, is the largest pump manufacturer in the world. In the semiconductor sector, Grundfos is committed to saving water through more energy-efficient equipment, and the reuse of water. Conceptually, they see that energy and water are tightly tied together, because to move water requires energy.

As one example of their innovative initiatives, Grundfos uses the same permanent magnet motors found in electric vehicles (EVs) for water pumps.[18] Water reuse systems applying these efficient pumps take dirty water and convert it into boiler or utility water. The alternative has been to take that dirty water and dispose of it externally. That dumping also has energy and pollution costs associated with its transportation. The Grundfos strategy for semiconductor firms could be described as making

---

[17] Cairncross, F. (1993) *Costing the Earth: The Challenge for Governments, the Opportunities for Business*, Harvard Business School Press, at 260. Cairncross published about the risks and business opportunities of sustainability over 30 years ago. The first environment editor of *The Economist* and former Dean of Exeter College, Oxford University. A mercurial journalist ahead of her time.

[18] Grundfos (2024) 'Water scarcity – an impending semiconductor crisis?', Seminar, 6 February 2024.

profit by focusing on solutions that use the least amount of energy to move the most amount of water.[19]

For readers consulting with architects with the aim of designing fabrication plants and offices to maximise the efficient use of water, two Spanish architects have produced a highly cited and rated primer. Their book provides clear summaries with diagrams explaining various ways to integrate the design factors of rain harvesting, fog harvesting and water recycling.[20]

6.6 Sustainable procurement

International lawyers maintain an in-depth understanding of climate change relevant to compound, photonic, and silicon products. The more climate change is factored into design and materials, the more likely original equipment manufacturers (OEMs) will procure for the long term, because EVs require far higher numbers of semiconductors. As EVs evolve the sustainability of semiconductors, from an energy use and recycling potential perspective, will be scrutinised by automotive groups.

For example, imagine a multinational confectionary group based in Switzerland. It has achieved and promotes its ISO 14001 Environmental Management (EMS) certification.[21] That certification relies on detailed scrutiny of how waste is managed in all its factories and offices.[22]

The Swiss multinational wants to transition from offering its employees the opportunity to lease petrol-only and hybrid cars as part of their benefits package, to encouraging EV leasing. The question previously posed by the procurement department of this Swiss multinational would have been simple. Primarily based on brand prestige, fossil fuel economy, dimensions, and price, the procurement function would ask itself, out of BMW,

19 See www.grundfos.com/.
20 Guitierrez, R. and L. Hidalgo (2020) *Elements of Sustainable Architecture*, Routledge, 104–13.
21 The formal title of this standard is ISO 14001:2015 Environmental management systems.
22 Globally, the practice of applying for quality management certification is widespread. Increasingly firms also seek to manage and audit their carbon footprint and wider sustainable practices.

Ford, Jaguar Land Rover, Honda, Hyundai, Kia, Toyota, Volkswagen, and Volvo, and all other competing brands, which cars are best for our employees?

But there is a new accompanying question. How can our employees know their EV is sustainable? Part of the answer to that question affects procurement decisions made daily around the world. Moreover, if automotive groupings, such as Honda and Nissan plan joint battery procurement and vehicle development, the more critical competition factoring in sustainability will become.[23]

There is a requirement to verify that the Swiss company's leased cars are sustainable. Part of the answer to that requirement is answered by the semiconductor choices for each vehicle. Further, as Rachel Oliver, Cambridge Professor and gallium nitride expert has pointed out 'how we charge EVs is a semiconductor issue…in a sustainability context'.[24]

6.7 Director liability

In the case of *ClientEarth v Shell Plc & Ors*, the English High Court looked at director duties under United Kingdom (UK) company law. The claimant, ClientEarth,[25] brought what is termed a derivative claim arising from an actual or proposed act or omission involving breach of duty by one or more of the Shell directors.[26] Under the UK Companies 2006, the applicant requires the court's permission to proceed to a full hearing.[27] ClientEarth owned 27 shares in Shell Plc (Shell).

Under English law, as a shareholder, ClientEarth was qualified to make a derivative claim against Shell and its directors.[28] The applicant in a derivative claim has an obligation to evidentially establish a prima facie

[23] Kawakami, A. (2024) 'Nissan weighs EV partnership with Honda', *Nikkei Asia*, 14 March 2024.
[24] Royal Academy of Engineering (2023) 'Critical Conversations: Semiconductors – a critical technology for a critical time?', 23 September 2023.
[25] ClientEarth is a non-profit environmental law organisation and UK charity.
[26] Section 260(1) Companies Act 2006.
[27] Section 260(3) Companies Act 2006.
[28] *ClientEarth v Shell Plc & Ors (Re Prima Facie Case)* [2023] EWHC 1137 (Ch).

case. Therefore, the evidential burden resided with ClientEarth. The practical aim of derivative actions is a quality control filter to capture unmeritorious claims.[29]

There were two key arguments made by ClientEarth. First, that the Shell directors failed to act in good faith in ways that would most likely promote the long-term success of the company for the benefit of all members. UK company law provides that a:

> director of a company must act in the way he considers, in good faith, would be most likely to promote the success of the company for the benefit of its members as a whole, and in doing so have regard to... (d) the impact of the company's operations on the community and the environment.[30]

The second argument was that the Shell directors failed to exercise the care skill and diligence that would be expected by a reasonably diligent person with (a) the general knowledge skill and experience that may reasonably be expected of a person carrying out the director-level functions, and (b) the general skill and experience of the individual director exercising reasonable care, skill, and diligence.[31]

The central argument for alleging director-level good faith breaches concerned failing to implement reasonable measures to mitigate the risks to the long-term financial profitability and resilience of Shell in its global temperature objective (GTO) of 1.5°C under the Paris Agreement.[32] That argument was based on the inadequacy of Shell's Scope 1, 2 and 3 target emissions set out in an annual report.[33] In particular, that there was no pathway for the Scope 3 absolute emissions.

Elsewhere in Europe, Shell directors have ended up in courts in the Netherlands. In the case of *Milieudefensie et al v Royal Dutch Shell*, the

---

[29] Hollington, R. (2022), *Hollington on Shareholder Rights*, 9th edition, London: Sweet & Maxwell, at paras 6-03 and 6-14.

[30] Section 172 Companies Act 2006. This is a subjective test. See *Regentcrest Plc v Cohen* [2001] 2 BCLC 80, per Jonathan Parker J at [120].

[31] Section 174 Companies Act 2006. This duty contains both subjective and objective elements.

[32] *ClientEarth v Shell Plc & Ors (Re Prima Facie Case)* [2023] EWHC 1137 (Ch) at [16].

[33] Ibid, at [38].

Hague District Court ordered Shell to reduce its group-wide CO_2 emissions by 45 per cent (net) compared with 2019 levels, by the end of 2030.[34] Milieudefensie is the organisation member of Friends of the Earth in the Netherlands. In this action Milieudefensie was the lead applicant supporting over 17,000 co-plaintiff individuals.

The Dutch high court placed significant focus on international treaties, so this case is relevant to semiconductor firm directors in many jurisdictions. Further, after the decision lawyers acting for Milieudefensie concluded 'we are convinced that other courts around the world will follow suit'.[35]

The *Milieudefensie et al v Royal Dutch Shell* judgment covers diverse legal points. However, two aspects deserve brief mention. First, the court ordered that the emissions reduction obligation extends over Shell's entire global value chain. Therefore, it covers all fossil fuel products from Scope 1, 2, and 3 emissions.

Second, the Dutch High Court took a negative view of Shell's corporate strategy, viewing the transition plan as 'intangible, undefined and non-binding for the long-term (2050)'.[36] Given directors are responsible for signing off transition strategies, there will be increased scrutiny on the pace, key performance metrics and traceability.

Subsequently, Shell appealed the 2021 decision. In late 2024, the Hague Court of Appeal held that under EU regulation, firms are free to choose their own approach to reducing emissions as part of their climate transition plans. As long as the transition plans are consistent with the Paris Agreement's climate goals. Specifically, Shell does not have an 'absolute [emissions] reduction' obligation of 45 per cent or any other percentage.[37]

---

[34] *Vereniging Milieudefensie et al v Royal Dutch Shell Plc*, Hague District Court, Decision of 26 May 2021.

[35] Milieudefensie and Paulussen Advocaten (2022) *Defending the Danger Line – A manual for climate litigators*, at 42.

[36] *Milieudefensie et al. v Royal Dutch Shell Plc*, at 4.5.2.

[37] *Royal Dutch Shell Plc v Milieudefensie et al.*, Hague Appeal Court, Decision of 12 November 2024, NL:GHDHA:2024:2100, available at https://uitspraken.rechtspraak.nl/details?id=ECLI:NL:GHDHA:2024:2100.

Turning to the US, in the ongoing lawsuit of *State of Rhode Island v Shell Oil Products & Ors*, the State of Rhode Island claims that Shell, along with more than ten other energy firms, has been burning fossil fuels knowing that such acts are damaging the Earth's atmosphere. A connected allegation concerned greenwashing by misleading public customers into purchasing increasing quantities of their products.

The Rhode Island causes of action include, among other things, public nuisance, and negligent failure to warn. Further, violations of that state's Environmental Rights Act are alleged. The plaintiff's case is based on eight causes of action – a contrast to the narrow UK ClientEarth lawsuit approach based only on director breaches under company law. While energy groups have far higher carbon emissions compared to even the largest semiconductor fabrication plant, these are relevant points to apply given the global nature, of GHG emissions.[38]

In sum, what English law, and other jurisdictions expect of directors is changing. Sustainability is likely to be a key requirement. In this sense there is a transition cost to make semiconductors as low carbon emitting and recyclable as possible.

6.8 Science and law

In the future, court decisions can more effectively balance the complexities of qualitative and quantitative factors by applying the precautionary principle. Indeed, pivotal European Union (EU)-derived legislation transposed into English law, requires just that in the context of environmental impact assessments.[39] This broad legal principle has increasing relevance to sustainability risk management. As a reminder, while there is no universally accepted definition of the precautionary principle, the Rio Declaration provides the following practical, respected, and succinct wording:

[38] *State of Rhode Island v Shell Oil Products & Ors*, Case Number: PC-2018-4716, filed 2018.

[39] EU Directive 54/2014, Recitals 2 and 7.

> Where there are threats of serious or irreversible environmental damage, lack of full scientific certainty shall not be used as a reason for postponing cost-effective measures to prevent environmental degradation.[40]

Put another way, if a project has (a) the potential for causing environmental damage, and (b) there is a degree of scientific uncertainty about the probability of damage, then that risk needs to be addressed.

However, the precautionary principle shifts the evidentiary burden onto the supporter of the project to prove the threat is negligible or non-existent. For instance, if a semiconductor firm promoted carbon capture and storage (CCS) strategies as a means of reaching net zero emissions, there is a compelling argument for requiring a reverse burden of proof. The aim would not be to ban CCS techniques that lack full scientific understanding. Instead to take a proportionate response on what is sustainable, and the degree of climate change mitigation and adaptation that can be attributed.

6.9 Sustainable semiconductor performance

The ambition to make sustainable semiconductors is consistent with the paradox of 'technological development'. First presented by a former leader of the Massachusetts Institute of Technology (MIT), the paradox states that business causes environmental damage but also provides methods to fix that damage.[41] However, the scale of the challenge cannot be underestimated. For instance, a Harvard research team calculated that approximately 33 per cent of Apple's mobile device CO_2 emissions derive from central processing units (CPUs), dynamic random access memory (DRAM), NAND flash storage and System on Chip (SoC) components.

[40] UN General Assembly (1992) Rio Declaration on Environment and Development, Principle 15, available at www.un.org/en/development/desa/population/migration/generalassembly/docs/globalcompact/A_CONF.151_26_Vol.I_Declaration.pdf.

[41] Gray, P. (1989) 'The Paradox of Technological Development', in Jesse, H. (1989) *Technology and Environment*, National Academy Press, at 92–204.

They logically conclude that future architecture and circuit researchers can make an impact on sustainable hardware design.[42]

In the context of graphics processing units (GPUs), Satya Nadella, Chairman and Chief Executive Officer (CEO) of Microsoft, commented at a Chatham House event that 'the most promising thing is to use AI and take 250 years of chemistry and accelerate it to achieve climate goals'.[43] GPUs are increasing carbon emissions, but they are also at the centre of such ambitions. While Microsoft's enthusiasm is not necessarily matched by current citizen level opinions about artificial intelligence (AI) as a sustainable source of innovation, in the pharmaceutical sector the use of GPUs or equivalent cutting-edge logic components are already accelerating progress. For example, research conducted by GlaxoSmith and AstraZeneca is already benefiting from Cerebras integrated circuits.[44]

For instance, a 2024 study found that only 30 per cent of citizen respondents from 28 countries had enthusiasm for AI innovation. The Edelman survey was based on 28 countries, 32,000 respondents, and each sample size varied between 1,109 and 1,500. The same survey revealed that enthusiasm for green energy innovation was significantly higher at 54 per cent.[45] Put another way, if AI is less trusted, proven green semiconductor innovations should emerge as a positive catalyst, assuming firms are adept at communicating the benefits of their products or services. Trust trumps marketing as the means to maximise that happening.

Yet given the energy demands of GPUs, there needs to be vigorous R&D on how best to produce more sustainable GPUs which will no doubt provide some incumbent and first mover firms with an opportunity to offer something new. The environmental threats and commercial opportunities are evident from a team of researchers who quantified the

---

42 Gupta, U. (2020) *Chasing carbon coal and the elusive environmental footprint of computing*, at 5, available at https://arxiv.org/pdf/2011.02839.pdf.

43 Chatham House (2024), 'Satya Nadella – A conversation on the opportunities and the impacts that AI will have on the global arena', 15 January 2024.

44 The record keeping and auditing of GPU or equivalent research needs to be of the highest standard.

45 Edelman (2024) Edelman Trust Barometer 2024, at 14, available at www.edelman.com/trust/2024/trust-barometer.

computational and environmental cost of training deep neural network models for natural language processing (NLP).

Their calculations focused on the energy required to train a mix of popular NLP models.[46] Their results showed that all the models emitted substantial carbon. Most memorably, they observed that using the ubiquitous pre-trained BERT model[47] with 64 Nvidia V100 GPUs produced carbon emissions comparable with one passenger taking a trans-American flight from New York to San Francisco.[48] A permanent column to populate on R&D spreadsheets is carbon emissions.

Some electronic design automation (EDA) will communicate to the market and policy makers that AI enables EDA tools to more effectively optimise for power and thermal performance with the possibility of achieving significant total power consumption savings compared with traditional EDA technology. Two points arise from these claims. First, there need to be clear, provable statistics for verification. Second, the equation for savings cannot omit the cost of running vast numbers of GPUs.

While environmental issues associated with semiconductor manufacturing are long established, the congruence of 190-plus nation-states signing the Paris Agreement, has triggered increasing regulation and lawsuits. Implementing sustainability makes this issue a higher compliance requirement and reputational issue.

---

46 Strubell, E., A. Ganesh and A. McCallum (2019) 'Energy and Policy Considerations for Deep Learning in NLP', available at https://arxiv.org/abs/1906.02243v1.

47 The Bidirectional Encoder Representations from Transformers (BERT) suite of language models was introduced in 2018 by Google. Since then, BERT has been applied in thousands of NLP experiments.

48 Strubell, Ganesh and McCallum (2019), at subsection 4.1. The BERT model expended 1,438 CO_2(lbs) compared with one passenger on a flight from New York to San Francisco consuming 1,984 CO_2(lbs).

6.10 Reframing the climate crisis as a commercial opportunity

It is logical for UK semiconductor strategies to prioritise on green production and products. There are two key reasons for this. First, for historic and geographical reasons the leading semiconductor economies of Japan, South Korea and Taiwan all share the challenge of producing sustainable semiconductors. They have high-density populations and their current investment in renewable energy supplies lags behind many other Organization for Economic Cooperation and Development (OECD) countries.

While each Asian economy seeks to adjust its renewable energy policy and implement change, the UK already has a comparatively advanced renewable energy sector. Based on 2024 statistics published by the International Renewable Energy Agency (IRENA), the UK's renewable energy share of electricity production is 41.7 per cent – nearly twice that of Japan (21.5 per cent) and the US (21.3 per cent). The UK also compares favourably with Germany (43.3 per cent). The leading semiconductor economies of South Korea (7.4 per cent) and Taiwan (7.6 per cent) are many years behind.[49]

Renewable use is a comparative advantage that benefits all types of semiconductor manufacturing. Each semiconductor firm will already or imminently be required to comply with TCFD and ISSB IFRS-S or equivalent disclosures. Further, the communication of comparatively more sustainable products especially compared with leading Asian centres is a valuable strategy.

6.11 Dissecting the environmental challenges

As mentioned at the beginning of this chapter, compared with other complex engineering sectors, such as oil and gas, making semiconduc-

---

[49] IRENA (2024) 'Renewable Energy Statistics 2024', at 97–8, available at www.irena.org/-/media/Files/IRENA/Agency/Publication/2024/Jul/IRENA_Renewable_Energy_Statistics_2024.pdf.

tors does not conjure up images of significant sustainability issues.[50] In fact, the use of electricity, chemicals and water can be vast. Further, the amount of non-recyclable waste is significant.

In GHG Protocol terms the current average semiconductor fabrication has considerable Scope 1 emissions from boilers and manufacturing equipment. An average firm is also going to have high Scope 2 emissions from purchased energy that has been produced on its behalf. Further, such a firm will also have indirect Scope 3 emissions from the products in which their designed or made components function. Figure 6.3 memorably captures the complexities of reporting disclosures,[51] although, software firms provide solutions to reduce the time-consuming nature of the calculation and disclosure challenges.[52]

6.12 Energy, chemicals and gases

A hugely impressive nine-month participant observation study of a leading US semiconductor manufacturer included the following succinct observation:

> Despite the relatively limited absolute scale of its environmental impacts, the semiconductor industry does present significant and specialised environmental challenges associated with its need to maintain a uniquely clean manufacturing environment and the manufacturing processes' reliance on small quantities of highly novel organic and inorganic chemicals to achieve desired chip properties.

---

[50] Queen Mary University of London asked me to contribute a chapter on sustainability litigation in the English High Courts. There were no lawsuits against semiconductor firms. However, the coverage of greenwashing is valuable to consider for any firm's strategy. See Mitsi, M. and B. Lim (2025) *Environmental, Social and Governance (ESG) Disputes: Litigation and Arbitration*, Kluwer, chapter on Climate Change (Sustainability) Litigation in the English Courts.

[51] World Resources Institute (2024) Greenhouse Gas Protocol – The global standard for companies and organisations to measure and manage their GHG emissions and become more efficient, resilient, and prosperous, available at www.wri.org/initiatives/greenhouse-gas-protocol.

[52] For example, IBM offers Envizi, an emissions management software product. See www.ibm.com/products/envizi/emissions-management.

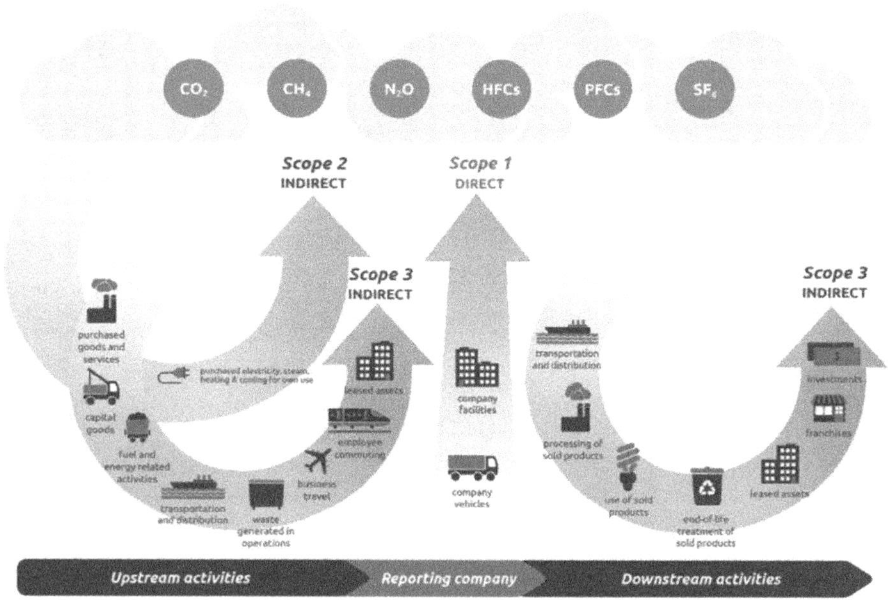

Source: World Resources Institute (2024) Greenhouse Gas Protocol, available at www.wri.org/initiatives/greenhouse-gas-protocol

Figure 6.3 *GHG protocol scopes and emissions across the value chain*

> Chip manufacturing is an immensely complex production process, made up of several hundred steps that use chemicals, gases, and energies of various forms to pattern, implant and build the layers that make up the finished product. To prevent dust particles from destroying the electrical properties of the chip during manufacture chemical solvents, gases and water are used to keep the silicon wafers on which the chips are created, the process equipment, and the fab in which the manufacturing takes place, scrupulously clean.[53]

6.13 Perfluorocarbons emissions

Semiconductor manufacturing uses many chemicals in both the etching and cleaning processes. These are classified as perfluorocarbons (PFCs). The risk with PFCs is that they are persistent in the environment because of their non-biodegradability and resistance to degradation potentially over 1,000 years. Hence, they are informally known as 'forever chemicals'.

Over the last two decades, firms have reduced PFC emissions by evolving manufacturing operations. Changes include applying alternative chemicals, deploying alternative manufacturing processes, improving abatement systems, and optimising processes. While PFCs have a minor impact on climate change, they still represent environmental risk to both citizens, communities, customers, and employees.[54]

The World Semiconductor Council (WSC) has led sector efforts to successfully achieve voluntary reduction goals in the emissions of PFCs.[55] Impressively, in 1999 WSC agreed to reduce PFC emissions by at least 10

---

[53] Howard-Grenville, J. (2007) *Corporate Culture and Environmental Practice: Making Change at a High-Technology Manufacturer*, Cheltenham, UK and Northampton, MA: Edward Elgar Publishing, at 24. Professor Howard-Grenville, Cambridge University, continues to research and publish forward-thinking articles on sustainability matters.

[54] In the UK PFCs are not banned from semiconductor manufacturing processes. In the EU under the Marketing and Use Directive (Directive 2006/122/EC) PFOS are not permitted, but the directive exempts photoresists and ARCs used in photolithography. See Annex, (3)(a) of the Marketing and Use Directive (Directive 2006/122/EC).

[55] WSC is made up of the semiconductor industry associations (SIAs) in China, Europe, Japan, South Korea, Taiwan and the US. See www.semiconductorcouncil.org/.

per cent by the end of 2010. By 2010, emissions were reduced by 32 per cent. WSC has also made voluntary commitments to eliminate the use of perfluorooctanyl sulphonates (PFOS).[56]

Currently, the process for substituting PFCs with other chemicals is too great a challenge. Further, even if non-harmful substitutes can be developed, the process of technology implementation, gaining approvals and final replacement may take many years.

The potential competitive advantage opportunities include establishing alternative, safer chemicals for use in semiconductor manufacturing processes. For government-funded research bodies there is an opportunity to make available and request more funding for established and start-up firms that take on this challenge. For individual firms, their competitive advantage may start with hiring talent that has both the prerequisite chemistry and sustainability expertise.

As illustrated in Figure 6.4, both the manufacturing processes and cleansing measures required to operate a fabrication facility use significant amounts of acids, electricity, gases and water. The main manufacturing processes include patterning, etching, implementation, deposition, diffusion and polishing. Cleansing measures include wafer cleaning, equipment cleaning and air recirculation throughout the fab. The environmental impacts of these processes and cleansing measures include:

1. Chemical waste
2. Hazardous waste
3. Global warming gases
4. Hazardous air pollutants
5. Volatile organic compounds
6. Wastewater[57]

---

[56] WSC (2024) 'Environment, Safety and Health', available at www.semiconductorcouncil.org/issuesactivities/environment-safety-and-health/.

[57] Wastewater must be treated on-site to neutralise acids and other harmful contaminants.

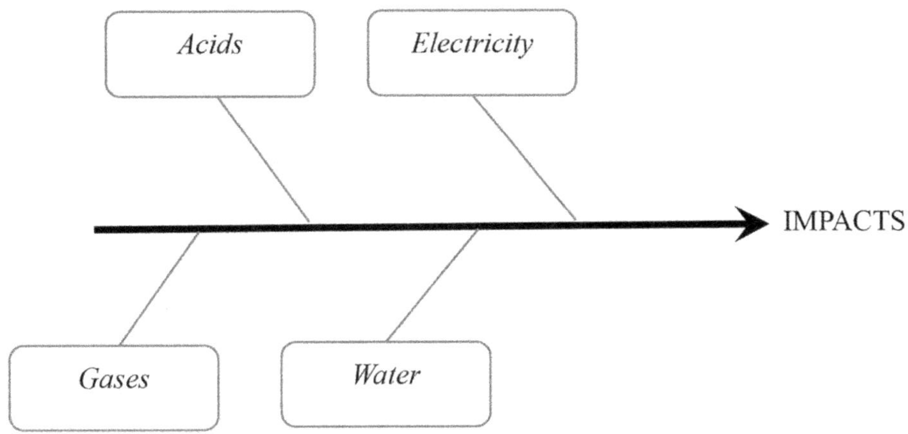

Source: © Iain Sheridan (2025)

Figure 6.4 *Environmental impacts of manufacturing process steps and cleansing tasks*

6.14 New entrant competitive advantages

Turning to new entrant firms, whether manufacturing or only designing, they have opportunities to make sustainable competitive advantages. Three strategies are especially promising. First, referencing the IPCC global warming mitigation framework. Second, investing in second-hand manufacturing equipment. Third, lobbying government for tax credits linked to environmental manufacturing efficiency.

The IPCC[58] provides a useful framework for analysis to facilitate combined actions towards limiting global warming to 1.5°C. This framework applies at the macro level of governmental management of systems for adaptation and mitigation decision making.

However, in my view the adjacent possible opportunity is that it provides equal relevance for each unique semiconductor firm. Further its application may provide added commerical success to align business plans with governmental support policies. The IPCC report summarises six feasibility dimensions of adaptation and mitigation that together can limit warming to 1.5°C within the context of sustainable development. These factors are set out in Table 6.1.[59]

6.15 Used manufacturing equipment

A demand surge at the beginning of the Covid-19 pandemic has made used semiconductor manufacturing equipment a growing market. For example, Moov Technologies (Moov), a US-based firm, also trades second-hand semiconductor making equipment in Asia and the EU. In 2023, Asia accounted for 50 per cent of its revenues, the US 35 per cent, and Europe and elsewhere 15 per cent. Moov has over US $4 billion of equipment, including from Advantest, ASML, Applied Materials, KLA, and Lam Research.[60] It seems logical for Moov and its competitor sup-

---

[58] www.ipcc.ch/.

[59] IPCC (2018) at 393.

[60] Ting-Fang, C. (2023) 'Demand for used chip equipment surging since COVID: Moov CEO', Nikkei Asia, 24 August 2023.

Table 6.1 *Feasibility framework*

Subject matter	Explanation
Environmental feasibility	Degree to which natural resource is, and systems are, available to support the various options for transitioning.
Technological feasibility	Extent to which the required technologies are available and developed.
Economic feasibility	Economic conditions and implications.
Social/cultural feasibility	Implications for human behaviour and health.
Institutional feasibility	Required types of institutional and political support.
Geophysical feasibility	Capacity of physical systems to support the option.

Source: IPCC (2018) *Global Warming of 1.5°C, Special Report*, at 393

pliers to experience increased demand based on the sustainability of its activities.

Further, it appears that Samsung and SK Hynix have stopped selling used semiconductor manufacturing equipment. Their reasoning is based on their risk assessment of falling foul of US export control policies on China. Existing and future US governments may decide to tighten policies. Hundreds of machines are owned by these two leading memory semiconductor manufacturers. This stockpile may present an opportunity for UK firms to buy them. It cannot be viable for them all to remain stored in South Korea and China.[61]

6.16 Energy efficiency

UK tax laws that factor in environmental impact are not a new policy maker innovation. For instance, company car tax is primarily determined

[61] *Financial Times* (2024) 'South Korean chipmakers halt old equipment sales over fears of US backlash – Samsung and SK Hynix have been storing used machines in warehouses as US-China tensions rise', 12 March 2024.

based on CO_2 engine levels and fuel type. A tax exemption for zero emission vehicles has been the catalyst for electric car sales.[62]

Tax credits could be provided for proof that semiconductor components are between 50 and 100 per cent recyclable. By which is meant it is not currently unlawful to make non-recyclable semiconductor components, but incentivising a significant reduction in them becoming landfill is a logical evolution for the whole sector.[63]

My past research has included considering how, in the manufacturing of smartphone batteries the use of rare earth elements (REE)[64] can be a measurable tax point metric for fiscal authorities.[65] REEs and the use of plastics may increase future tax costs for the customers of semiconductor designers and producers.

A sensible tax strategy at the individual firm level is to offset such increases with deductions from circular policies for as many materials as possible. Although to be clear, the circular economic principle encompasses not only eliminating waste and pollution, but also maximising the lifetime of products and materials as well as regenerating natural systems.[66]

---

62 See Vehicle Excise and Registration Act 1994 and its related statutory instruments.

63 Note there is recycling subject matter overlap with other chapters in this book, especially Chapter 5 Strategic issues, Chapter 11 Taxation law, and Chapter 12 Conclusions on achieving growth.

64 Rare Earth Elements are defined as 'any member of the group of chemical elements consisting of three elements in Group 3 (scandium [Sc], yttrium [Y], and lanthanum [La]) and the first extended row of elements below the main body of the periodic table (cerium [Ce] through lutetium [Lu])'. See www.britannica.com/science/rareearth-element.

65 Sheridan, I. (2016) 'Smartphones, Research and Development and Corporation Tax: Current Treatment and Future Possibilities' 44(11) *Intertax* 831–7.

66 Schröder, P. and J. Barrie (2024) 'How the circular economy can revive the Sustainable Development Goals Priorities for immediate global action, and a policy blueprint for the transition to 2050', Chatham House, Research Paper, at 9.

6.17 Recycling efficiency

ASML, the world leader in photolithography, has invested in sustainability policies for several years. It has adopted impressive recycling targets and has revised these. ASML has repair centres at its global headquarters and stores used components. It is also expanding repair centres in China, South Korea, Taiwan, and the US. In 2022, ASML claims to have reused 87 per cent of the parts in its machines. Further it has set the ambitious target of reusing 95 per cent of its components by 2025.[67]

6.18 Cooperative industry associations

Given sustainability is high up on the collective agenda of leading semiconductor firms, there is logic in increasing sector-wide pooling of best practice and knowledge. For instance, Global Semiconductor Alliance (GSA), an industry association, has established a Semiconductor Interest Group that signals the sector's worldwide acknowledgement it must focus more on climate change.[68] GSA has regular workshops discussing, among other issues, Scope 3 emissions in the semiconductor value chain.

6.19 Conclusions

Thanks to NASA's technology we all know that, from space, currently Earth looks beautiful. Semiconductors played a pivotal role in making that happen. However, we have yet to collectively commit to sustain our habitation on Earth. One IPCC report, weighing in at 3 675 pages, has reached the conclusion that there are already 'locked-in' impacts of climate change.[69] By which is meant we cannot even get back to the climatic position Earth was in in 1968 when the Apollo team first looked

---

[67] *Financial Times* (2023) 'ASML says decoupling chip supply chain is practically impossible', 27 June 2023.

[68] See at www.gsaglobal.org/sustainability.

[69] IPCC is a body of the United Nations. Widely respected by scientists worldwide, in 2007 it shared a Nobel Peace Prize with Al Gore for its climate change contributions. The IPCC has pre-eminent technical authority on climate change in the context of its science-based predictions. See www.ipcc.ch/.

back home. We may yet end up reading a future NASA transcript like 'We see the Earth now...I think that's the Florida coastline'.

In a speech entitled 'The purpose and future of the corporation', Colin Mayer, former Dean of Saïd Business School, Oxford University, reframed firms in the following thought-provoking people, planet, profit way: 'The purpose of business is not to produce profits. The purpose of business is to produce profitable solutions to the problems of people and planet. And in the process, it produces profits'.[70] In his 2024 book, Mayer evolves these earlier arguments by promoting business activity based on what he terms 'Moral Law'.[71] He argues that the current Companies Act 2006 or equivalent legislation fails to prevent profiting from detriments.

It is difficult to disagree with Mayer's conclusion that 'corporate purposes of profiting from solving problems without creating them should be the basis on which corporate law establishes the duties of directors'.[72] From this moral viewpoint, his treatise follows the established English law principles of equity that focus on fairness and rebalancing unjust enrichment scenarios.[73]

Ultimately, CEOs, boards, and legal advisers can make important contributions via their respective firms and by influencing policy decisions across the semiconductor sector. Balancing profit-making with transition planning. All relevant stakeholders will be watching, and each presents unique legal risks: environmental activists, business-to-business customers, constituents, consumers, employees, government departments, lobbyists, OEMs, regulators, and shareholders.

---

[70] Harvard University, Kennedy School (2019) 'The Purpose and Future of the Corporation', speech by Colin Mayer, CBE, on 21 February 2019. He has expanded on this change in philosophy in his latest book. See Mayer, C. (2024) *Capitalism and Crises: How to Fix Them*, Oxford University Press.

[71] Mayer (2024).

[72] Ibid at 17.

[73] *Banque Financière de la Cité v Parc (Battersea) Ltd* [1999] AC 221; and *Bank of Cyprus v Menelaou* [2015] UKSC 66. See also Mitchell, C. (2022) *Goff & Jones: The Law of Unjust Enrichment*, 10th edn, London: Sweet & Maxwell. Unjust enrichment derives from the Roman Law principle of *nemo locupletari postet aliena iactura* – no one can be enriched by another's loss.

7. Competition law

Mergers and acquisitions in the semiconductor sector are a continuous opportunity and threat. The motivations for this activity seem as varied as the types of firms involved. However, the commercial value of semiconductors will only increase competitive acquisitions or mergers, especially in the race to do 'more than Moore' and leverage artificial intelligence (AI)/machine learning (ML). The recent acquisitions of the Finnish firm Silo AI by AMD, and the Israeli firm Run:ai by Nvidia, reflect this trend. Additionally, not only tensions between China and the United States (US), but also more ambitious competition from the Global South mean all business decision makers must have an acute grasp of rapid changes in geopolitics.

This chapter sets out the legal issues and risks associated with a United Kingdom (UK) semiconductor strategy in the context of English law, regulation, and regulatory approach. Given the global nature of semiconductor markets there are also references to court and regulator decision making in China, the European Union (EU) and the US. Most of the analysis has relevance to any other jurisdiction given the cross-border nature of semiconductor business.

7.1 Acquisition activity

Table 7.1 captures a sample of significant strategic acquisitions since 2015 across the whole product cycle, from design to packaging. There are four broad acquisition trends. First, increased expenditure on cars, PCs for gaming, smartphones and computer networks relying on increasing numbers of semiconductors are driving activity. Second, ML applications or at least the ambition to do more ML, can account for other decisions. Third, acquisitions based on growth where one underperforming firm is acquired by a more successful competitor. Fourth, private equity portfolio acquisitions, exemplified by SoftBank's acquisition of ARM.

Table 7.1 Semiconductor acquisitions

Acquisition event	Product or service advantage	Year	US$
Nvidia acquired Run:ai	Software that speeds up graphics processing unit (GPU) initiatives	2025	700 million
AMD acquired Silo AI	Open-source AI models	2024	665 million
Renesas acquired Altium	Electronic design automation (EDA) software	2024	5.9 billion
Microchip acquired Neuronix AI Labs	Neural network acceleration architectures	2024	Undisclosed
Vishay Intertechnology acquired Newport Wafer Fab	Compound, photonics, and silicon production	2023	177 million
Broadcom Inc. acquired VMware	Cloud computing	2023	61 billion
AMD acquired Xilinx	Field programmable gate array (FPGA)	2022	60 billion
Renesas acquired Dialog Semiconductor	Application Specific Standard Products (ASSP) including Power Management Integrated Circuits (PMIC).	2021	5.9 billion
Analog Devices acquired Maxim Integrated	Analog, mixed signal integrated circuits (ICs)	2021	20 billion
SK Hynix acquired Intel's NAND plant in Dalian, China[1]	NAND foundry and NAND intellectual property (IP)	2021	9 billion
Infineon acquired Cypress	NOR	2020	9.7 billion

Acquisition event	Product or service advantage	Year	US$
Cadence Design Systems acquired OpenEye Scientific	EDA - Computational modelling and simulation software used by pharmaceutical sector	2020	0.5 billion
NVIDIA acquired Mellanox[2]	Data centre network technology	2019	6.9 billion
ON Semiconductor acquired Global Foundries 300mm fabrication facility	300mm foundry dedicated to power, analog and sensing products	2019	0.4 billion
Intel acquired Mobileye	ADAS, sensors for vehicular automation, including aircraft, car, and watercraft	2017	15.3 billion
Amkor Technology acquired NANIUM	Wafer-level packaging for smartphones, tablets, and other applications	2017	TBC
ON Semiconductor acquired Fairchild	Diverse, but especially metal-oxide-semiconductor field-effect transistor (MOSFET)	2016	2.4 billion
The Analog Devices acquired Linear Technology	Analog ICs	2016	14.8 billion
Microchip acquired Atmel	Microcontrollers, RF/ wireless, memory products	2016	3.5 billion
Renesas acquired Intersil	Microcontrollers and System on Chip (SoC)	2016	3.2 billion
SoftBank acquired AMD	Design	2016	24.3 billion
ASML acquired Hermes Microvision	Lithography	2016	3.1 billion

Acquisition event	Product or service advantage	Year	US$
Avago acquired Broadcom	Diverse, including design and manufacturing	2015	37 billion
Infineon acquired International Rectifier	Analog and mixed-signal ICs	2015	3 billion

Notes: [1] The first phase of the SK Hynix acquisition was 2021, but the final phase is scheduled for 2025. [2] In Q4 2024, the Chinese state administration of market regulation opened an investigation into Nvidia concerning suspected competition law breaches. The focus concerned commitments made by Nvidia during its acquisition of Mellanox. The investigation appears to be a response to tougher export controls issued less than ten days before by the US Government. See *Financial Times* (2024) 'China launches antitrust probe into Nvidia', 9 December 2024.
Source: © Iain Sheridan (2025)

Both external and in-house legal counsel dedicated to semiconductor firms will inevitably find themselves at some point working to support an acquisition or a merger. In either scenario, they need to have some understanding of current and likely future competition law that may affect expansion plans with different risk issues, timescales, and board-level strategic decision making.[1] In the UK, semiconductor sector competition activity is investigated and enforced by the Competition and Markets Authority (CMA).[2] Although Brexit places the UK outside of the requirement to cooperate with EU member state competition authorities and the European Commission, UK courts and regulators are generally expected to maintain consistency with principles provided by the EU's Court of

1 An authoritative and in-depth work on all aspects of competition is Scott, A. et al (2023) *Encyclopaedia of Competition Law*, London: Sweet & Maxwell.
2 Section 25 Enterprise and Regulatory Reform Act 2013; ss.32–38 Competition Act 1998.

Justice of the European Union (CJEU).[3] The list below captures the functions and areas of responsibility and focus of the CMA.[4]

- Competition powers across all sectors of the economy.
- Promoting competition for the benefit of consumers by leading investigations into businesses, investigating all market sectors, taking action against businesses and producing policy papers.
- Providing directions concerning agreements.
- Providing direction concerning conduct.[5]

7.2 The CMA's approach to competition

The CMA 'has powers to initiate market investigations, gather and appraise evidence and also impose structural and behavioural remedies'.[6] It is not just a matter of good law and guidelines, given that the CMA needs access to independent information on pricing along with insights to make balanced decisions on when anti-competitive practices exist. Absent the CMA's role, there is a real risk 'that sector regulators, even the most dedicated ones, may fail to understand and predict market dynamics'.[7]

However, evidence from the CMA's responses to a House of Lords investigation into digital platforms reveals an organisation aware that

3 Section 60A Competition Act 1998. Although note s.60(A)(7) provides exceptions that allow for deviation from this rule. For example, changes in forms of economic activity since the time when the European principle or CJEU decision was made.

4 Payment Systems Regulator (PSR) (2021) 'Consultation Paper - Our Proposed PSR Strategy', CP21/7, at 1.13, sets out the PSR's proposed five-year strategic plan. One of its four strategic priorities is to promote competition in the payment systems sub-sector. See www.psr.org.uk/publications/general/our-proposed-strategy/.

5 Sections 32 and 33 Competition Act 1998.

6 CMA (2013) 'Guidelines for Market Investigations: Their Role, Procedures, Assessment and Remedies', CC3 (Revised) (April 2013). See www.gov.uk/government/organisations/competition-and-markets-authority.

7 Ezrachi, A. and M. Stucke (2016) *Virtual Competition – The Promise and Perils of the Algorithm-Driven Economy*, Harvard University Press, at 216.

over-zealous regulation may stifle innovation.[8] This online platform report recorded that 'the CMA focused on the potentially anti-competitive effects of "disproportionate regulatory mechanisms", which could have "the counterproductive effect of 'locking-in' a particular market structure", and thereby "insulate incumbent on-line firms from dynamic competition that would otherwise benefit consumers"'.[9] The semiconductor sector is equally vulnerable to stifling innovation.

There has already been CMA scrutiny of semiconductor firms, namely the planned acquisition by Broadcom Inc of VMware Inc.[10] In March 2023, the CMA started investigating whether this merger would 'result in a substantial lessening of competition within a market or markets in the United Kingdom'.[11]

As part of a merger process, instead of applying its own anti-competitive remedies to a merger scenario,[12] the CMA has the power to accept appropriate 'undertakings in lieu' aimed at mitigating or preventing the substantial lessening of competition expected to occur from the impact of the merger.[13] Existing undertakings already published by the CMA may assist counsel working with semiconductor firms during the planning phase of a merger.[14] More generally, they can assist any regulated firm in gaining insight into the 'undertakings in lieu' process.

---

8 House of Lords, *Online Platforms and the EU Digital Single Market*, 10th Report of Session 2015–16 (20 April 2016), HL Paper 129.

9 HL Paper 129, 'Competition and Markets Authority—Written evidence (OPL0055)', at para.45.

10 UK Government (2023) Broadcom/VMware merger inquiry, available at www.gov.uk/cma-cases/broadcom-slash-vmware-merger-inquiry.

11 Section 33 Enterprise Act 2002.

12 Sections 22 and 33 Enterprise Act 2002. See www.legislation.gov.uk/ukpga/2002/40/section/22; and www.legislation.gov.uk/ukpga/2002/40/section/33.

13 Section 73 Enterprise Act 2002. See www.legislation.gov.uk/ukpga/2002/40/section/73.

14 CMA (2016) 'Undertakings given by *Tullett Prebon plc* and *ICAP plc* to the Competition and Markets Authority pursuant to section 73 of the Enterprise Act 2002', available at https://assets.publishing.service.gov.uk/media/57da7601ed915d6c2f000056/tullett-icap-final-undertakings.pdf.

If the CMA concludes it has a case of anti-competitive behaviour, it has powers to impose a penalty of up to 10 per cent of annual worldwide group turnover.[15]

7.3 The CMA's Subsidy Advice Unit

Of additional relevance to semiconductor firms growing in the UK, since 2023 the CMA has operated a Subsidy Advice Unit (SAU). It forms part of the new regime for governing the provision of subsidies within the UK following its exit from the EU. Any UK authority planning to provide a subsidy to a firm, must first request a report from the CMA.[16]

A subsidy in this new UK regime context includes:

> financial assistance which…confers an economic advantage on one or more enterprises…is such that it benefits one or more enterprises over one or more other enterprises with respect to the production of goods or the provision of services, and…is capable of having, an effect on competition or investment within the United Kingdom, trade between the United Kingdom and a country or territory outside the United Kingdom, or investment as between the United Kingdom and a country or territory outside the United Kingdom.[17]

The scope of 'financial assistance' is wide, covering grants, loans, guarantees, tax breaks and the purchase of good or services.[18]

7.4 UK competition law

From a UK perspective, the concept of dominance has its roots in EU case law. Dominant market position has been consistently defined as 'a position of economic strength enjoyed by an undertaking which enables it to prevent effective competition being maintained on the relevant market by affording it the power to behave to an appreciable extent independently of

---

[15] Section 36(8) Competition Act 1998. See www.legislation.gov.uk/ukpga/1998/41/section/36.

[16] Made operational under s.52 of the Subsidy Control Act 2022.

[17] Section 2(1) Subsidy Control Act 2022.

[18] Section 2(2) Subsidy Control Act 2022.

its competitors, customers and ultimately of its consumers'.[19] Further, it is also important to emphasise that based on CMA guidance, dominance is inextricably linked to substantial market power.[20]

In the context of semiconductors, there is the initial logic of thinking about market economic strength and substantial market power as relevant to a handful of market leaders, such as ARM, Intel, Qualcomm, Samsung and so forth. However, as technology becomes a central part of competitive advantage, it is likely that diverse firms will come under the scrutiny of the CMA. For instance, if any semiconductor firm enters a joint venture with Ali Baba, Amazon, Apple, Facebook, Google, or Microsoft.

7.5 Consequences of anti-competitive behaviour

The CMA has wide powers of enforcement that can cause significant cost and loss of corporate time. It possesses the power to publish a notice of an investigation, which would be potentially harmful for any firm's short-term reputation.[21] Whilst carrying out investigations, the CMA can impose interim measures stopping potential anti-competitive behaviour until a final decision is made.[22] Further, the CMA's options include accepting appropriate commitments from a firm under investigation to take specific action or refrain from taking such action.[23]

---

19 *United Brands v Commission* (C-27/76) [1978] ECR 207; [1978] 1 CMLR 429. See https://op.europa.eu/en/publication-detail/-/publication/32bf3aa2-d8b1-4201-81eb-a238062fcd37/language-en.

20 At the risk of being accused of pedantry, the CMA guidance was in fact that of the Office of Fair Trading (OFT), the predecessor to the CMA. See OFT (2004) 'Abuse of a Dominant Position – Understanding Competition Law', at 13, available at https://assets.publishing.service.gov.uk/government/uploads/system/uploads/attachment_data/file/284422/oft402.pdf.

21 Section 25A Competition Act 1998. See www.legislation.gov.uk/ukpga/1998/41/section/25A.

22 Section 35 Competition Act 1998. See www.legislation.gov.uk/ukpga/1998/41/section/35.

23 Section 31A Competition Act 1998. See www.legislation.gov.uk/ukpga/1998/41/section/31A.

7.6 Merger activity involving specific technologies

The merger threshold for an entity targeted for acquisition being referred to the CMA for investigation, is a turnover exceeding £1 million, for the following activities[24]:

- AI research;
- cryptographic authentication research;
- ownership, development or supply of IP covering the functional capability of computer processing units, instruction set architecture units and any code that provides low level control for such units;
- quantum computing research;

any services employing quantum computing communication or simulation; or quantum resistant cryptography;

- any services employing AI;
- any services employing cryptographic authentication.

For most semiconductor firms, the aspects of most importance are the ownership and development, or supply, of intellectual property, concerning computer processing units and instruction set architecture units. However, given disruptive activity is also where some future activity will be, AI research and acquisitions are likely to be increasingly relevant areas.

Additionally, semiconductor firms with a turnover below the £1 million threshold may still be investigated at the discretion of the Secretary of State on the grounds of public interest. Therefore, it likely that AI projects may experience special attention regardless of their turnover level.[25]

There is also a merger test based on 'share of supply'. Specifically, the threshold is based on services supplied in the UK amounting to at least 25 per cent of the UK market or a 'substantial part of the UK'.[26] This

---

[24] The Enterprise Act 2002 (Turnover Test) (Amendment) Order 2020 (SI 2020/763). See www.legislation.gov.uk/uksi/2020/763/article/2.

[25] Section 42 Enterprise Act 2002. See www.legislation.gov.uk/ukpga/2002/40/section/42.

[26] Section 23(4A) Enterprise Act 2002. See www.legislation.gov.uk/ukpga/2002/40/section/23.

second share of supply test may seem an unlikely consideration in the UK semiconductor market. However, with central processing unit (CPU) or memory unit supply in the automotive sector this could present a risk for some firms.

There are also scenarios where niche providers in small markets could fall foul of this test. For example, logic processing units provided for drones used in narrow markets such as agriculture or defence. By which is meant the 'substantial part of the UK' test may affect a successful niche firm as much as high-volume providers, such as Qualcomm, Texas Instruments or Samsung. For example, Mobileye, the advanced driver assistance systems (ADAS) firm, and subsidiary of Intel, is estimated to have 70 per cent of the market driver-assist technology cameras.[27]

7.7 Comparing the UK with China, the EU, and the US

Given the global nature of the semiconductor sector, it is useful to see how UK law compares with China, the EU, and the US. Table 7.2 provides the key principles for each jurisdiction.

It not necessarily always politics that drives decisions, legal principles and jurisprudence can have equal influence. Consequently, knowing this may assist legal counsel anticipating if proposals made by clients are likely to be approved by leading regulators.[28]

7.8 The National Security and Investment Act 2021

The National Security and Investment Act 2021 (NSIA 2021) is also of potential relevance to semiconductor firms.[29] The NSIA 2021 creates a new regime for vetting both foreign and national investment in the UK.

[27] *Financial Times* (2023) 'UK chip designer raises millions from Agnelli fund', 17 July 2023.

[28] The comparison table of UK, China, EU and US regulation does not include reference to state aid principles.

[29] The NSIA 2021 came into effect on 4 January 2022.

Table 7.2 Key Aspects of competition law in China, the EU, the UK, and the US

Jurisdiction	Aspects relevant to the semiconductor sector
UK	• Prohibition on the abuse of a dominant position within the UK. The abuse may include, among other things, unfair pricing or other unfair trading conditions, applying dissimilar conditions to equivalent transactions, and making contracts subject to acceptance by the counterparty of supplementary obligations which commercially or practically have no connection with the contract subject matter.[1] • Prohibition on agreements or practices in the UK that potentially affect or effect to distort, prevent or restrict competition.[2] • A completed merger may result in a substantial lessening of competition within any UK market.[3] • An imminent merger may result in a substantial lessening of competition within any UK market.[4] • A turnover test - based on >£70 million turnover of the target entity.[5] • If a proposed acquisition or merger is considered to pose an unacceptable risk to national security, the National Security and Investment Act 2021 (NSIA 2021) provides the power to block the transaction. The relevant percentage share ownership or voting rights tests are from 25% or less to more than 25%, from 50% or less to more than 50%, or from less than 75% to 75% or more.[6] In addition, there are another two acquisition situations that require mandatory notification. First, where the acquisition of voting rights enable a person to 'secure or prevent' the passing of any class of resolution under the entity's constitution.[7] • A turnover test - based on >£1 million to £70 million turnover for specifically listed technology activities, including AI, cryptographic authentication and quantum computing.[8]
China	• Prohibition on the abuse of a dominant position based principally on control of price, quantity, or terms of trade, or to influence the ability of another entity to enter a market.[9] • Special turnover threshold tests apply to the financial services sector.

Jurisdiction	Aspects relevant to the semiconductor sector
EU	• Prohibition on the abuse of a dominant position within the EU internal market.[10] Note there is no attempted monopolisation law. • Prohibition on agreements or practices within the EU that potentially affect or effect to distort, prevent or restrict competition.[11] • Likely future decision to make a centralised EU budgetary allocation for semiconductors supported by a new 'fast-track' Important Projects of Common European Interest (IPCEI).[12]
USA	• Prohibition on every contract, combined arrangement, or conspiracy in restraint of trade.[13] • Prohibition on monopolising or attempting to monopolise or conspiring to monopolise.[14] • Mergers and acquisitions that substantially lessen competition.[15]

Notes: [1] Section 18 Competition Act 1998. See www.legislation.gov.uk/ukpga/1998/41/section/18. [2] Section 2 Competition Act 1998. See www.legislation.gov.uk/ukpga/1998/41/section/2. [3] Section 22 Enterprise Act 2002. See www.legislation.gov.uk/ukpga/2002/40/section/22. [4] Section 33 Enterprise Act 2002. See www.legislation.gov.uk/ukpga/2002/40/section/33. [5] Section 23(1)(b) Enterprise Act 2002. See www.legislation.gov.uk/ukpga/2002/40/section/23. [6] Section 8(2)–(5) NSIA 2021. The NSIA 2021 is covered in detail later in this chapter. [7] Section 8(6) NSIA 2021. [8] UK Government (2024) 'Guidance: National Security and Investment Act; details of the 17 types of notifiable acquisitions', available at www.gov.uk/government/publications/national-security-and-investment-act-guidance-on-notifiable-acquisitions/national-security-and-investment-act-guidance-on-notifiable-acquisitions. [9] Article 17 Anti-Monopoly Law, applying throughout the People's Republic of China with the exception of Hong Kong (SAR) and Macau. An authoritative book on this subject is Kikkoris, I., S. Maniatis and X. Wang (2019) *Competition Law and Intellectual Property in China*, Oxford University Press. In Chapter 10, entitled 'Abuse of Dominance and Intellectual Property in China', at 196, the authors point out that 'China is still a comparatively new player in the antitrust world but it has grown quickly and it is currently one of the most important emerging jurisdictions for antitrust enforcement… Intensifying enforcement action in China over recent years suggests that IP-centred, or related, business models and practices will face growing antitrust scrutiny over the next few years'. Readers may logically assess IP-centred businesses to include patent-driven semiconductor providers. Firms are advised to take legal advice in both their home jurisdiction and China before implementing long-term strategies. [10] Article 102 Treaty on the Functioning of the European Union (TFEU). See https://www

.legislation.gov.uk/eut/teec/article/102. [11] Article 101 TFEU. See https://www.legislation.gov.uk/eut/teec/article/101. [12] Draghi, M. (2024) *The future of European competitiveness: Report*, European Commission. at 54. This decision would be legally viable because Article 107(3)(b) TFEU allows 'aid to promote the execution of an important project of common European interest or to remedy a serious disturbance in the economy of a Member State'. [13] Section 1 Sherman Antitrust Act 1890. [14] Section 2 Sherman Antitrust Act 1890. [15] Section 7 Clayton Antitrust Act 1914, as amended.
Source: © Iain Sheridan (2025)

While the main political driver behind the NSIA 2021 is national defence and security, it will certainly play a role in the make-up of actors supplying technology to, not only established regulated firms, but also start-ups.

The NSIA 2021 introduces a mandatory notification regime for 17 sectors. Some of these sectors, such as AI and cryptographic authentication, are intuitive areas for notification. However, many of the remaining are less obvious.[30] For example, dual-use applications covering both military and other applications. This significantly broadens the pool of semiconductor firms. In sum, many types of planned merger or acquisition can be scrutinised by the Secretary of State, who in turn has the power to block the transaction.

7.9 Nvidia attempted acquisition of ARM: case study

Nvidia's attempted acquisition of ARM is, in my view, a valuable case study, because it raises some important insights for the future for other established technology behemoths seeking growth through acquisitions of semiconductor firms. For instance, it is likely that any planned acquisitions by Amazon, Apple, Google, and Meta may experience similar regulatory scrutiny. That may seem a lateral point to make, but the market capitalisation of the most dominant technology firms that are all dedi-

[30] The UK Government provides helpful detail guidance on the boundaries of each sector: www.gov.uk/government/publications/national-security-and-investment-act-guidance-on-notifiable-acquisitions/national-security-and-investment-act-guidance-on-notifiable-acquisitions.

cated to advancing AI makes them natural future acquirers of the most advanced semiconductor designers and manufacturers.

7.9.1 Background to Nvidia's approach

In September 2020, Nvidia announced its intention to acquire ARM from SoftBank. It is an interesting case to examine because it attracted the attention of regulators in China, the UK and the US. Further, many sector incumbents were unhappy with the implications of such a successful acquisition. The cash and equity total cost to Nvidia, if it had succeeded, would have been in the region of US $75 billion.

The CMA's 2021 response to the proposed acquisition, set out in its report to the Secretary of State for Digital, Culture, Media and Sport, concluded that the transaction would result in a realistic prospect of a 'substantial lessening of competition' and, as such, foreclosure in the supply of 'CPUs, interconnect products, GPUs, and SoCs' especially in the contexts of data-centre, internet-of-things, automotive and gaming console applications.[31]

7.9.2 China's likely response

In China, the key competition regulator is the State Administration for Market Regulation (SAMR). The Chinese Anti-Monopoly Law (AML) includes not only competition-related factors, but also public interests and the impact on the development of the national economy.[32] When reviewing semiconductor cases, the SAMR usually seeks opinions from the leading trade body, the China Semiconductor Industry Association (CSIA). Further, it communicates with the Ministry of Industry and Information Technology (MIIT), the Ministry of Science and Technology (MST) and the National Development and Reform Commission (NDRC).

---

[31] CMA (2021) *CMA NVIDIA-ARM Summary of the CMA's report to the Secretary of State for Digital, Culture, Media & Sport on the anticipated acquisition by NVIDIA Corporation of Arm Limited*, at 1.4–1.8.

[32] Under Article 27 of the AML, the SAMR assesses on the basis of: (1) market shares and controlling power; (2) degree of concentration in the relevant market; (3) impact of the concentration of undertakings on market entry and technical progress; (4) impact on consumers; (5) impact on the national economy; and (6) any other anti-monopoly factors designated by the State Council.

The Chinese Ministry of Commerce (MOFCOM), the predecessor regulator, had a track record of making decisions congruent with the European Commission and the US Federal Trade Commission (FTC). However, in the strategically important semiconductor sector the SAMR blocked Qualcomm's attempt to buy NXP in 2018. The SAMR's decision not to approve the Qualcomm acquisition of NXP in 2018 marked a new direction.[33] Therefore, it seems that the SAMR's decision was politically motivated, albeit it was publicly expressed in terms of technical reservations.

Approximately eight months after announcing its intended acquisition of ARM, Nvidia submitted an application to the SAMR to review the transaction.[34] Throughout 2021, the Covid-19 pandemic greatly slowed down SAMR progress in assessing the merits of the application. In early 2022, before the SAMR was able to complete its work, Nvidia announced the termination of the previously announced transaction to acquire ARM.

7.9.3 The EU's response

Under EU merger regulation, in 2021 the European Commission opened an in-depth investigation to assess the proposed acquisition of ARM by Nvidia. The Commission's conclusion matched the UK CMA's, mirroring some but not all of the UK reasoning. What is striking is that the Commission's reasoning was more expansive, a fact that legal counsel involved in presenting cases that nullify or mitigate accusation of foreclosure strategies may find helpful to analyse in more detail. The European Commission list included: SmartNICs; ADAS for autonomous driving; infotainment, including, among other things, USB and Bluetooth connectivity, internet access and Wi-Fi; SoCs equipping high-performance IoT devices; SoCs used in gaming consoles; SoCs used in general-purpose PCs.[35]

---

[33] SAMR concerns revolved around Qualcomm's baseband semiconductors, and NXP's MIFARE technology, NFC technology and SE semiconductors. Both the European Commission and the US FTC approved the deal.

[34] *Financial Times* (2021) 'Nvidia asks Chinese regulators to approve $40bn Arm deal'.

[35] European Commission (2021) 'Mergers: Commission opens in-depth investigation into proposed acquisition of Arm by NVIDIA', 27 October 2021. Available at https://ec.europa.eu/commission/presscorner/detail/en/ip_21_5624.

7.9.4 The US's response

Regulators in the US, to some extent, reached the same conclusion as the UK. The US highlighted three areas, namely (a) Advanced Driver Assistance Systems (ADAS) products, an enabler of autonomous driving, (b) cloud computing CPUs, and (c) data centre products, especially Data Processing Unity (DPU) smart network interface cards (SmartNICs).[36]

The FTC's director of competition justified suing as a way:

> to block the largest semiconductor chip merger in history to prevent a chip conglomerate from stifling the innovation pipeline for next-generation technologies... This proposed deal would distort ARM's incentives in chip markets and allow the combined firm to unfairly undermine Nvidia's rivals. The FTC's lawsuit should send a strong signal that we will act aggressively to protect our critical infrastructure markets from illegal vertical mergers that have far-reaching and damaging effects on future innovations.[37]

7.10 Identifiable patterns to factor into future semiconductor acquisitions

In the UK, the CMA's detailed conclusions are important for future proposed acquisitions, because they assessed the joining of ARM as a design firm and Nvidia as a leading GPU manufacturing specialist

[36] FTC (2021) *Complaint 9404: Nvidia Corporation, Softbank Corporation and ARM Ltd*, at 11, para.56. Available at www.ftc.gov/system/files/documents/cases/d09404_part_3_complaint_public_version.pdf.

[37] FTC (2021) 'FTC Sues to Block $40 Billion Semiconductor Chip Merger', Press Release, 2 December 2021, available at www.ftc.gov/news-events/news/press-releases/2021/12/ftc-sues-block-40-billion-semiconductor-chip-merger.

would result in a substantial lessening of competition in the following markets:

(a) global datacentre CPU supplies;
(b) global SmartNICs supplies;
(c) global datacentre GPU supplies;
(d) the global supply of SoCs for high performance internet-of-things applications;
(e) global SoCs supplied to the automotive sector for ADAS applications, infotainment applications; and
(f) global supply of SoCs for gaming consoles.[38]

7.11 Nvidia in retrospect

In hindsight, the collective key regulators' conclusion that Nvidia acquiring ARM could not be approved, albeit for their detailed different reasons, was the right decision. It is interesting that in 2023 the *State of AI Report Compute Index* revealed that Nvidia's A100 GPU model was found in significant numbers in public, private and national high performance computing (HPC) clusters.[39] Coupled with Nvidia's developed brand loyalty among engineers to its Compute Unified Device Architecture (CUDA) toolkit for programming its GPUs this means it is increasingly dominant in this market sub-sector.

Second, the combining of Nvidia's GPU semiconductor manufacturing with ARM's instruction set architecture (ISA) design capabilities had potential significance for capital markets. The vision that algorithms driven by computers should be essential components of markets has been the focus of leading researchers for several decades.[40] However, the

[38] CMA (2021) *CMA NVIDIA-ARM Summary of the CMA's report to the Secretary of State for Digital, Culture, Media & Sport on the anticipated acquisition by NVIDIA Corporation of Arm Limited*, at 1.32.

[39] State of AI (2023) See www.stateof.ai/compute.

[40] For instance, in his 1975 Nobel Prize lecture entitled 'Mathematics in Economics: Achievements, Difficulties, Perspectives', the Russian economist Leonid Kantorovich shared his understanding and ambition for algorithms optimising the market challenges of prediction and allocation. See www

combination of GPUs, ISA and ML knowhow in the merged Nvidia-ARM firm would have caused a substantial lessening of competition across UK capital markets.

7.12 Intel's annulled US $1 billion fine

The experience of Intel over a period of more than 20 years of operations in the EU provides both lessons and surprises. In 2000, a formal complaint was lodged by its competitor Advanced Micro Devices (AMD) with the European Commission. Among other allegations, AMD alleged Intel breached Article 102 of the TFEU.

Article 102 TFEU states that 'any abuse by one or more undertakings of a dominant position within the internal market or in a substantial part of it shall be prohibited as incompatible with the internal market in so far as it may affect trade between Member States'.[41] Abuse is defined as (a) directly or indirectly imposing unfair prices or other unfair trading conditions; (b) prejudicing consumers by limiting production, markets or technical development; (c) putting other trading parties at a competitive disadvantage by dissimilar conditions to equivalent transactions with other trading parties, thereby placing them at a competitive disadvantage; (d) making the conclusion of contracts subject to acceptance by the other parties of supplementary obligations which, by their nature or according to commercial usage, have no connection with the subject of such contracts.

This original complaint was supplemented with a secondary set of allegations in 2003. In May 2004, the European Commission launched investigations to determined if Intel's conduct was abusive behaviour based on a dominant position. Assisted by national authorities, the Commission conducted on-the-spot checks in Germany, Italy, Spain, and the UK.

In 2009, the Commission decided that under Article 102 TFEU and Article 54 of the EEA Agreement, Intel was implementing, between 2002 and 2007, a foreclosing strategy on its competitor AMD in the x86 CPU

.nobelprize.org/nobel_prizes/economic-sciences/laureates/1975/kantorovich-lecture.html.

41 See https://www.legislation.gov.uk/eut/teec/article/102.

microprocessors (x86 CPUs) market.[42] The Commission levied a fine of €1.2 billion on Intel. The strategies adopted by Intel were twofold. First, conditional rebates to original equipment manufacturers (OEMs) based on buying all or almost all of its supply needs from Intel. Second, naked restrictions in the form of payments conditional on OEMs postponing or cancelling the launch of AMD-based products or putting restrictions on the distribution of AMD-based products.[43]

In reaching its decision, the European Commission applied prior case law that no showing of competitive harm was required. However, applying its own guidelines, on enforcement priorities in exclusionary abuse cases the Commission did complete an 'as efficient competitor' (AEC) test. The AEC test measures whether a competitor of comparable efficiency to Intel could have competed with Intel despite the exclusivity rebates.

Intel appealed the Commission's decision to the EU General Court (GC). In 2014, the GC, dismissed the appeal and upheld the Commission's finding that the exclusivity rebates were per se abuses of dominance. Subsequently, Intel appealed the GC decision to the CJEU.

In 2017 the CJEU ruled that exclusivity rebates are not per se abuses under Article 102 TFEU. Additionally, the CJEU held that where a dominant undertaking submits evidence that its conduct was incapable of restricting competition, and in this context producing the alleged foreclosure effects, the European Commission must analyse as a minimum the effects of the conduct applying the following five criteria:

(a) the extent of the undertaking's dominant position on the relevant market;
(b) the share of the market covered by the contested practice;
(c) the conditions and arrangements for granting the rebates in question;
(d) the duration and their amount; and
(e) the possible existence of a strategy aiming to exclude competitors that are at least as efficient as a dominant undertaking from the market.[44]

---

[42] [2009] OJ C 227/13. See https://eur-lex.europa.eu/legal-content/EN/TXT/PDF/?uri=OJ:C:2009:227:FULL&from=EN.

[43] Ibid at 16–19.

[44] *Intel Corporation Inc v European Commission* (C-413/14 P) EU:C: 2017:632, judgment of 6 September 2017, at [139].

Because the GC had failed to consider Intel's arguments concerning the Commission's application of the AEC test, the CJEU remitted the case to the GC for reconsideration.

In 2022 the GC concluded that the European Commission had made an error of law by treating Intel's rebates as automatically anti-competitive. Conditional rebates are not a per se infringement that relieves the Commission of its obligation to conduct an effects analysis where the investigated firm challenges the presumption. Further, a no effects analysis was required to establish an abuse. The fine was totally annulled.

In its 102-page 2022 judgment, the GC stated that, as a minimum, the Commission was required to examine the five criteria mentioned in the CJEU 2017 appeal decision as set out in an earlier paragraph in this chapter. Further, the GC ruled that the Commission made an error in law in its infringement decision by inferring:

> ...from the Hoffmann-La Roche case-law, first, that the rebates at issue were by their nature anticompetitive, with the result that there was no need to demonstrate foreclosure capability in order to establish an infringement of Article 102 TFEU. Second, although the contested decision contains an additional analysis of the foreclosure capability of those rebates, the Commission took the view that, in accordance with that case-law, it was not required to take that analysis into account in order to conclude that those rebates were abusive. Third and lastly, still on the basis of that same case-law, the Commission held, inter alia, that a number of factors were irrelevant for determining whether there was abuse.[45]

7.13 Key lessons for dominant semiconductor firms in the EU

In terms of specific lessons from the 2022 GC decision, the first concerns evidential standards. The second, the ongoing application of AEC tests. First, the GC confirmed that the Commission must produce 'sufficiently precise and consistent evidence to support the firm conviction that the alleged infringement took place'. However, it is important to note that it

[45] *Intel Corporation v Commission* (T-286/09 RENV) EU:T:2022:19, judgment of 26 January 2022, at [144].

is sufficient if the body of evidence relied on analysed as a whole meets that requirement.[46]

Second, the GC clarified that the Commission's AEC analysis should not have been 'less efficient than Intel in terms of the costs it would incur whilst competing'. Intel alleged that the Commission's AEC calculations contained numerous errors. The GC examined the Commission's AEC analysis in significant detail, finding:

(a) errors in contestable share calculations;[47]
(b) errors in the conditional portion of the rebates;[48]
(c) unsubstantiated extrapolations of rebate figures from one single quarter-year period applied to the entire infringement period;[49] and
(d) errors in the quantified assessment of the non-cash advantages at issue.[50]

Given the scale of the fine imposed on Intel and then annulled in its entirety, it would be easy for a cynic or political analyst to be surprised by the GC decision. Despite the length of time elapsing between decisions from 2009 to 2022, the application of rigorous legal analysis to a dominant US semiconductor firm operating across the EU presents the EU competition law judicial system in a positive light for other dominant semiconductor firms. The European courts will challenge Commission decisions that lack rigorous evidential support and legal analysis.

7.14 Final points

When analysing the outcomes for both Nvidia in its attempted acquisition of ARM, and Intel's long running saga with the European Commission, it is evident that regulators invest time and considerable effort analysing how semiconductor markets operate. Regulators are also stimulated to act by semiconductor firms approaching them with complaints or concerns.

---

46 Ibid at [163].
47 Ibid at [256].
48 Ibid at [389].
49 Ibid at [411].
50 Ibid at [455].

For example, for the foreseeable future, it is rational to expect continued global dependence on TSMC foundries, especially so given this firm's expansion plans in Germany and the US. However, competitors of TSMC exist, albeit not in the most cutting-edge CPUs, namely GlobalFoundries, United Microelectronics, and Samsung.

A likely scenario is that in some markets, threatened firms will challenge TSMC's dominant influence. By which is meant existing competition law adjusted to the exceptional role of cutting-edge semiconductors will allow national champions to flourish. It will be important for legal counsel to monitor this dynamic. The influence of business competitors protecting their established market presence and long-term ambitions may also play a role in shaping global competition.

8. Contract law

Oft expectation fails and most oft there where most it promises, and oft it hits where hope is coldest and despair most fits.[1]

English commercial courts are always busy, partly because English law carefully evolves contract law precedent to provide a high degree of predictability. Lord Mansfield has pointed out that in contract law the key element is certainty, that 'it is of more consequence that a rule should be certain, than whether the rule is established one way or the other'.[2] Further, he observed that daily contract negotiations should be based on 'rules easily learned and retained'.[3] These judicial comments sound as if they were written yesterday. In fact they are over 250 years old.

8.1 Introduction

Given the detailed nature of both standard commercial contracts, and even more so master services agreement (MSA), semiconductor legal professionals regularly find the best answers in the leading voluminous general commercial practitioner publications. This chapter draws on those leading texts.[4] It also attempts to cover recurring key risk clauses of special relevance in the semiconductor sector. Brevity and clarity of drafting might be the assumed contribution of external and in-house counsel, but some High Court cases suggest otherwise.

1 Shakespeare, W. (1623) *All's Well That Ends Well* Translation, Act 2, Scene 1, https://shakespeare.mit.edu/allswell/allswell.2.1.html.

2 *Vallejo v Wheeler* (1774)1 Cowp 143, at 153.

3 *Hamilton v Mendes* (1761) 2 Burr 1198, 1214.

4 Beale, H. (ed) (2023) *Chitty on Contracts*, 35th edn, London: Sweet & Maxwell; Treitel, G. (2014) *Frustration and Force Majeure*, 3rd edn, London: Sweet & Maxwell; and Peel, E. (2021) *Frustration and Force Majeure*, 4th edn, London: Sweet & Maxwell.

From one angle, the main topics covered in this chapter in part reflect the era we live in that they present the most challenges and uncertainties for semiconductor business growth. A combination of unexpected events, sudden macroeconomic, geopolitical changes and climate change, mean eagle-eyed, pedantic contract negotiation is as important as ever. Of particular focus are choice of law risks, *force majeure*, impracticality, quality control breaches, price renegotiation, sanctions compliance and sustainability issues.

Given readers have different buyer and supplier roles, along with multiple product or service offerings, examples are provided from across the sector. Therefore, most examples could apply to electronic design automation (EDA) tool providers, disposition machines, photolithography machines, removal chemicals and gases, physical property alteration materials, wafer manufacturing equipment and semiconductor component suppliers. The final section provides ideas on how even experienced professionals may look to improve their already high-level contributions. This last section is especially valuable to parties that have stronger bargaining power.

The task of ensuring supplied products are protected under enforceable contracts is a vital one. There are also a variety of purchase agreements covering chemicals, components, machinery, and technology. Bargaining power inevitably influences the outcomes of many contract negotiations. However, advanced negotiation must allow for long-term relationships that include a win-win for both parties.

Given the expense and time-consuming nature of litigation and arbitration, the ideal is to negotiate and draft contracts that avoid all disputes. An ideal that will remain, but there are several aspects of contract negotiation under English law that deserve reiteration to maximise contract robustness. Apparently, they often say in scuba diving and skydiving that there is a risk that the most advanced expert participants can, over time, become complacent. At that point mistakes are more likely to occur.

This chapter sets out the legal issues and risks associated with a United Kingdom (UK) semiconductor strategy in the context of English law. Most of the analysis has relevance to any other jurisdiction given the cross-border nature of semiconductor business.

Lawyers provide vital independent thinking, understanding and careful drafting for short-, medium- and long-term risk management. The hope is that a *force majeure* clause will never be scrutinised because commercial relations are able to manage any unexpected or unusual changes. Lawyerly caution has been especially valuable in the last few years in the UK: Brexit, then the Covid-19 pandemic, then Ukraine, and so forth. Events of significant change for any semiconductor firm require well thought out *force majeure* clauses.

The nature of increasing uncertainty concerning events beyond the control of parties is increasingly an issue for integrated device manufacturers (IDMs). Many IDMs, including Intel, Texas Instruments, Freescale Semiconductor, STMicroelectronics, and Renesas Electronics, outsource their manufacturing to fabrication plants in East Asia. Especially to South Korea and Taiwan and, once again, Japan.[5] A recent example is the 7.4 magnitude earthquake in Taiwan that caused semiconductor manufacturers to halt production.[6]

IDMs are often reliant on a capacity reservation contract. Under such an agreement, the IDM reserves capacity from the foundry by paying a reservation fee per unit. The reservation fee is refundable, which means the IDM pays to the foundry a wholesale price deducted by the reservation fee for a unit of product. The Covid-19 pandemic showed how quickly one issue, worker health and safety, can negatively affect global supply. Increasing occurrences of extreme weather events, especially flooding, are lower impact compared with pandemics, but are still more frequent *force majeure* events.

Cautious, longsighted lawyering is pivotal here. What is required is a balance combination of imagination, clear drafting skills and an understanding of law – in equal measures. If you deliver a cocktail of excessive words in law and an afterthought of imagination, worry! Consider if a lawyer was negotiating a semiconductor supply contract in December 2019 what did they envisage as a possible event? On the one hand you cannot draft to risk manage everything, on the other hand you need to

---

5 *Nikkei Asia* (2024) 'Silicon Island', 29 February 2024. This article reported on TSMC's first factory in the southwestern prefecture of Kumamoto, Japan.

6 *Financial Times* (2024) 'Quake is a reminder of seismic risk to global chip supply', 3 April 2024.

imagine what might be. Relevancy and clarity of drafting might be the assumed contribution of external and in-house counsel. Some of the potentially unforeseen risk issues could include the supply of disposition machines, photolithography machines and physical property alteration materials. Additionally, the removal of chemicals and gases.

Imagine the parties to a semiconductor supply contract have agreed on a *force majeure* clause that includes earthquakes as a qualifying *force majeure* event. In many civil law systems *force majeure* is defined in statute. Under English law, it is undefined in statute, but generally treated as a broad concept of 'events beyond the control' of the parties that entitle the cancellation or suspension of the contract. For example, any level of earthquake tremors could close a fabrication plant, because of safe access to buildings, disruption to electricity supplies, injured staff, or closed ports.[7] The fact that such a risk may occur in Japan, Taiwan and certain states of the United States (US) cannot be overlooked.

Interpretation of *force majeure* clauses is not an exercise of looking for all events that are beyond the reasonable control of a contracting party. The process requires looking for inclusion of an event from the list of *force majeure* events.[8] Based on well-established case law, a *force majeure* 'should be construed in each case with close attention to the words which preclude or follow it, and with due regard to the nature and general terms of the contract'.[9]

Common sense or experience can lead an observer to conclude an event is within the control of a contracting party. However, if an event is recorded in a list of *force majeure* events, that specific event may qualify as a *force majeure* event.

7 See *Chitty on Contracts* (2023), 35th edn, at 15-152. The effect of a *force majeure* clause is a matter of construction. See Treitel (2014), 3rd edn, at 12-026. For a very detailed treatment of the *force majeure* see Peel (2021), 4th edn, a book that provides expert analysis on not only English law treatment but also American law cases.

8 *Chitty on Contracts* (2023), 35th edn, at 27-062.

9 *Lebeaupin v Crispin & Co* [1920] 2 KB 714, per McCardie J at 720.

A point worth emphasising is that extreme storms[10] may be an event beyond the control of a contracting party, but technology may increasingly make even severe typhoons and tornadoes manageable events. Recently, as part of my contribution of a machine learning (ML) contracts chapter to an all-sector artificial intelligence (AI) law practitioner book, my research included looking at how ML models can provide accurate early warning of incoming severe storms. If such models become accessible beyond meteorological offices, which is quite possible given cloud computing services, contracting parties might be expected to monitor and mitigate for such meteorological events.[11]

8.2 Practical steps required

A contracting party actually or potentially affected by the event has an obligation to take reasonable steps or make reasonable endeavours to overcome the event. A recent English High Court case emphasised that the meaning of 'overcome' includes a means of overcoming the event that may include performance not envisaged and specified in the terms of the contract.[12]

8.3 Interpretation

The case of *Classic Maritime Inc v Limbungan Makmur Sdn* has provided recent guidance on *force majeure* clause interpretation and drafting from the Court of Appeal.[13] The background facts concerned a long-term contract of affreightment providing for shipments of iron ore from Brazil to Malaysia between the claimant shipowner and the defendant charterer. The contract covered seven shipments over a period of 13 months. The defendant failed to deliver the first two shipments and accepted liability in

---

10 As *Chitty on Contracts* (2023), 35th edn has also highlighted, 'abnormal weather conditions' can be too general and cause uncertainty over their application. See at 27-071.

11 Kerrigan, C. (2022) *Artificial Intelligence – Law and Regulation*, Cheltenham, UK and Northampton, MA, USA: Edward Elgar Publishing, Chapter 7, at 109.

12 *MUR Shipping BV v RTI Ltd* [2022] EWCA Civ 1406.

13 *Classic Maritime Inc v Limbungan Makmur SDN BHD & Anor* [2019] EWCA Civ 1102 (27 June 2019).

that respect. However, before the remaining five shipments the Samarco Dam burst, resulting in the flooding of the iron ore mine. It was accepted that because the dam burst that made it impossible to deliver the iron ore. However, the trial judge also determined that, even if the dam has not burst, it was more likely than not that the defendant was going to default on the five remaining deliveries.

The defendant argued it was protected against liability relying on the list of exceptions in the contract. The exceptions list included, among other things, 'acts resulting from…accidents at the mine' beyond the control of the charterer 'always provided that any such events directly affect the performance of either party, protected it against liability'.[14]

However, the trial judge held the defendant could not rely on the exceptions clause, because it could not prove that, but for the dam burst, it would have performed the contract. Therefore, the defendant's failure to perform had not conclusively 'resulted from' the dam bursting, nor that the dam bursting had 'directly affected' its performance. The Court of Appeal unanimously agreed with the trial judge that there was an issue of causation. Lord Justice Males summarised the exceptions clause in this way:

> I agree with the judge that the words 'resulting from' together with the requirement that the events in question 'directly affect the performance of either party' import a causation requirement… These are not merely 'events' which happen to have occurred, but 'causes' which impact on performance. This is not necessarily conclusive as the causation requirement could be merely that the event renders performance impossible, but the combined effect of these phrases suggests a more demanding requirement. It is a valid use of language to say that a failure to supply the cargo (or even a cargo) does not 'result from' an event if in fact the event makes no difference because the charterer was never going to supply a cargo anyway. Similarly, the proviso refers in my view to the performance which would have been rendered if the event or cause had not occurred. If the accident at the mine did not cause the charterer to do anything different because it had no intention of supplying a cargo anyway, it is fair to say that its performance was not 'directly affected'.[15]

Lord Justice Males also made an important statement of practical importance to drafting clauses dealing with events that impact contract perfor-

[14] Ibid, at [11].
[15] Ibid, per Lord Males at [45].

mance. He concluded 'what matters is not whether the clause is labelled a contractual frustration clause, a force majeure clause or an exceptions clause, but the language of the clause. As with most things, what matters is not the label but the content of the tin'.[16] In short, the courts will construe the context and purpose above the labelling of clauses.

8.4 Force majeure and government policies

The number of sanctions imposed by the EU, the US and other individual nation states mean that long-term semiconductor supply contracts are agreed in a context of potentially multiple changes. Consequently, seeking specialist trade law advice on an ongoing basis may be required. Further, the supplier or the buyer or both can encounter a contractual or permanent state of disadvantage triggered by government policies. For example, if a UK virtual reality headset device producer enters a contract for semiconductors supplied from China, it is likely, regardless of the UK political party in power, that UK policies will remain congruent with EU and US policies. As both EU and US policies change in their detail there is a consequent need to allow for contractual flexibility. Current case law provides scope for a party to be prevented from making a purchase or supply choice because of an export embargo.[17]

8.5 Frustration

If a contract under English law does not include an express *force majeure* clause, then either party may be able to apply the doctrine of frustration. The qualifying event is one when for either party 'a contractual obligation has become incapable of being performed because the circumstances in which performance is called for would render it a thing radically different from that which was undertaken by the contract'.[18]

---

[16] Ibid, per Lord Justice Males at [62].

[17] *C. Czarnikow v Centrala Handlu Zagranicznego Rolimpex* [1979] AC 351.

[18] *Davis Contractors Ltd v Fareham UDC* [1956] 1 AC 696 at 729 per Lord Radcliffe.

A court may judge that an event makes further performance of the contract impossible. However, before reaching that conclusion, as a minimum, the judge is required to review five factors:

- the contractual terms;
- the context;
- at the time of the contract formation the parties' assumptions, expectations, and knowledge, especially concerning risk;
- the nature of the supervening event;
- the possibilities of future performance in the new circumstances based on the parties' objective and reasonable calculations.[19]

Suddenly, in the twenty-first century this multifactorial approach is adopted consistently in the English High Court. While these factors seem comprehensive as a judicial decision-making framework, contemplated risks by both parties may always create uncertainty over whether frustration is excluded or not. The English judiciary has put the complete task in this way:

> Since the subject matter of the doctrine of frustration is contract, and contracts are all about the allocation of risk, and since the allocation assumption risk is not simply a matter of express or implied provision but may also depend on less easily defined matters such as 'the contemplation of the parties', the application of the doctrine can often be a difficult one. In such circumstances, the test of 'radically different' is important: it tells us that the doctrine is not to be lightly invoked; that mere incidence of expense or delay or onerousness is not sufficient; and that there has to be as it were a break in identity between the contract as provided for and contemplated and its performance in the new circumstances.[20]

8.6 Degree of foreseeability

When assessing the foreseeability of frustrating events, Covid-19 is an example of a pandemic which was arguably a foreseeable event. A future pandemic could be drafted into a contract as a foreseeable event, but if the duration is radically different from the specified duration or typical

[19] *Edwinton Commercial Corporation v Tsavliris Russ (Worldwide Salvage & Towage) Ltd (The Sea Angel)* [2007] 2 Lloyds Rep 335 per Rix LJ at [111].

[20] Ibid, per Rix LJ at [111].

duration of a pandemic – if there can be such a typical time period – that extended pandemic may not be judged as foreseeable.

The English judiciary has encapsulated it in this way:

> Even events which are not merely foreseen but made the subject of express contractual provision may lead to frustration: as occurs when an event such as a strike...last for so long as to go beyond the risk assumed under the contract and to render performance radically different from that contracted for... The less that an event, in its type and its impact, is foreseeable, the more likely it is to be a factor which, depending on other factors in the case, may lead onto frustration.[21]

In some cases the practical question the court must answer is "in what circumstances did the parties intend the contract to operate?"

8.7 Changes in law or regulation

In an era of increasing geopolitical uncertainty the issue of a supervening illegality is a likely scenario for semiconductor contracting parties to carefully assess. Under English law, the issue of a supervening illegality qualifying as an instance of frustration is well established.[22] Importantly, the nature and the duration of a change in law need to be assessed. Changes in law or regulation that interrupt commercial engineering activity are likely '...of such a character and duration that it vitally and fundamentally changed the conditions of the contract, and could not possibly have been in the contemplation of the parties to the contract when it was made'.[23]

It was most recently reconfirmed as a common law precedent in the context of Brexit. The brief facts were that European Medicines Agency (EMA) signed a contract for a 25-year lease to rent a Canary Wharf office. The lease did not contain a break clause, but it did contain the right to sub-lease. EMA sought a declaration from the High Court that Brexit

21 Ibid, per Rix LJ at [127].

22 See especially *Metropolitan Water Board v Dick, Kerr & Co Ltd* [1918] AC 119 at para.119. Other authorities include *Sir Arnold McNair* (1944) 60 LQR 160, 1623; *Twentieth Century Fox Film Corporation v British Telecommunications Plc (No.2)* [2011] EWHC 2714 (Ch); [2012] 1 All ER 869 at [47].

23 Ibid, at [126].

qualified as a frustrating event. The practical motivation of EMA was its decision to relocate its headquarters from Canary Wharf to Amsterdam.

One of the two main arguments put forward was that the UK's departure from the EU changed the legal landscape in the UK. Specifically, EMA's past lawful obligations had become unlawful because of Brexit. However, the High Court ruled that the lease was not frustrated. The supervening illegality was a fiction, because EMA continued to have the capacity to use the office in return for paying the rent. A different event is not necessarily a frustrating one.[24]

8.8 Enforceability of sums paid or payable

For contracts governed by English law, statute states that 'sums paid or payable to any party in pursuance of the contract before the time when the parties were so discharged... Shall, in the case of the sum so paid, be recoverable... and, in the case of some so parable, cease to be payable'.[25] The structure also provides judges with the flexibility to allow set-off for expenses generated before the time the contract was discharged. However, the recoverability of such expenses is discretionary given that the statute provides that the court may allow recovery of expenses 'if it considers it just to do so'.[26] Notably, the carriage of goods by sea is an excluded category of contract under this statute.[27]

8.9 Price renegotiations

Force majeure clauses under English law will not excuse non-performance because performance would be uneconomic for one of the parties. There are many case law examples to support this view. In an era that has experienced greater geopolitical instability, varying inflation rates and pandemics, the costs of semiconductor manufacturing or shipping rates or both

---

[24] *Canary Wharf (BP4) T1 v European Medicines Agency* [2019] EWHC 335 (Ch).

[25] Section 1(2) Law Reform (Frustrated Contracts) Act 1943.

[26] Ibid. Notably, under s.1(2) the carriage of goods by sea are an excluded category of contract.

[27] Section 2(5) Law Reform (Frustrated Contracts) Act 1943.

are unlikely to be judged *force majeure* factors. As one High Court judge succinctly put it 'the fact that a contract has become expensive to perform, even dramatically more expensive is not a ground to relieve a party on the grounds of force majeure or frustration'.[28]

An alternative way of allowing parties to continue working on the same terms of a contract, but altering price and delivery, is to draft a variation clause. As long as consideration exists when a contract is varied, the new contract will validly concern the same subject matter. By which is meant there must be consideration for the recission of the original contract. This is well established in case law: 'the same consideration which existed for the old agreement is imported into the new agreement, which is substituted for it'.[29]

It is only arguable that a factual benefit for one party to a variation of contract amounts to consideration. In the leading High Court case on this point, a factual benefit in the form of a promise to complete work, qualified as consideration under the original contract between the parties. Party B, an architect firm, promised to make extra payments to Party A, a carpentry firm. These extra payments by Party B were supported by consideration in the shape of actual performance by Party A rather than Party B resorting to suing for non-performance.[30]

A drafting solution to ensure that factual benefit qualifies as consideration is to allow for a price renegotiation clause. For high-volume, long-term semiconductor supply contracts this should suit both parties in most scenarios. The price renegotiation would be based on the subsequent shipment. Therefore, the current, latest shipment would provide evidential justification for a price change. In my view, a price renegotiation clause would include text along the following lines:

> In the event that the manufacturing costs or delivery costs of components are so different from the originally contracted terms, the parties will vary the contract by reference to some or all of the following evidence:
> - inflation rates in the manufacturing costs of the country of origin;
> - currency rate changes in the specified currency for payment;
> - currency rate changes in the manufacturing country of origin;

---

[28] *Thames Valley Power v Total Gas & Power Ltd* [2006] 1 Lloyd's Rep 441.

[29] *Stead v Dawber* [1839] 10 A & E 57.

[30] *Williams v Roffey Brothers & and Nicholls (Contractors) Ltd* [1991] 1QB 1.

- changes in shipping rates caused by the threat or use of force along sea lanes or routes.

One means of managing the additional workload and inefficiencies created by the triggering of a price renegotiation clause is to make such a mechanism periodic. For example, 'every 36 months from the signing of this agreement by the parties'. Further, to additionally allow for an exceptionally harsh or special change of circumstances to be also addressed by drafting a 'wildcard review' which can be triggered outside of the usual 36-month cycle of price renegotiation. The more exceptionally harsh or special circumstance are based on a quantitative trigger, such as a specific percentage change, the fewer interpretative challenges should arise.[31]

8.10 Joint venture agreements

Innovation often occurs by mixing different nationalities together, and this has formed part of long-term semiconductor firm strategies. Joint ventures, discussed later in this chapter, also benefit from the blending of cultures and nationalities.[32] Readers only have to reflect on the fact that the metal-oxide-semiconductor field-effect transistor (MOSFET) was advanced by the collaborative research of an Egyptian and a Korean.[33] Access to markets and engineering talent are also primary motivations in making long-term investments in semiconductor joint ventures. Therefore, the drafting of joint venture clauses that allow for long-term cooperation and meet the evolving ambition of all parties are not only commercially valuable legal contributions, but vital risk management frameworks.[34]

---

[31] My own professional experience working on arbitration cases in Vienna included price renegotiation cases. With exceptionally high-value contracts, the degree of care taken over the drafting of triggering events is based on considerable detail.

[32] Joint ventures are also considered in Chapter 9 Intellectual property law.

[33] Mohamed Atalla and Dawon Kahng.

[34] An authoritative work on all types of joint ventures with extensive case law referencing is Hewitt, I. (2024) *Hewitt on Joint Ventures*, London: Sweet & Maxwell. In its eighth edition, this practitioner book provides an immense volume of detail on, among other things, planning a joint venture, contractual alliances, equity joint ventures, governance and dispute resolution.

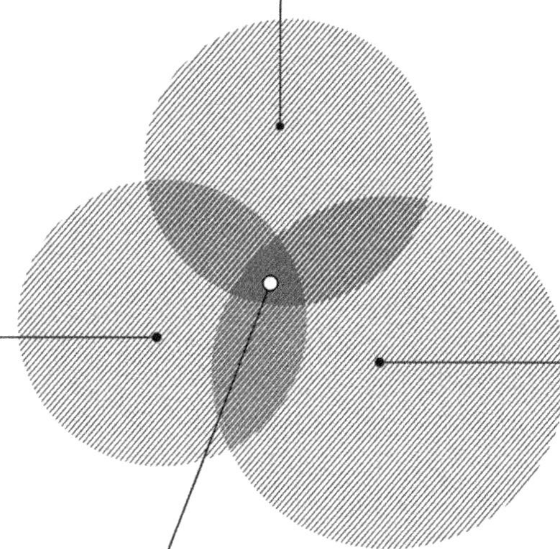

Source: © Iain Sheridan (2025)

Figure 8.1 *Joint venture essentials*

As set out in Figure 8.1, the signed detail of a joint venture (JV) agreement is unlikely to have long-term success without managing factors that are fundamental to building trust and a spirit of common endeavour. While a JV can be based on a contract between the parties, a corporate JV will include a JV agreement or shareholders' agreement or framework agreement. Whatever the preference, the core documents will record the issue of shares and details for valuing each party's contribution.

8.10.1 Cultural awareness

First, there is the need for cultural awareness both at the JV contract negotiating phase and throughout the life of the JV contract. An experienced general counsel (GC) has remarked that 'culture governs how negotiators understand, communicate, and conduct themselves when operating across cultures. Most aspects of our cultures are subconscious, but have a profound impact on how we interpret information and act when negotiating, as well as outcomes we achieve'.[35] Consequently the degree to which culture has or has not been considered during contract negotiations surrounding a planned JV is of special importance.

With the support of documentation, including visual charts and diagrams, the aim is to minimise frictions and risks. Insufficient cultural awareness is often overlooked and yet is often the fundamental reason JV parties experience inefficient frictions or in some cases disputes that lead to the abandonment of plans.

Professor Erin Meyer of INSEAD has devised a well respect cultural comparison tool.[36] Based on eight dimensions, this tool allows parties to visually compare aspects of culture relevant to negotiating a JV and enabling it to continue to work once the agreement is signed. Therefore, all parties can choose to apply this tool as part of due diligence and preparation before operating a JV. The tool addresses stereotypical cultures so differences between national characteristics and each firm's unique corporate culture have to be factored in.[37]

---

35 Leathes, M. (2017) *Negotiation – Things Corporate Counsel Need to Know but Were Not Taught*, Kluwer, at 53.

36 Meyer, E. (2016) 'The Culture Map (PublicAffairs)'.

37 The Culture Map tool is available at www.erinmeyer.com. The website also contains access to a 24-section questionnaire to enable leaders to self-assess

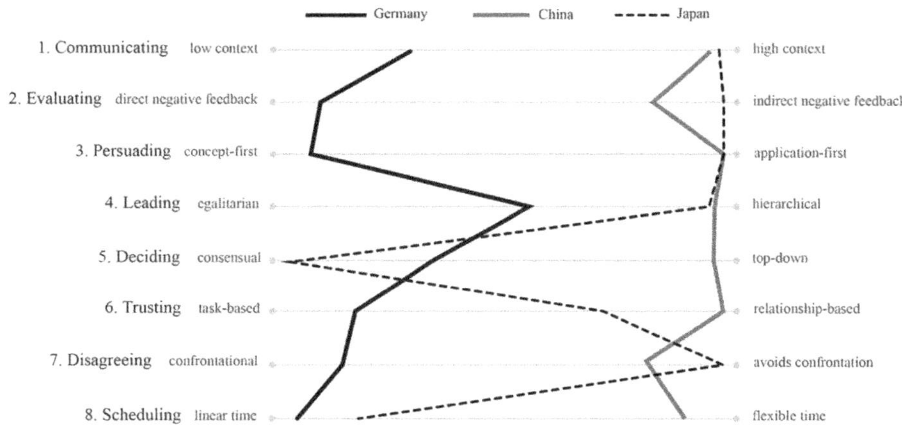

Source: Meyer, E. (2016) 'The Culture Map (PublicAffairs)', available at www.erinmeyer.com

Figure 8.2 Culture map of three countries

Taking the example of a British semiconductor firm forming a JV with German and Korean parties, Figure 8.2 illustrates how negotiations can benefit from having cultural awareness of the similarities and differences. Note Professor Meyer's website allows over 65 country cultures to be analysed in this way, so on each occasion of a planned JV all parties can examine the cultural nuances. In the short term, this approach should reduce the cost and time spent negotiating, and in the long term reduce communication, decision making, leadership activity and disagreements that damage relationships.

In my experience of building a China legal practice focused on Beijing and Northeast China which included drafting JV framework agreements, it is evident planning and negotiating a JV requires the additional awareness of local cultures. Northeast China is quite different from Beijing, and radically different when compared with Shanghai. There is a need to negotiate terms with these local cultural factors in mind and mistakes could be made if lawyers and leaders omit to invest effort and time in local areas to adjust behaviour and risk management decisions.

8.10.2 Leadership rotation

Second, there is the importance of rotating leadership amongst the JV company entities incorporated in different countries and typically led by nationals from each country. Specifically, constitutional documents and employment contracts that ensure the Chief Executive Officer (CEO) and Chief Financial Officer (CFO) leadership roles change between the JV entities every 36 to 48 months. Clearly two years is too short a period for a CEO to make an impact. For example, in a British, German, Chinese and Korean JV structure, the first CEO might be British with the first CFO German. Thereafter, the second CEO could be German with the second CFO changing to a Chinese executive.

Readers will recall that the UK firm ARM sold a 51 per cent stake in its Chinese subsidiary, ARM Technology (China) Co Ltd. (ARM China), to an investor group to form a JV for ARM's existing semiconductor technology intellectual property (IP) business in China. The CEO of ARM China unilaterally took control of decision making despite a seven to one

their own cultural profile and then compare that with their stereotypical country culture and other country cultures.

board vote in favour of his removal from the CEO role. Two years passed before a new company legal representative and CEO could be signed off by local authorities.[38]

If a leadership rotation clause had existed in this JV framework it would have been more certain that a Chinese court would have been supportive of deciding on the legitimacy of a new Chinese CEO for ARM China, a new company legal representative and the return the company seal.

If the chosen JV structure includes a separate chairman, then that would be an additional role to consider making mandatory for rotation. However, that could be based on a long period, for example five years. Conversely, a longer serving chairman brought in with no shareholding or country of origin conflicts of interest may prove to be the best approach. Given the appointment of a chairman is not a compulsory or customary occurrence in all countries, each project requires careful assessment on whether a chairman needs appointing at all and if so on what basis.

8.10.3 Equal equity ownership

Third, there is value in a JV shareholding structure based on an equal equity. My proposed idea is for three JV partners to agree to commence cooperation and investment on a semiconductor facility, with each party holding 33.3 per cent equity. The constitutional documentation, such as any articles of association, would prohibit the increase of the shareholding of any of these three original JV partners.[39]

If a fourth JV partner joined, the constitutional documents would permit the reduction of the original 33.3 per cent equity holdings. In that scenario each JV partner would own 25 per cent of the equity. In both scenarios of 33.3 per cent equity held by three JV partners and 25 per cent equity held by four JV partners, the risks of a hostile takeover or even milder political manoeuvrings are illuminated. From the beginning the JV parties realise they cannot gain control of the whole venture, and equally do not waste

[38] *Financial Times* (2022) 'Arm takes action to regain control at its renegade China unit', 27 April 2022.

[39] © Sheridan 2012.

energy and time assessing if a JV partner has specific ambitions to change the balance of gain between the parties.[40]

The above equal equity ownership structure seems, in my view, to be an effective practical way by which a JV can sustain its existence and continue to benefit all parties.[41] At a China-UK City event where the main speaker was Sir Vince Cable, a former UK Minister for Business, and the chair was the former Lord Mayor of London, Michael Mainelli, there was a consensus that this equal equity ownership structure was an effective solution.[42]

The risks associated with both the rotating leadership and equal equity ownership structures is how best to manage disputes. Dispute resolution escalation clauses are well established, but the challenge is to maintain the positive relationships developed within the life cycle of a JV project.[43] Executives and workers may have spent thousands of hours learning to work together in research and development (R&D) or manufacturing contexts. The investment value on this level can be enormous.

8.10.4 Dispute prevention and management

Formal dispute resolution structures so often prove to be the beginning of the end for JVs. As common to all disputes managed by lawyers, arbitrators or judges, the focus is no longer on commercial longevity but on the

[40] Termination clauses would have to cover the options available to any existing JV parties.

[41] My original thought was this structure would enable Australian, Chinese and Japanese firms to collaborate on very high-value infrastructure projects.

[42] China Insight Foundation (2022) 'How Can UK Financial Services Take Advantage Of The Chinese Market In Today's Political Climate', Seminar at Lloyd's Of London, 21 November 2022.

[43] One valuable approach is to draft, agree and maintain a relationship management plan (RMP). A high-quality RMP is drafted with thought put into maintaining a spirit of continuous improvement. British Standard BS 11000, a framework specification for Collaborative Business Relationships promotes such a document as 'a working platform for relationship management through the life of the collaboration, ensuring that relationship management is effect communicated at all levels and integrated into execution and delivery for all stakeholders'. See www.bsigroup.com/LocalFiles/en-GB/bs-11000/resources/BSI-BS11000-Product-Guide-UK-EN.pdf.

detail of the contract and the technicalities of the adversarial processes. One potentially effective option is draft a mediation clause where all the JV parties agree to allow an independent mediator to attempt to resolve differences in an environment that has less formality and relies less on legal arguments.[44]

The presence of a neutral person with no affiliations to any JV party facilitates an atmosphere of commercial dialogue. If readers liken a formal dispute mechanism such as a court or arbitral hearing as a cure to a problem, a mediator may avoid the problem altogether, allowing all parties to continue focusing on future mutually beneficial revenue generation.

8.11 Governing law and jurisdiction risks

A mistake common to both supply contracts and JV agreements is a choice of law that reflects the greater bargaining power of one party or more than one party. While choosing the governing law of the most influential party enables negotiations to proceed without delay, in the event future disputes involving courts that choice can be a source of regret. A preferable approach is to make English law the choice of law of the contract and subject to the jurisdiction of English courts.

The main and pivotal reason to opt for English law is the established doctrine of good faith in contracts. In essence, English courts do not overrule or contradict the express terms of contracts between business entities on the grounds of expressing a judicial view of fairness. A key factor that has developed English courts under English law to consistently apply this doctrine of good faith is a strong business orientation that respects the freedom of business parties to contract on the terms that they choose.

Further, the large sums of money involved and interdependence between parties, mean contract predictability is judged to be of pre-eminent importance. It should also be acknowledged that the notion of good faith is also found in the laws of China, Japan and South Korea. However

---

[44] In *Churchill v Merthyr Tydfil County BC* [2023] EWCA Civ 1416, 29 November 2023, the UK Court of Appeal ruled that courts can stay proceedings and order parties to engage in alternative dispute resolution (ADR), including mediation.

English law has arguably an almost unique predictability given the extensive amount of judicial precedent whereby lower courts are bound to follow the decisions of higher courts.[45]

8.12 Final points

Increasingly, semiconductor firms heavily rely on cloud service providers to process and store their data. For instance, detailed EU regulation addresses the critical nature of such service providers.[46] This may seem a far-fetched scenario, given the competence and financial resources of the main cloud service providers, yet it is also a highly complex topic.[47]

A priority should be placed on managing cloud service provision by renegotiating existing contracts and assessing carefully how data is distributed across several providers given the risk that prolonged malfunctions could be catastrophic for any semiconductor firm. My own advice on outsourcing and third-party relationships relevant to cloud computing: Chief Operating Officers (COOs) and Chief Technology Officers (CTOs) need to follow an agreed rule of thumb to mitigate individual and systemic risks. The use of cloud computing requires contractual relationships based on:

- one-third (33.3 per cent) of total annual expenditure is with companies in the jurisdiction in which the headquarters of the regulated firm is located;
- one-third (33.3 per cent) of total annual expenditure is based on intra-group outsourcing which can be in the same jurisdiction as the headquarters of the regulated firm or distributed globally;

---

[45] Wood, P. (2022) *Governing Law Risks in International Business Transactions*, London: Sweet & Maxwell, at 77–81. Written by a former Allen & Overy partner with more than 40 years' experience, it also points out that while New York courts apply the doctrine of judicial precedent, it can be undermined by the unpredictable decisions reached in jury trials.

[46] See the Digital Operational Resilience Act (DORA), Regulation EU 2022/2554.

[47] Institute of Electrical and Electronics Engineers (2016), 'Systemic Risks in the Cloud Computing Model: Complex Systems Perspective', available at https://ieeexplore.ieee.org/document/7820361.

- one-third (33.3 per cent) of total annual expenditure is with companies globally excluding the jurisdiction in which the headquarters of the regulated firm is located.

Clearly this rule of thumb is most appropriate for global businesses with huge resources, such as Infineon, Intel or Samsung. However, it is important to highlight that regulator expectations on operational resilience still require proportionate focus and investment by all sizes of semiconductor small- and medium-sized enterprises. In short, diversification of cloud service providers based on location of data centres is an essential part of any procurement plan.[48]

[48] An authoritative practitioner book on cloud computing is Marchini, R (2015) *Cloud Computing: A Practical Introduction to the Legal Issues*, 2nd edn, British Standards Institute. Additionally, see Ruparelia, N.B. (2016) *Cloud Computing*, MIT Press.

9. Intellectual property law

9.1 Introduction

A balanced innovation protection mindset revolves around three areas, namely confidentiality, trade secrets, and intellectual property (IP) law.[1] These are the trio of foundational ways to either licence or protect products or both.[2] This chapter predominantly focuses on these foundations as applied in the UK. There is also some reference to European Union (EU) law and United States (US) law to make comparative points.[3]

The nature of implementing semiconductor innovation means there is normally uncertainty about which technical advance has a direct impact on revenues. That means a considerable amount of innovation protection runs the risks of wasting precious capital and time. The rule-based think-

1 I'm grateful to two exceptional patent attorneys for reviewing the patent law section. Andrew Thompson, Partner, UK and European patent attorney and UPC representative at the law firm EIP (see https://eip.com/us/people/andrew-thompson); and Howard Sands, Partner, UK and European patent attorney at the law firm Boult (see www.boult.com/people/howard-sands/).

2 Most IP relevant to semiconductors simultaneously performs both functions: it enables licensing to others and protects against unlicensed use. An authoritative and in-depth work on all types of IP with extensive case law referencing is Cornish, W., D. Llewelyn and T. Aplin (2019) *Intellectual Property: Patents, Copyright, Trademarks and Allied Rights*, 9th edn, London: Sweet & Maxwell.

3 My own China, EU, UK and US patent law research was hugely enriched by attending the 25th Annual Berkeley-Stanford Advanced Patent Law Institute (APLI). The APLI attendees included government officials, judges, litigators, patent prosecutors, professors, and senior in-house IP counsel. It was a highly insightful two-day event covering patent law and practice across the leading jurisdictions. Among other topics, participants discussed venue considerations, injunctions, discovery, dispute resolution strategies, and damages.

ing relied on by all legal counsel requires a counter-balancing judgement to know when to choose protective measures or alternative options, and when to proceed to litigation.

Innovation protection also requires close, continuous professional cooperation between legal counsel, board members, and engineers. To use the professional ice hockey metaphor referred to in the introductory chapter, to anticipate the vector of change, to envisage the sliding position of the puck.

9.2 Confidentiality

Breaches of confidentiality by current or former employees and third parties are commonplace in the semiconductor sector. An essential way of maximising protection is to manage how these individuals are held accountable for maintaining confidentiality. English law on confidentiality is multifaceted.[4] The requirements to prove breach of confidentiality are threefold:[5]

- The information is confidential in nature.[6]
- The information was communicated in circumstances indicating an obligation of confidence.[7]
- There is unauthorised use of the information to the detriment of the person communicating it.[8]

---

4 For an authoritative exploration of all aspects, see Phipps, C. and W. Harman (2019) *Toulson & Phipps on Confidentiality*, 4th edn, London: Sweet & Maxwell.

5 *Coco v A N Clark (Engineers) Ltd* [1968] FSR 415.

6 In the context of inventors, and potential commercial acquirers of innovation, it can never be presumed that information is being given freely. See *Seager v Copydex Ltd* [1967] 1 WLR 923.

7 There is no generally established precise test provided by the High Court to decide if circumstances indicate an obligation of confidence. However, in the *Argyll v Argyll* case cited by Megarry J in *Coco v A N Clark (Engineers) Ltd*, an objective test was proposed based on when a reasonable person would realise information was given in confidence: *Argyll v Argyll* [1967] Ch 302.

8 The Trade Secrets (Enforcement, etc.) Regulations 2018 (SI 2018/597) came into force in 2018. They operate in parallel with the common law. Case law indicates that common law principles are unaffected. See www.legislation.gov

9.3 Mitigating information leakage

While both English civil and criminal sanctions provide deterrent value for semiconductor-based trade secrets, human nature means that some individuals are still going to risk stealing then divulging confidential information. However, respecting confidential information is a cultivatable habit. For example, it is sensible to ask the Chief Executive Officer (CEO) to meet all new joiners and politely remind them about the importance of preserving confidentiality. While on first reflection it is unreasonable to ask a busy a CEO to support the legal function in this way, especially in a large business, in my experience, this leadership input is a practical five-minute time investment with a potentially enduring influence.

9.4 Characterising trade secrets

The World Intellectual Property Organization (WIPO) defines trade secrets as any confidential business information that provides an entity with a competitive advantage. Further, the Agreement on Trade-Related Aspects of Intellectual Property (TRIPS), produced by the World Trade Organization (WTO), provides the following three general standards to determine if something is a trade secret:

- The information must be secret, which means its substance is only accessible or known to a restricted circle of people.
- The information must be valuable.
- The owner must have taken reasonable steps to keep the information secret.[9]

Despite the pre-eminent position of the English High Court in the context of protecting mainstream IP, such as copyrights and patents, it cannot be assumed that trade secrets are equally protected. For example, for trade secrets protection rankings, five countries were at the apex of the 50-plus jurisdictions under annual assessment. These top five countries were

.uk/uksi/2018/597/regulation/. See also *Shenzhen Senior Technology Material Co Ltd v Celgard LLC* [2020] EWCA Civ 1293.

9 World Trade Organization (WTO) (1994) Article 39.2 of the Agreement on Trade-Related Aspects of Intellectual Property.

Germany, Netherlands, Spain, Sweden, and Switzerland – all with a score of 100. However, the UK scored only 75. While this placed it in the top fourth set of jurisdictions, the UK has a lower score than Ireland (83.33) and Italy (91.67).

In all jurisdictions, the challenge of trade secret management is a mixture of insufficient civil regulation, court experience, and effective deterrent criminal law. As the IP Index report concluded, courts 'have limited experience ruling on cases involving the misappropriation, improper acquisition, use, or disclosure of trade secrets or confidential business information. This gap is especially pronounced for criminal sanctions'.[10]

9.5 Treatment of trade secrets under English law

Under English law, trade secrets are managed in three contexts, namely breach of confidence, breach of contract and industrial espionage. Listed below are some aspects relevant to a semiconductor firm managing trade secrets:

- Algorithms that contribute to greater semiconductor efficiency.
- Business strategies, for example the decision to use an overlooked process, that is currently unpatented.
- Charts or flow diagrams.
- Company procedure manuals, for instance policies on developing, monitoring and registering IP-based on the contributions of several in-house functions.
- Commercial IP valuation based on internal and external legal function audits.
- Designs and drawings of inventions some of which, whether in draft or final version form part of a semiconductor design.

Figure 9.1 provides a checking process to assist in the decision making on (a) filing a patent, (b) attempting to keep innovation as a trade secret, or (c) tactically publishing an innovation as a defensive measure to prevent a future lawsuit. The legal function must contribute to an assessment on whether the granting of a patent is a realistic prospect, so this flowchart

[10] US Global Innovation Policy Center, International IP Index (2020) *Art of the Possible*, 8th edition, at 62.

decision making process has special value when there is no patent filing, because even the most robustly protected trade secret may still have some vulnerability to being leaked.

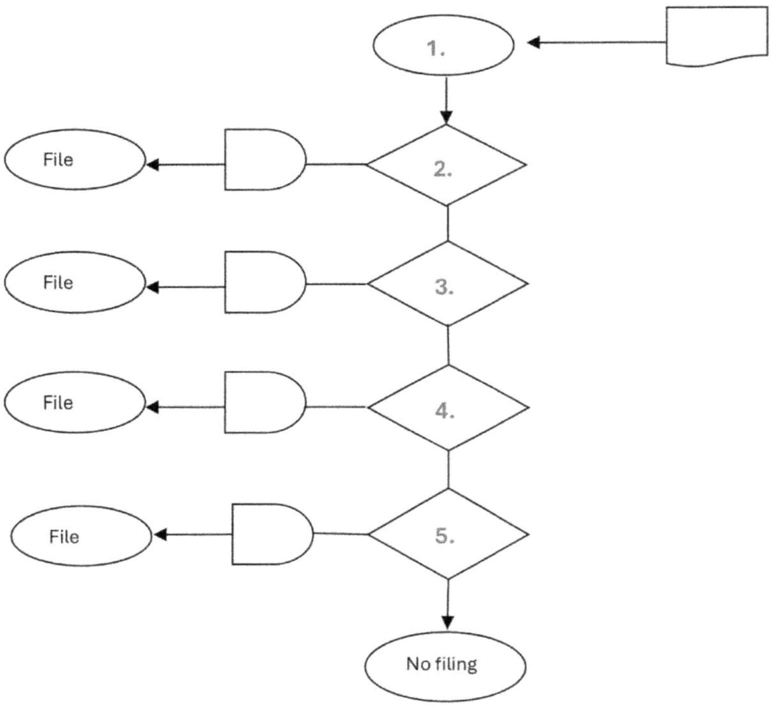

Source: © Iain Sheridan (2025)

Figure 9.1 Trade secret decision tree

The five steps in Figure 9.1 are:

1. Development team starts the process by providing information to the legal function on a new commercially valuable concept.
2. Is the trade secret vulnerable to being intentionally or unintentionally revealed to a third party? If yes, then file.
3. Can the method or product be reversed engineered? If yes, then in most instances file.
4. Is it likely that a competitor will invent the new concept or product with a consequential impact on the firm? If yes, then file.
5. Is maintaining the trade secret impractical or too costly? If yes, then file for a patent. Alternatively, as a defensive measure, consider publishing the innovation on the firm's website.

9.5.1 Trade secrets litigation

A memorable example is the lawsuit won by TSMC against a former employer who communicated details about TSMC's 28nm process technology to Samsung. Mr Liang Mong-song, a former senior research and development (R&D) director with 17 years' service, left TSMC in 2009. After moving to Taiwan's National Tsing Hua University, he started working for a private Korean institute, Sungkyunkwan, which was funded by Samsung. Thereafter, Liang started working directly for Samsung.

TSMC alleged that Liang's leak of its 28nm process designs helped Samsung gain a competitive edge it would not otherwise have achieved. Even despite Liang having left TSMC two years before TSMC started its lawsuit, and the fact his non-compete clause had run out, in 2015 the Taiwan Supreme Court still ruled that Liang was forbidden from working for any competitor of TSMC.[11]

More recently, Korean prosecutors indicted a former Samsung executive who allegedly attempted to replicate Samsung's Xian semiconductor plant with a copycat plant only 1.5km away. The sophisticated theft relied on the former Samsung executive hiring in the region of 200 employees from

[11] *Electronic Engineering Times* (2015), 'TSMC Wins Lawsuit Against Ex-Employee Now at Samsung', 25 August 2015.

Samsung and SK Hynix, then tasking them with obtaining trade secrets from their former employers.[12]

To some degree, the publicity surrounding both these court cases has a deterrent effect on current and future employees within the sector. For in-house legal functions it is valuable to include these case studies in training sessions with both new starter and long-serving employees.

9.5.2 TSMC's trade secrets register

In addition to putting in place confidentiality agreements with employees with knowledge of trade secrets, it is sensible to establish and maintain a trade secrets register. An effective trade secrets register could include specific reference to a number or code that is the record of the trade secret. Such an administrative process reduces the chance of an individual running a court defence based on accidental disclosure.

The adoption of a trade secrets database with positive recognition to staff for innovative contributions has already succeeded in Taiwan. For example, TSMC has already built such a database and implemented a complementing staff reward system. TSMC's 'Trade Secret Registration and Management System' records and tracks trade secrets that contribute to the firm's technological advancement.

The TSMC system, has over 100,000 trade secrets registered that are recorded by 30,000 employees. Annually, TSMC presents its 'Golden Trade Secret Award' for registered trade secrets that have the most significant impact on the firm's competitiveness. Further, special awards are presented to inventors who have earned numerous awards.[13]

---

[12] *Financial Times* (2023), 'Ex-Samsung executive alleged to have stolen tech to recreate chip plant in China', 12 June 2023.

[13] TSMC (2021), 'TSMC Continues to Use Artificial Intelligence (AI) for Trade Secret Management to Sustain Innovation and Strengthen Competitiveness', available at https://esg.tsmc.com/en/update/innovationAndService/caseStudy/29/index.html.

9.5.3 The impact of increased cyber security vulnerabilities

As cyber attacks increase on an annual basis, trade secrets, especially commercial tactics to prevent or at least slow down others from reverse engineering semiconductors, may become the most effective way to maintain a competitive advantage.[14] Innovation needs the protection of cyber security. As Bill Bryson has eloquently put it 'We're all precariously dependent on elaborate [Internet] networks… It is crucial to optimise the resilience of such systems against accidental malfunction or against wilful disruption by individuals or small groups empowered by technology'.[15]

A report commissioned by the international law firm CMS, written by *The Economist Intelligence Unit*, covers the degree to which firms identify intangible assets as trade secrets. The report was based on a survey of 314 senior corporate executives located in China, France, Germany, Singapore, the UK and the US, and across six sectors, including manufacturing and technology.[16] The results indicated that cyber security is perceived as the main way trade secrets are revealed.[17]

9.6 Patents

The legal justification for patents is the promotion of innovation with the reward of a monopoly right for a limited period.[18] The 'patent bargain'

[14] For a summary on how best to protect against cyber attacks, see Sheridan I (2022) *Financial Regulation and Technology*, Northampton, MA, USA: Edward Elgar Publishing, Chapter 5.

[15] Bryson, B. (2011) *Seeing Further – The Story of Science and the Royal Society*, William Collins, at 443.

[16] CMS (2021) *Open Secrets? Guarding Value in the Intangible Economy*, at 9.

[17] Sheridan (2022), Chapter 5 Cyber security also provides important general risk guidance relevant to accidental, negligent and malicious situations. Readers will recall that in July 2024 Microsoft operating systems crashed, resulting in US $10 billion financial loss. The cause was faulty CrowdStrike security software updates.

[18] *Actavis Group PTC EHF v ICOS Corporation* [2019] UKSC 15; [2019] Bus LR 1318, [53].

between each inventor and government is a social contract in which knowledge is shared in exchange for exclusive rights.[19]

The management of patents requires long-term cooperation between in-house legal counsel and the instructed patent attorney, until each patent right lapses. Although this section provides an accurate high-level summary, it is always necessary to obtain specialist patent attorney advice before lodging any application.[20]

Under English law, the protection of IP plays a vital role in attempting to reward innovators for their hard work and persistent applications of creative talent. It is easy to be cynical, but generally IP protection, certainly as practised in the English High Court, attempts to maximise commercial fairness.

In terms of legal principles, the UK has its own established case law and statutory framework.[21] It also refers to many EU court decisions. However, when business leaders discuss with legal counsel how best to tactically protect innovation, most realise that not all computer-driven innovations, for example computer programs, can be patented.[22] The same barrier to patentability applies to business methods.

---

19 European Patent Office (EPO) (2024) 'What to expect', available at www.epo.org/en/new-to-patents/what-to-expect.

20 The probability of obtaining a commercially useful patent is significantly increased by instructing a registered patent attorney. This is because the drafting of a patent specification requires a mix of legal and technical skills. For an objective summary on this topic produced by the UK Intellectual Property Office see www.gov.uk/guidance/why-you-should-use-an-ip-attorney.

21 Section 1(2) Patents Act 1977 provides that the grant of a patent excludes: '(i) a discovery, scientific theory or mathematical method; (ii) a literary, dramatic, musical or artistic work or any other aesthetic creation whatsoever; (iii) a scheme, rule or method for performing a mental act, playing a game or doing business, or a program for a computer; (iv) the presentation of information'. See www.legislation.gov.uk/ukpga/1977/37/section/1.

22 *Aerotel Ltd v Telco Holdings Ltd & Ors Rev* 1 [2006] EWCA Civ 1371, 27 October 2006. The EPO provides a succinct summary of the key challenges of hardware and software patentability. See www.epo.org/news-events/in-focus/ict/hardware-and-software.html.

Under English statute,[23] a patent may be granted for an invention[24] only when (a) the invention is new,[25] (b) it involves an inventive step,[26] (c) it is capable of industrial application,[27] and (d) it does not fall within an exception.[28] Computer programs that provide a technical effect, which most used in industrial applications do, are patentable.

For semiconductor start-up firms, the cost-benefit analysis of attempting to obtain one or more patents can form part of a funding strategy and medium-term success. Many firms can expect to pay up to £10,000 to file a patent with the support of a patent attorney. Patenting is not a low-cost form of protection but, given the power and signalling of the monopoly it provides that makes sense, albeit it is not without risk.

---

[23] Section 1(1)(a)-(d) Patents Act 1977. See www.legislation.gov.uk/ukpga/1977/37/section/1.

[24] The concept of an invention is not a defined term forming part of any initial judicial analysis. See *Biogen Inc v Medeva Plc* [1996] UKHL 18, (1997) 38 BMLR 149, [1997] RPC 1, per Lord Hoffmann at [46] advised all judges to 'put on one side their intuitive sense of what constitutes an invention until they have considered the questions of novelty, inventiveness and so forth'.

[25] Section 2(1) Patents Act 1977 states that 'an invention shall be taken to be new if it does not form part of the state of the art'. Section 2(2) elaborates that the state of the art includes any invention made public in any way, so including oral and written communication, before the priority date. For any readers new to English patent law, it is crucial to note that novelty is lost if the invention is divulged before filing. Many inventors have made this mistake. See www.legislation.gov.uk/ukpga/1977/37/section/2.

[26] *Pozzoli SpA v BDMO SA* [2007] F.S.R. 37 at [23].

[27] This is broadly construed and certainly covers any practical or useful innovation that forms all or part of a service.

[28] Section 1(2) Patents Act 1977 the exceptions are: anything which consists of:

(a) a discovery, scientific theory or mathematical method;
(b) a literary, dramatic, musical or artistic work or any other aesthetic creation whatsoever;
(c) a scheme, rule or method for performing a mental act, playing a game or doing business, or a program for a computer;
(d) the presentation of information;

but the foregoing provision shall prevent anything from being treated as an invention for the purposes of this Act only to the extent that a patent or application for a patent relates to that thing as such.

The words 'as such' are especially important and are elaborated on later in this chapter.

If the patent application fails, there are sunken legal patent attorney costs and a considerable loss of time. The invention will also be disclosed upon publication. However, as a long-term strategy the fact that individual rights might fail must be considered as part of overall investment in potentially tens or hundreds of rights.

Patent examiners are bound by legal precedent and must follow the decisions of the higher courts. Each examination is expected to be judged on its own merits. Different cases decided on different facts and inventions may not assist, and whether a patent application is granted is an inherently uncertain process.[29] For instance, there can be flaws in examiner assessments because they follow internal guidelines that miss specific case law or statute. In the event a patent application is rejected, patent attorneys are adept at spotting any gaps between patent office guidelines and current law with the aim of appealing the decision.

9.6.1 Patent tactics

Under UK statute the patent monopoly is granted for 20 years.[30] However, the commercial motivations driving firms to make patent applications are more realistically anchored in shorter timeframes. If granted, a patent might provide 24–36 months'-plus protection to the patent owner before competitors are able to work around the patent or advance the state of the art and have their own patent granted. However, the degree to which patents restrict competitors can vary hugely and depend on a wide variety of factors. In the specific context of many semiconductor patents there is the added complexity of an invention sitting as just one of many layers of innovation with numerous firms owning the patent for one or more layers.

For semiconductor start-ups seeking more funding there is certainly a pattern of venture capital firms assessing a patent portfolio as a reliable metric on which, among other evidence, to make investment decisions. To be clear, that portfolio might initially be one patent given it is often one very clever idea that needs protection. From an initial action to take

[29] *Research In Motion UK Ltd v Inpro Licensing SARL* [2006] EWHC 70 (Pat) per Pumfrey J at [186].

[30] Section 25 Patent Act 1977. See www.legislation.gov.uk/ukpga/1977/37/section/25.

viewpoint, an invention disclosure report needs to be produced. An invention disclosure report is a confidential document written by the in-house inventor for exclusive reading by the in-house legal counsel and external patent attorney. This confidential document is used to decide if patent application should be lodged or if an alternative type of protection should be deployed.

9.6.2 Patent applications in the UK and Europe

Compared with other jurisdictions, such as Japan, South Korea and the US, the strategic process of making patent applications to protect innovation in the UK has an extra advantage. Namely, the UK is a member of the European Patent Convention (EPC).[31] The EPC allows any signatory country to file a patent application with the European Patent Office (EPO) in Munich with the aim of having a patent granted for one or more EPC member states.[32] If granted, a bundle of national patents is obtained, with the applicant selecting the countries in which they require protection.[33] For example, by choosing the EPO option a semiconductor firm could efficiently achieve patent cover in not only the UK, but also France and Germany.

An interesting trend in IP strategies for both design and manufacturing firms is that the evolving global semiconductor market is predicted to place more focus on patent filing in Europe covering many countries. In the past, the trend was for the overwhelming quantity of patent filings relating to semiconductor technology to be made directly with the German Patent Office.

[31] The 17th edition of the European Patent Convention is available at www.epo.org/law-practice/legal-texts/epc.html.

[32] Current EPC member states include all the EEA members, Albania, North Macedonia, Monaco, San Marino, Switzerland, Turkey and the UK. To check for future additional member states, see www.epo.org/about-us/foundation/member-states.html.

[33] For an authoritative article-by-article analysis of the EPC, see Convention updated to 1 March 2024: Suominen, K. et al (2024) *Visser's Annotated European Patent Convention*, Kluwer Law International. Note that an inventor may simply choose to file a patent application at the UK Patent Office. It is not mandatory to use the EPO.

However, the EU CHIPS Act is likely to see an expansion in the relevance of protecting manufacturing processes in other European countries, especially France and Italy. Further, cross-border joint venture activity, with R&D in one EU member state and manufacturing in another, should make EPO filings a more logical choice, rather than solely relying on the German Patent Office.

An important reason there is more European semiconductor manufacturing, and therefore more European patent filing, is the increased importance placed, within the EU, on supply chain sovereignty. The Covid-19 pandemic caused firms to think about supply chain security, which requires increasing local supply and decreasing global supply chain vulnerabilities.

A second noteworthy change predicted for IP strategies concerns an increase in Integrated Design Manufacturers (IDMs) filing patents in Europe as a defensive strategy in response to a general increase in Europe-based manufacturing, including TSMC's increased activity in the region. In the past, TSMC manufacturing overwhelmingly occurred in East Asia. Most Western IDM activity takes place in Germany and North America. However, as Figure 9.2 illustrates, TSMC has altered its international patent filing strategy over the last few years from East Asia to place more emphasis on patent filings in Europe as well.[34]

Andrew Thompson, is a patent partner at the leading European IP law firm EIP. This firm is known for its high-profile patent lawsuits and patent portfolio management consulting. Thompson believes:

> IDMs will need to carefully consider their approach to protecting manufacturing processes. Techniques that at one time would have been better off as trade secrets, may need to be patented to provide the IDMs with some defence against the pure-play foundries...we expect that the dial will shift further towards patents, and away from trade secrets.[35]

[34] EIP (2022) 'Changes in the semiconductor industry: how patent strategies need to adapt', available at https://eip.com/uk/insights/article/changes_in_semiconductor_industry_how_patent_strategies_need_to_adapt/.

[35] EIP (2022) 'Changes in the semiconductor industry: how patent strategies need to adapt', available at https://eip.com/uk/insights/article/changes_in_semiconductor_industry_how_patent_strategies_need_to_adapt/.

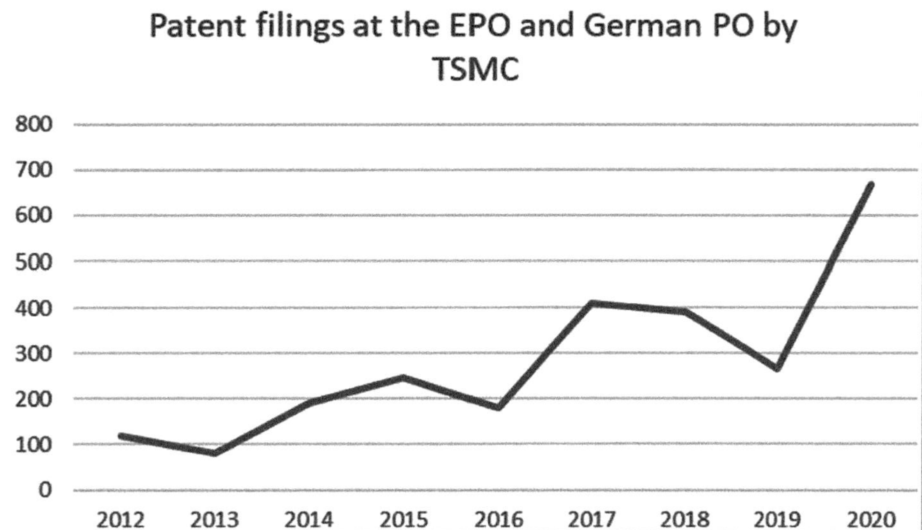

Source: EIP (2022) 'Changes in the semiconductor industry: how patent strategies need to adapt', available at https://eip.com/uk/insights/article/changes_in_semiconductor_industry_how_patent_strategies_need_to_adapt/

Figure 9.2 *TSMC patent filings at the EPO and German patent office*

The 2023 decision by TSMC to invest US $3.88 billion in a new Dresden semiconductor plant is likely to accelerate this trend of significant increases in its European patent filings. The specific use of the EPO for patent filings because of this TSMC investment is also likely to increase because the Taiwanese group will be a 70 per cent equity owner in a joint venture with Infineon Technologies, Robert Bosch and NXP Semiconductors.[36] With support from both the EU and the German Government, total investment in this project will exceed US $11 billion.[37] Other joint ventures based on similar Asian multinational participants, with European and US IDMs, are also likely to expand patent filing activity at the EPO.

9.6.3 The Unified Patent Court

Since June 2023, 17 member states of the EU provide a supranational patent court.[38] The Unified Patent Court (UPC) has been created under the UPC Agreement (UPCA). With a Court of First Instance in Paris as well as a Court of Appeal in Luxembourg, the UPC provides an efficient framework for patent litigation for both infringement and revocation actions.[39]

A significant advantage of the UPC is that its judgments are directly applicable in the member states that have ratified the UPCA.[40] Importantly for Asian and US firms that rely on English as one of their professional working languages, the language of proceedings before any local or regional division of the Court of First Instance includes English.[41]

---

36 These two German firms and one Dutch firm will each own a 10 per cent equity stake.

37 Ting-Fang, C. (2023) 'TSMC reveals $11 billion deal to build first European chip plant', *Nikkei Asia*, 8 August 2023.

38 To clarify, 24 member states have agreed to participate in the UPC, but to date only 17 have ratified the UPCA.

39 UPC (2024) Unified Patent Court Structure, available at www.unified-patent-court.org/en/court/presentation.

40 EU Regulation No 1257/2012 Unitary patent protection.

41 UPC (2024) Language of Proceedings, available at www.unified-patent-court.org/en/court/language-proceedings.

9.6.4 FRAND

The concept of a patent owner giving an undertaking to licence their patents on fair, reasonable and non-discriminatory (FRAND) terms, merits brief coverage. For some readers FRAND terms may represent a recent pattern of commercial negotiations. In fact, such undertakings have existed, albeit in less developed forms, for decades.[42]

The existence of FRAND terms stems from the benefit of developing industry standardisation. The efficient creation of standards affects many sectors, including automotive, computer hardware and mobile telecommunications and all other semiconductor components integral to other equipment. For example, 4G and subsequent standards for mobile telecommunication networks facilitate competition by allowing governmental bodies and commercial firms to work on the same technical level. Such partnerships are known as Standard Setting Organisations (SSOs).

In the telecommunications sector, one of the SSOs is the 3rd Generation Partnership Project (3GPP) which is made up of both national and regional partners, as well as market representative partners.[43] The 3GPP focuses on the 5G standard. One of its market representative partners is the 5G Automotive Association (5GAA) which promotes automative standards. The 5GAA membership includes major semiconductor patent holders, such as Ericsson, Huawei, Infineon, Intel, Nokia, Qualcomm, Vodafone, and ZTE.[44] These firms, and many others, are the owners of many Standards Essential Patents (SEPs).

The reason FRAND undertakings exist is that the standardisation of technology is facilitated by their existence. Any holder of SEPs is rewarded with licence royalties. Simultaneously, FRAND undertakings reduce anti-competitive behaviour and litigation. The aim is to strike a balance between the owners of patents and implementing firms that must incorporate the patents.

---

[42] *Terrell on the Law of Patents* has been the leading authority on UK patent law since 1884. Its editors point out that the reasonableness and non-discriminatory nature of royalties has been a feature since 1994. See Campbell, D. et al (2024) *Terrell on the Law of Patents*, 20th edn, London: Sweet & Maxwell, at vii.

[43] See www.3gpp.org/about-us/partners.

[44] See https://5gaa.org/members/.

Under English law, if a patent owner has established that a valid patent has been infringed, it is, until proved otherwise, entitled to prevent further infringement by seeking an injunction.[45] In the UK, the legal consequences of agreed FRAND undertakings temper the patentor's tactics to threaten an injunction as part of negotiating exorbitant fees.

The High Court position has been succinctly summarised this way:

> If a worldwide licence is not FRAND then a putative licensee should not be coerced into accepting it by the threat of an injunction in one state. However, if a worldwide licence is FRAND then the situation changes. The logic of the FRAND undertaking...should present the licensee with a simple choice either to take a FRAND licence or stop dealing in the products.[46]

The UK common law principles on FRAND have recently been covered in detail at the UK Supreme Court level.[47] These include a principle of global relevance given it makes clear how UK courts will deal with FRAND terms in the future – based on 'real world' commercial practice. That English courts have jurisdiction to determine the terms of a FRAND licence where the implementer enters into a global licence covering an international patent portfolio. Put another way, if the intellectual property rights (IPR) policy of an SSO stipulates FRAND contractual terms, the High Court may set global FRAND licence terms based on a finding of infringement of one patent in the UK.[48]

Lastly, for the semiconductor sector a significant commercial advantage was gained in 2022 when Huawei and Nordic Semiconductor entered into a global FRAND licence agreement. Although specifically dealing with a sub-set of Huawei's 4G standard, namely LTE-M and NM-IoT, it means

---

45 Under Scots law an interdict provides a similar presumption of entitlement to seek a restraining order against the implementer of the patent.

46 *Unwired Planet International Ltd & Anor (Respondents) v Huawei Technologies (UK) Co Ltd & Anor (Appellants)* [2020] UKSC 37, *per omnes iudices*, at [165], quoting Birss J.

47 *Unwired Planet International Ltd & Anor (Respondents) v Huawei Technologies (UK) Co Ltd & Anor (Appellants)* [2020] UKSC 37. This Supreme Court decision was in fact made up of three appeals. The second respondent was a Patent Assertion Entity (PAE) called Conversant Wireless Licensing SÀRL (Conversant).

48 Ibid at [58].

that Nordic Semiconductor can access standardised cellular technology across its range of products. The FRAND agreement allows licensing at the component level, which had been rare in the Internet of Things (IoT) industry.[49] Nordic Semiconductor has at least 1,000 customers so this is a significant commercial advantage.

9.7 Semiconductor topography rights

Globally, the underlying IP protection provided to semiconductor topologies derives from the application of principles found in the unratified mid-1990s WTO TRIPS Agreement.[50] Article 36 of TRIPS specifies that:

> Members shall consider unlawful the following acts if performed without the authorization of the right holder: importing, selling, or otherwise distributing for commercial purposes a protected layout-design, an integrated circuit in which a protected layout-design is incorporated, or an article incorporating such an integrated circuit only in so far as it continues to contain an unlawfully reproduced layout-design.[51]

In the UK, The Design Right (Semiconductor Topologies) Regulations 1989 (SI 1989/1100) (UK Topography Regulations) provide for a special form of unregistered design right.[52] The scope of semiconductor topography protection includes (a) the pattern fixed, or so intended to be fixed, or (b) upon a layer of a semiconductor product, or (c) in or upon the layers of a semiconductor product.[53] In this specific context, the UK Topography Regulations define a semiconductor product as:

---

[49] Sandys, A. (2022) 'Huawei and Nordic FRAND deal important step for IoT licensing', Juve Patent, 21 June 2022, available at www.juve-patent.com/people-and-business/huawei-and-nordic-frand-deal-important-step-for-iot-licensing/.

[50] TRIPS Agreement members include all 164 WTO members.

[51] WTO (2005) Agreement on Trade-Related Aspects of Intellectual Property Rights as Amended by the 2005 Protocol Amending the TRIPS Agreement. See www.wto.org/english/docs_e/legal_e/trips_e.htm#art6.

[52] The Design Right (Semiconductor Topologies) Regulations 1989 (SI 1989/1100).

[53] Regulation 2(1)(a) and (b) The Design Right (Semiconductor Topologies) Regulations 1989 (SI 1989/1100).

> 'semiconductor product' means an article the purpose, or one of the purposes, of which is the performance of an electronic function and which consists of two or more layers, at least one of which is composed of semiconducting material and in or upon one or more of which is fixed a pattern appertaining to that or another function.[54]

Two aspects of the UK Topography Regulations present potential sources of competitive advantage. First, in contrast to the US Semiconductor Chip Protection Act 1984, reverse engineering is permissible.[55] Therefore, a UK entity or individual can analyse an existing protected semiconductor topography and, with sufficient originality, create a new topography with significantly diminished risk of litigation.[56]

Second, the UK Topography Regulations allow for the reproduction of a protected design when carried out privately for non-commercial aims, or the motivation of reproduction is based on analysing or evaluating the design or enables teaching the concepts, processes, systems, or techniques embodied in it.[57] This defence should facilitate cost-effective R&D in universities and other institutions where the aim is to developed semiconductor talent with minimal licensing costs and litigation concerns.

From a strategic viewpoint, the risks associated with licensing Instruction Set Architecture (ISA) can affect even the most long-standing contractual relationships. A recent example is the Delaware lawsuit filed by ARM against Qualcomm. Despite a 22-year relationship, ARM argued that in connection with Qualcomm's acquisition of Nuvia in 2021, there has been a subsequent breach of ARM Licencing Agreements (ALAs) and trade mark infringement.

The ALAs allow Qualcomm to develop custom core designs on top of ARM's ISA. Qualcomm's planned market strategy is to compete with cutting-edge semiconductor technology to operate in future laptops and smartphones. This court action, placed uncertainty on the implementa-

54 Ibid reg.2(1).

55 Ibid reg.8(4).

56 Article 5(3) of EU Directive 87/54 [1987] OJ L24/36, from which the UK Topography Regulations originate, provides for the same freedom to reverse engineer.

57 Ibid reg.8(1)A(a)–(b).

tion timing of Qualcomm's strategy.[58] Lessons for general counsel include the need to have as much detail as possible on the strategic direction of the firm, including how acquired entities may change terms of contracts and access to IP.

9.8 Copyright protection

Under the Berne Convention for the Protection of Literary and Artistic Works (the Berne Convention), 176 UN member states apply the same standards of national treatment to copyright authors.[59] Copyright protection will be of most value to electronic design automation (EDA) software providers, and fabless design firms that offer design augmentation programs as part of their licensing services.[60]

Semiconductor entrepreneurs increasingly focus on logic units that exploit machine learning. Therefore, the successful combination of hardware and software present a competitive advantage. Semiconductor firm R&D and product development will increasingly include software development. However, as Jim Keller, CEO of Tenstorrent and former architect at AMD, Apple, Intel and Tesla, has observed, the software element is hard.

An example of successful software protection linked to semiconductor hardware is Nvidia's copyrighted compiler, CUDA. As early as 2006, Nvidia's leaders sought to optimise graphics processing unit (GPU) performance, including improving frame rates, and reducing crashing

---

[58] *Arm Ltd v Qualcomm Incorporated and Nuvia Incorporated* (2022) Delaware District Court, CA No. 22-1146 (MN). In December 2024 a jury was asked three questions. Their answers are in brackets: 1. If Nuvia breached its licence with ARM? (No); 2. If Qualcomm breached its licence with ARM? (No); 3. If Qualcomm's licence included semiconductor technology that ARM argued it did not cover? (Undecided).

[59] Berne Convention for the Protection of Literary and Artistic Works (1979). See https://wipolex.wipo.int/en/treaties/textdetails/12214. Note: this came into effect in 1984.

[60] Ibid at Section 3A(2) on the treatment of databases. To gain copyright protection any database needs to be original and based on 'the author's own intellectual creation'.

or freezing during game play. Nvidia achieved this by introducing its unified driver architecture (UDA). Customers can download the Nvidia UDA from the internet based on GPU type, version, and computer operating system.[61] To date, Nvidia has expanded the copyright protection to a range of CUDA components. Nvidia is synonymous with semiconductor hardware, but also software services.

The pivotal element of code will be novel algorithms that allow one semiconductor firm to offer greater efficiencies, or unique features, compared with competitors. Generally, for an algorithm to be patentable it must contribute to the solution of a real-world technical problem. However, this is a complex area for judicial interpretation. Therefore, copyright is a key extra defensive weapon for algorithms that form part of software. While copyright infringement occurs when a substantial part of a creative work is copied, to determine if an algorithm is a 'substantial' is a complex task.

For engineers this vulnerability of algorithms forming part of copyrighted software may present a sense of puzzlement. As the pioneering Dutch software engineer Djistra put it 'if a drawing can be worth 1,000 words, a formula can be worth 1,000 drawings'. Unfortunately, IP law on copyright is less sensitive to the realities of coding.

9.9 Employer and employee relations

The role of employees as inventors is a complex issue.[62] Dynamic leadership revolves around trust. Further, the employee needs to be incentivised, but simultaneously the firm has invested salary and other benefits which mean a balance needs to be struck between fair treatment of employees versus revenue. Common law provides many relevant cases on the issue of employee inventions. However, for many decades statute

---

[61] The original UDA has since expanded to be a platform that includes a compiler, libraries, and an application programming interface (API). It was renamed the Compute Unified Device Architecture (CUDA).

[62] A recent Supreme Court decision dealt with the issue of the s.40 Patents Act 1977 requirement to compensate employee patents that have contributed an outstanding benefit to the employer. See *Shanks v Unilever Plc & Ors* [2019] UKSC 45, available at www.bailii.org/uk/cases/UKSC/2019/45.html.

has also governed.[63] In a leading English High Court case it was also made clear that while employee duties are primarily captured in contracts of employment, the reality is that, over time, roles evolve making it unsafe to rely on only contractual terms.[64]

Non-compete clauses are a global phenomenon. A balance needs to be struck. Based on employment tribunal cases and media coverage, employers run the risk of creating rather than mitigating societal problems. On the one hand it is reasonable for a non-compete clause to require a leaving employee not to exploit knowledge and contacts that principally derive from that existing employer. On the other hand, there is a risk of creating societal stresses that amount to mental and physical abuse.

As an example, in the technology sector a worker that had left the Chinese firm Pinduoduo was asked to sign a confidentiality, non-compete and intellectual ownership agreement. An attached notice letter restricted the employee from working at a rival firm for 4–9 months. The employee left Pinduoduo looking for a new role and was immediately in breach of a sum of money that amounted to 24 months' salary. Consequently, she committed suicide.

There is also a wider need to consider the role innovation plays in motivating engineers and other science, technology, engineering and mathematics (STEM)-based innovators in the semiconductor sector to remain creative and motivated. For instance, allowing some moonlighting on projects that maybe be semiconductor-based but do not compete directly with the main employer firm's current product lines.[65]

---

[63] The Patents Act 1977 was made law on 1 June 1978. For an in-depth analysis of the Patents Act 1977 in this context, see Johnson, P. (2021) 'From Banks to Shanks; the History of Employee Awards for Patented Inventions under the Patents Act 1977', *Queen Mary Journal of Intellectual Property* (*Elgaronline*), 11(2).

[64] *LIFFE Administration and Management v Pavel Pinkava* [2007] RPC 30.

[65] Zhou, C. (2024) 'China's Tech Workers Trapped in Jobs by Non-compete Contracts', *Nikkei Asia*, 3 April 2024.

In 2023, I asked Sir Tim Berners-Lee how he thought the challenge of innovation and employer flexibility could be solved? He jokingly replied, 'work in a university'. Perhaps many a partly true word is spoken in jest.[66]

One possibility is for an employer to provide employment contract clauses that permit an employee to, not work for, but alongside, a university[67] for a limited number of hours per month. In short, extending the young person's day-release concept to all innovative career professionals.

If we further imagine that individual productivity is increased because all employees are permitted to dedicate one day per week to an innovative project that is different from their other four days, there may be a point when such models of employment become part of law, at the level of a right to request an innovation day.

Asynchronous compliance refers to the pattern of technology-driven business strategies and operations that are moving at markedly different speeds compared with regulation.[68] This mismatch creates a negative impact on firms. By which is meant asynchronous timing creates uncertainty that dynamic business initiatives meet regulatory requirements. In my view, there is also a current asynchronous compliance issue for employees working in engineering and science-led businesses. The nature of semiconductor research and the realities of effective employee stimulation present a strong case for employment law to adjust to this form of 'innovation day release' as part of a solution to grow more entrepreneurial activity.

---

66 This book is focused on hardware, but it cannot be lost on any reader that Sir Tim is another product of both British innovative culture and a world-class STEM university education.

67 London School of Economics (2023) 'WEB 3.0 Technology and Policy', Seminar, 25 May 2023.

68 In 2017, I coined the term 'asynchronous compliance'. See Sheridan, I. (2017) 'MiFID II in the context of Financial Technology and Regulatory Technology', *Capital Markets Law Journal*, 12(4), 417–27.

9.10 Employer versus employee innovation ownership

It is worth reflecting on a case concerning patents made to protect an electronic trading system. The brief facts were that a Dr Pavel Pinkava (Pinkava) was employed by the LIFFE, the former operator of the London Futures Exchange, as a manager in its Interest Rate Product (IRP) Management Team. In July 2004 he invented a novel electronic trading system for various financial instruments. He was promoted to senior manager in the same team on 13 September 2004.

In January 2005 Pinkava was advised by the LIFFE that he was entitled to be the owner of the invented IRP trading system. On 23 April 2005 Pinkava filed four applications for US patents covering the trading system.[69] Thereafter, the LIFFE terminated Pinkava's employment on 13 July 2005. One week later, LIFFE also started proceedings claiming to be entitled to the confidential information relating to the system devised by Pinkava and the patent applications based on it. Subsequently, at a first instance hearing instigated by Pinkava claiming ownership of the four US patents, the judge concluded that:

- The inventions were not made in the course of the normal duties of Pinkava as an employee of the LIFFE.
- The inventions were made as part of duties specifically assigned to him.
- The circumstances were such that an invention might reasonably be expected to result from the carrying out of the specific duties.[70]

At first instance, the LIFFE was held to be the owner of the inventions claimed in the US patent applications. The appeal by Pinkava was dismissed. However, a different conclusion was reached, specifically that

---

[69] As discussed earlier in this chapter, s.1(2)(c) Patents Act 1977 excludes such patents under English law. But they are available under US law. For example, in 1999 Amazon was granted a patent for its one-click buying invention (US Patent US5960411A). The granting of US patents for business methods and computer programs is increasingly harder, so EDA firms rely on other IP strategies.

[70] Section 39(1)(a) Patents Act 1977. See www.legislation.gov.uk/ukpga/1977/37/section/39.

the US patents belonged to the LIFFE because each invention was made during Pinkava's normal duties.

The issues in the LIFFE case can be found in the semiconductor sector where software developers may have a portfolio of work with more than one employer. In sum, if the employee activity is part of their general duties or specially assigned duties, the patent belongs to the employer. For example, a software developer dedicated to EDA tool advances, any patent linked to either type of duties is the property of the employer. As the statute makes clear, 'any other invention made by an employee shall, as between him and his employer, be taken for those purposes to belong to the employee'.[71]

9.11 Auditing

The starting point for protecting the IP of any firm is to understand and record precisely what a company owns, what trade secrets it needs to protect, what patents it has filed and what other IP it has registered. Therefore, the legal function, in cooperation with research, product development and other front-office business functions, needs to conduct regular audits of its IP. The way to conduct an IP audit is to (a) first answer internal audit questions, and then (b) go on to answer external audit questions that focus on licensing and third-party IP. The questions that need to be answered for the internal audit are set out in Figure 9.3.

Regularly answering seven questions can act as the most effective form of IP protection by deterring or preventing disputes. Amongst these questions there is no hierarchy of importance. For example, checking that all contracts with subcontractors adequately cover ownership can be valued as the most key concern for semiconductor firms developing products and systems with proprietary information. However, many of the most valuable corporate IP assets are protected by trade secrets, therefore, rigorous procedures for keeping commercially sensitive information within a firm and setting out clearly what can and cannot be externally disclosed, potentially matter even more.

[71] Section 39(2) Patents Act 1977. See www.legislation.gov.uk/ukpga/1977/37/section/39.

Internal audit questions	Document, policy or person confirming answer
Who owns the IP?	
Has the firm any obsolete IP?	
Which granted patents do not justify the fees required to maintain them?	
If others use the firm's IP what are the terms?	
Do contracts with employees or subcontractors adequately cover ownership?	
Has the firm proper procedures in place when disclosing confidential information?	
Has the firm sufficient protection where it matters most, especially core IP?	

Source: © Iain Sheridan (2025)

Figure 9.3 Internal audit questions

There needs to be constant monitoring of IP law, including litigation rules, in the countries in which the semiconductor firm markets products or services. It is also important to watch competitors' patent filings and grants to avoid inadvertently infringing a patent. These activities may reduce the risk of disputes and on the occasions when litigation cannot be avoided, the cost of litigation. For instance, currently the registration of European patents is granted by the EPO in Munich, Germany providing patent protection across the 39 contracting countries that apply this continental system.[72] However, infringements are litigated on a country-by-country basis, often resulting in unpredictable outcomes because each jurisdiction may reach a different outcome.

Turning to external auditing, the legal function needs to answer at least seven external audit questions that focus on third-party IP and licensing. The questions that need to be answered for the external audit phase are listed in Figure 9.4.

Potentially the most valuable external audit questions are the last two questions because considerable IP expense can be saved by researching, and then using, lower cost IP, rather than entering or extending IP licensing agreements made with more expensive third parties. Costs are sec-

[72] EPO (2024) member states, available at www.epo.org/en/about-us/foundation/member-states/date.

External audit questions	Document, policy or person confirming answer
Does your firm use or intend to use third-party IP?	
Is the IP properly protected?	
Are proper licensing agreements in place?	
What precisely has been licensed?	
Is all non-core IP being fully exploited?	
Is it possible and safe to lower the cost of IP?	
Are regular searches conducted of IP databases relevant to the firm's existing and planned products?	

Source: © Iain Sheridan (2025)

Figure 9.4 External audit questions form

ondary to effective legal advice, contract formation and risk management by the legal function, but such measures make incremental contributions to sustaining competitiveness.

9.11.1 Practical implementation

A sample confidential in-house checklist for signing-off by both the legal counsel conducting the audits and the Head of Legal function is set out in Figure 9.5. The Head of Legal will look to ensure the process of internal audit is regularly completed and remains confidential.

> This confidential document and the attached summary are for the view of the following staff only: [insert name]; [insert name]; [insert name].
> I confirm that all the above checks have been carried out. Any necessary action has been taken or the date of any future action has been recorded before the next scheduled review.
> ...., Legal Counsel
> Signed................
> I have discussed the process and completion of this audit with the above Legal Counsel. I am satisfied that checks have been carried out and that any appropriate action has been taken.
> ...., General Counsel
> Signed....................
> *WARNING: This checklist and attached summary are the confidential property of [insert full firm name]. Its contents must not be sent or communicated to any person or entity that is not listed at the top of this page. If you have any query concerning this document please* contact the Legal Department at email address [ ] or on telephone number [ ].

The legal counsel or team of lawyers conducting the audit should state the objective of the audit. For example, that the task is the '8th Formal annual

IP audit task	Type of evidence	Date reviewed	Action to take
• Patents held and filed.			
• Patent renewals.			
• Review of patent licensing arrangements.			
• Search for patents dealing with the same activity.			
• Check trademark names are registered, including all internet-based domain names.			
• Check all relevant trademark names are renewed.			
• Discuss future product plans and launches with business units.			
• Review trademark and design right licensing arrangements.			
• Check legitimate trademark and design right usage.			
• Search registers for similar marks or design rights registered by competitors.			
• Check copyright notices comply with the Company standard.			
• Identify copyrights of commercial value.			
• Confirm ownership of copyrights.			
• Review copyright licensing arrangements.			
• Review confidentiality agreements with employees, subcontractors, and joint-venture partners.			

Source: © Iain Sheridan (2025)

Figure 9.5 Quarterly intellectual property audit

audit'. They should also sign off the report attaching a one-page executive summary explaining what has been audited, the IP issues the audit has raised and recommended ways of improving both the exploitation and protection of the firm's IP, as well as stating the timescale for the implementation of suitable improvements.

The completion, signing and circulation of a succinct executive summary to senior management will also play a useful role in highlighting this valuable preventative role played by the legal function. To whom this executive summary is circulated needs to be stated precisely, indicating that the summary is highly confidential and not to be forwarded electronically or on paper to any employee, director or external adviser or consultant without the prior permission of the general counsel.

9.12 Final points

Perhaps what makes the semiconductor sector the most dynamic sector of all is the pivotal role of innovation. To advance humanity with infinite possibilities based on STEM-based research. The success of ARM, and more recently Imagination Technologies, suggests the UK remains a highly innovative environment. In the 2024 annual report of the US Chamber of Commerce's Global Innovation Policy Center International IP Index, the UK and all other leading countries were assessed on their overall systemic efficiency based on the following five criteria:

- National efforts at coordinating IP rights enforcement.
- Stakeholder consultation mechanisms during the IP law-making process.
- Awareness-raising and educational activities on the importance of IP rights and benefits.
- Targeted incentives for small- and medium-sized enterprises (SMEs) concerning the creation, registration, and use of IP assets.
- The degree to which authorities in an economy aim to map and measure the economic impact and importance of IP-intensive sectors to their national economies.[73]

Encouragingly, based on this global comparison of systemic efficiency, the UK scored 95 out of 100, ranking only below South Korea.[74] Other countries also scored 95, including France, Japan and the US.

From a global perspective, IP protection is imperfect, especially in the context of Patent Assertion Entities (PAEs) not actively involved in advancing the state of the art. PAEs do not invent, develop, or manufacture anything. In contrast semiconductor firms survive by advancing

[73] US Chamber of Commerce (2024) Global Innovation Policy Center, *International IP Index* (2024), 12th edition.

[74] Ibid, at 72. South Korea scored 100. Germany, the Netherlands, and Taiwan all scored 90.

real innovation.[75] A US Federal Trade Commission (FTC) study on PAEs concluded that, on the one hand judicial systems positively function to promote respect for patent laws. However, on the other hand PAE litigation is often a nuisance, draining judicial resources and diverting attention away from productive business.[76]

Turning to new initiatives, the US Patent and Trademark Office (USPTO) initiative to accelerate the time taken to process patent applications is something that could be successfully copied in the UK. This USPTO scheme aims to fast track non-provisional utility patent applications for certain apparatuses and processes focused on manufacturing semiconductor devices, by advancing them out of turn for examination. This pilot programme deserves ongoing scrutiny by entrepreneurs, lawyers, and policy makers.[77]

Finally, as AI-based systems are increasingly applied it will be even more important that commercial fairness is facilitated by the ability of both patent examiners and courts to dissect the connections between hardware, firmware, and software.[78] Consequently, semiconductor firms will increasingly be part of court litigation, whether as a litigating party or by providing witnesses who explain how AI-augmented devices function. Semiconductor firms will find that the 'inventive step' requirement will be impacted by AI. For example, patent examiners and courts concluding

[75] In contrast, a study of inventors made up of labs, SMEs and universities, that used PAE intermediation, found they produced greater numbers of inventions. But the inventions tended to lack 'commercialization capabilities', and only incrementally advanced the state of the art. See Chari, M. et al (2022) 'The influence of patent assertion entities on inventor behaviour', *Strategic Management Journal*, 43(8), 1662–90.

[76] FTC (2016) *Patent Assertion Activity – An FTC Study*, at 9.

[77] USPTO (2023) 'USPTO announces Semiconductor Technology Pilot Program in support of CHIPS for America Program', Press Release, 30 November 2023.

[78] The UK Supreme Court has confirmed that an AI-driven program cannot currently be an 'inventor' of a patent, because an inventor must be a natural person as made clear under ss.7 and 13 of the Patents Act 1977. See *Thaler v Comptroller-General of Patents, Designs and Trade Marks* [2023] UKSC 49 at [56]–[59]; applying *Rhone-Poulenc Rorer International Holdings Inc v Yeda Research and Development Co Ltd* [2007] UKHL 43.

that a patent is obvious based on AI-related skills evolving as an established component of common knowledge.[79]

[79] Shemtov, N. and G. Gabison (2024) *Intellectual Property and Artificial Intelligence – The Inventive Step Requirement and the Rise of AI Machines*, Cheltenham, UK and Northampton, MA, USA: Edward Elgar Publishing, at 423–42.

10. National security law

We must not make a scarecrow of the law, setting it up to fear the birds of prey, and let it keep one shape, till custom make it their perch and not their terror.[1]

During the Cold War, United States (US) computer manufacturing firms were allowed to sell their mainframes to the USSR, although this permission excluded cutting edge machines. Therefore, when thinking about current national security law in the United Kingdom (UK), the European Union (EU), or elsewhere, managing the business of computer hardware with geopolitics is not a new challenge. However, it has become considerably more complex to manage, because the possibility of asymmetric warfare between countries presents a wider range of risks.

Today, international semiconductor firms expanding in the UK undergo greater vetting compared with a few years ago. This stricter approach to semiconductor acquisition is especially logical if the design, device or equipment is at the advanced end of the nanometre spectrum. The challenge is to not erroneously impede commercial growth across areas of semiconductor activity that present low or manageable security risk.

10.1 Introduction

Since January 2022, the National Security and Investment Act 2021 (NSIA)[2] creates a new regime for vetting both foreign and national investment in the UK. While the main political driver behind the NSIA is national defence and security, its reach has broad implications. The

---

1 Shakespeare, W. (1623) *Measure for Measure*, Act 2, Scene 1, https://shakespeare.mit.edu/measure/measure.2.1.html.

2 NSIA 2021 came into effect on 4 January 2022.

UK Government provides helpful detailed guidance on the boundaries of each sector. As set out in Table 10.1, the NSIA introduces a mandatory notification regime for 17 areas that require government clearance before acquisition activity can occur.[3] Some of these areas, such as artificial intelligence (AI) and cryptographic authentication, are intuitive areas for notification.

The main semiconductor area is Advanced Materials. This category covers, among other things, semiconductors, photonic and optoelectronic materials and devices, graphene, other two-dimensional (2D) materials, and nanotechnology. However, Figure 10.1 captures the overlapping areas that require special attention.

Dual-Use applications mean those covering both military and other applications. A recurring example here would be semiconductor devices used in drones. For all dual activities, it is advisable to seek out dedicated UK legal counsel, because there are complex, multiple regulatory lists that require scrutiny.[4]

The UK Cabinet Office guidance also provides numerous examples of what would typically be outside of the boundaries for each area. For example, components with broader applications beyond Advanced Robotics, such as complementary metal-oxide-semiconductor (CMOS) sensors, are out of scope.

---

3 UK Cabinet Office (2024) 'Guidance National Security and Investment Act: details of the 17 types of notifiable acquisitions', available at www.gov.uk/government/publications/national-security-and-investment-act-guidance-on-notifiable-acquisitions/national-security-and-investment-act-guidance-on-notifiable-acquisitions.

4 This list includes, among others: the UK Military List, Schedule 2 to the Export Control Order 2008 (SI 2008/3231); the UK Dual-Use List, Schedule 3 to the Export Control Order 2008 (SI 2008/3231); the UK Radioactive Sources List, Schedule to The Export of Radioactive Sources (Control) Order 2006 (SI 2006/1846); and the Dual-Use List, Annex I to Council Regulation (EC) No. 428/2009. There is also a consolidated UK Department of Business and Trade Strategic Export Control List. It runs to 385 pages and was last updated in July 2023: available at https://assets.publishing.service.gov.uk/media/64ef1c7e13ae15000d6e305f/uk-strategic-export-control-lists.pdf.

Table 10.1 *NSIA mandatory notification regime for 17 areas*

Area	Activities Covered
Advanced Materials Advanced Robotics Artificial Intelligence Civil Nuclear Communications Computing Hardware Critical Suppliers to Government Cryptographic Authentication Data Infrastructure Defence Energy Military and Dual-Use Quantum Technologies Satellite and Space Technologies Suppliers to the Emergency Services Synthetic Biology Transport	• Research • Development or production • Development or production of anything designed as an enabler • Development or production of anything designed to be used for the purpose of production • Provision of qualified or certified designs, materials, parts or products • Owning, creating, supplying or exploiting intellectual property • Provision of knowhow or services of enablers • Recycling or re-using[1]

Note: [1] Semiconductor recycling and reuse are considered in Chapter 6 Sustainable innovation.
Source: © Iain Sheridan (2025)

Under the NSIA, if a proposed acquisition or merger poses an unacceptable risk to national security in the UK, the Secretary of State in the Cabinet Office has the power to block the transaction. Currently, the NSIA does not provide a definition of 'national security'.[5] From a foreign direct investment viewpoint, uncertainty over the scope of national security has

[5] The City of London Law Society and the Law Society of England and Wales provided joint evidence on this weakness as part of the consultation phase of the NSIA 2021. See the City of London Law Society/the Law Society (2020) House of Commons Public Bill Committee, 'Joint Response of the Company Law Committees of the City of London and the Law Society', at section 2; https://publications.parliament.uk/pa/cm5801/cmpublic/NatSecurity/memo/NSIB03.pdf.

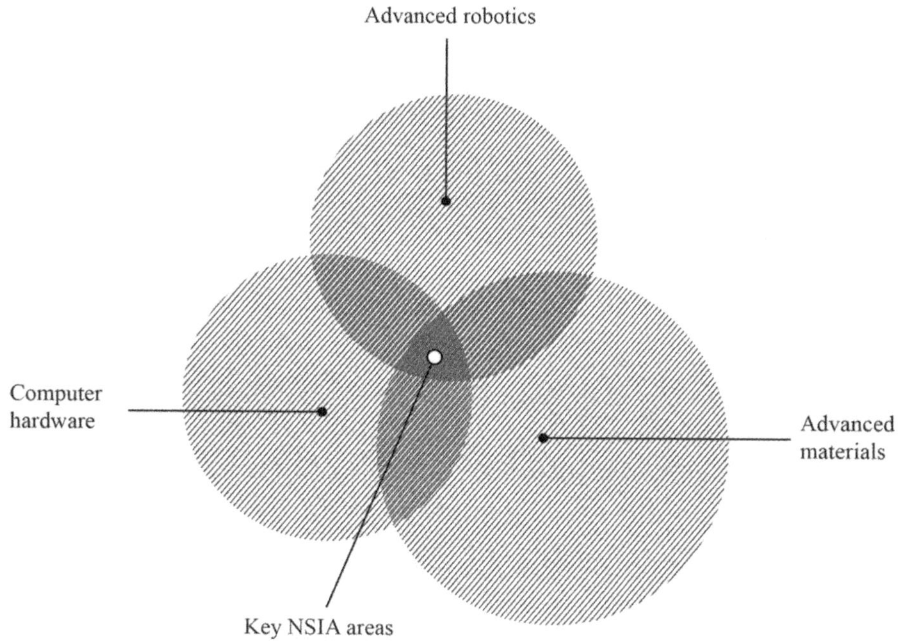

Source: © Iain Sheridan (2025)

Figure 10.1 Key NSIA areas for semiconductor firms

already affected ownership of one of the UK's two largest semiconductor manufacturing facilities, namely Newport Wafer Fab.[6]

If a proposed acquisition or merger is considered to pose an unacceptable risk to national security, the NSIA provides the power to block the transaction. When proposing an acquisition or merger, resulting in changed thresholds of percentages for share ownership or share voting rights, mandatory notification is required.[7] The thresholds of percentages of an entity requiring mandatory notification are from 25 per cent or less to more than 25 per cent; from 50 per cent or less to more than 50 per cent; or from less than 75 per cent to 75 per cent or more.[8]

There are another two situations that require mandatory notification. First, where an acquisition enables the person to materially influence the strategic planning of the entity. Material influence may be achieved alone or in combination with other interests or rights held by the person.[9] Second, where the acquisition of voting rights enables a person to 'secure or prevent' the passing of any class of resolution under the entity's constitution.[10]

6 The UK's other large semiconductor manufacturer, with a planned significant expansion between 2023–28, is owned by Pragmatic in Durham, Northeast England. Pragmatic's expansion is funded by a diverse group of investors, including M&G Investments and UK Infrastructure Bank, Northern Gritstone, a trio of English universities' investment fund, British Patient Capital, a division of the UK Government's British Business Bank, and Prosperity7 Ventures, part of the Saudi energy group Aramco. See *Financial Times* (2023) 'UK backs chipmaker Pragmatic to boost domestic tech manufacturing', 6 December 2023.

7 'The City Code on Takeovers and Mergers' (the Code), deriving its statutory basis under Chapter 1 of Part 28 (ss.942 to 965) of the Companies Act 2006, does not have specific amendments covering interplay between the NSIA 2021 and the Code. However, the Code Committee has produced valuable guidance of what it expects professional advisers, including lawyers, to advise clients to do. This guidance is summarised in Takeover Panel RS 2020/1 (2021) 'Conditions to Offers and the Offer Timetable', at 1.18. See www.thetakeoverpanel.org.uk/wp-content/uploads/2021/03/RS-2020_1-FINAL-31-March-2021.pdf.

8 Section 8(2)–(5) NSIA 2021.

9 Section 8(8) NSIA 2021.

10 Section 8(6) NSIA 2021.

Under these two broader acquisition scenarios the declaring party may be the person or entity that originally held a low percentage shareholding or percentage voting rights. Thereafter, their shareholding or voting rights time increase, and consequently their power to secure or block voting decisions or change in corporate policy.

An important aspect to highlight is that the NSIA acts as a filter for all acquirers in the 17 areas, including UK firms. In 2023, the UK Government reported that, of the 57 final notifications issued 2022–23, 40 per cent involved China-linked acquirers, 30 per cent were UK-linked acquirers, and 19 per cent were US-linked acquirers.[11]

A notable difference between the NSIA and other leading jurisdictions, is its reach includes control of assets, such as intellectual property (IP) licences. In summary form, under the NSIA a 'qualifying asset' includes all 'ideas, information or techniques which have industrial, commercial or other economic value'.[12] Most relevant to semiconductor activity, the types of assets are algorithms, databases, designs, drawings, formulae, plans, software, source code, specifications, and trade secrets.[13] The use of any qualifying asset includes its 'exploitation, alteration, manipulation, disposal or destruction'.[14]

The US Committee on Foreign Investment in the United States' (CFIUS) remit does not extend to IP transfers.[15] However, for the UK semiconductor sector, the NSIA has already imposed significant influence over who owns which firm, or who is attempting to own which semiconductor firm or IP asset.

---

11 UK Cabinet Office *National Security and Investment Act 2021 Annual Report 2022–2023*, at para.12, 6.

12 Section 7(4)(c) NSIA 2021.

13 Section 7(5) NSIA 2021.

14 Section 9(2) NSIA 2021.

15 The US Foreign Investment Risk Review Modernization Act of 2018 can trace its roots to the Exon–Florio Amendment of 1988 (Exon-Florio Amendment) was enacted in 1988. CFIUS was empowered at that time under the Exon-Florio Amendment to reject the acquisition of Fairchild Semiconductor by Fujitsu. State intervention in the semiconductor sector is not a new phenomenon.

Table 10.2 *UK semiconductor prohibitions*

Acquirer [Target]	Context	Location
Nexperia [Newport Wafer Fab]	Divestment of 100% shareholding in the target. At the relevant time, Newport Wafer Fab (NWF) was a 200mm SMIF Wafer-fab, with a current capacity of 32 000 wafer starts per month of 0.18µm, wide range of semiconductor technologies ranging from MOSFETs/TIGBTs using wafer thinning methods to CMOS, analog and compound semiconductors. NWF transfers and enhances MOSFET/TIGBT processes, and develops photonic and compound processes.	Newport, South Wales
SiLight (Shanghai) Semiconductor [HiLight Research]	HiLight specialises in the design and supply of analog and mixed-signal CMOS ICs.	Southampton, Southern England
Super Orange HK Holdings [Pulsic Limited]	Pulsic provides EDA tools covering analog circuit, DRAM, NAND design.	Bristol, Southwest England

Source: © Iain Sheridan (2025)

Table 10.2 records three decisions along with the type of activity and the timescale of the Investment Security Unit (ISU) decision.[16] The average time the ISU takes to decide is 30 days.[17]

10.2 Case study on Nexperia

In November 2022, the UK Government ordered Nexperia to divest 86 per cent of its 100 per cent shareholding in the Inmos factory in Newport

[16] The ISU is the department that advises the UK Government under NSIA 2021.

[17] UK Cabinet Office *National Security and Investment Act 2021 Annual Report 2022–2023*, at Annex A, records that in the year 2022–23, the mean number of days between the ISU calling in an acquisition and issuing a final notification was 31.

(Newport Wafer Fab) in South Wales.[18] Nexperia acquired Newport Wafer Fab in 2021 for £60 million, having owned 14 per cent of the firm before the NSIA came into force. Readers will appreciate that the NSIA came into force in January 2022, but this statute also provides the UK Government with retrospective powers.[19]

In 2021, the initial UK Government decision was that the sale to Nexperia could proceed. So, there had already been an extensive review of the Newport Wafer Fab acquisition before the sale was initially approved.[20] However, the UK Government requested an additional review by its national security adviser, Stephen Lovegrove. He also approved it.

At the time of the divestment order, Nexperia, a Dutch firm whose roots can be traced back to Philips Semiconductors, was 100 per cent owned by the Chinese firm Wingtech Technology.[21] Wingtech Technology is a Chinese semiconductor group listed on the Shanghai Stock Exchange, and is partially state-owned by the State-owned Assets Supervision and Administration Commission of the State Council (SASAC) of the People's Republic of China (PRC). SASAC's key role is to invest PRC state capital into strategic economic sectors.

Ultimately, the reasoning provided by the UK Government to prohibit the acquisition did not provide Nexperia or any other future semiconductor firm with much detail to learn from for future commercially acceptable strategic acquisitions. The Secretary of State concluded in the order letter that a risk to national security concerned:

---

[18] This order was issued by the Secretary of State of the Department for Business, Energy & Industrial Strategy (BEIS). However, since 7 February 2023, responsibility for NSIA 2021 acquisition assessments and orders is managed by the Secretary of State in the Cabinet Office. See UK House of Commons (2023) 'Memorandum of Understanding on Scrutiny of the Investment Security Unit'.

[19] BEIS (2022) National Security and Investment Act 2021 Publication of Notice of Final Order, 16 November 2022, available at https://assets.publishing.service.gov.uk/media/6375ef068fa8f5771111bd60/NWF_Final_Order_Public_Notice_16112022.pdf.

[20] *Financial Times* (2021) 'Welsh silicon wafer plant review highlights security fears Downing Street rethink about takeover reflects China jitters as UK seeks to enhance chip production', 28 July 2021.

[21] HC Foreign Affairs Committee (2022) *Sovereignty for sale: follow-up to the acquisition of Newport Wafer Fab*, Sixth Report of Session 2021–22, at 5.

> i. technology and know-how that could result from a potential reintroduction of compound semiconductor activities at the Newport site, and the potential for those activities to undermine UK capabilities; and ii. the location of the site could facilitate access to technological expertise and know-how in the South Wales Cluster ('the Cluster'), and the links between the site and the Cluster may prevent the Cluster being engaged in future projects relevant to national security.[22]

Newport Wafer Fab was a unique situation, because it represented the largest established fabrication plant in the UK that operated at a scale of production and design flexibility to facilitate numerous manufacturing orders. Nexperia was unfortunate because the South Wales Cluster is the key pillar, or at least a central pillar of any future industrial strategy. No UK national or local government can afford for this cluster to not grow. Put another way, it was logical, sensible risk management to order the divestment.

Readers will be familiar with the English saying 'to compare apples with oranges'. It would be simplistic to compare the Dutch Government's decision to approve Nexperia BV's acquisition of Nowi Energy BV (Nowi), a firm focused on energy harvesting integrated circuits (ICs), with the UK decision on Newport Wafer Fab but Nowi was a start-up and its products have no dual-use potential.[23]

The medium-term commercial damage of the UK Government's decision was caused by a protracted investigations by the ISU. The duration from when the acquisition was announced to the final BEIS notice order prohibition was 15 months. Nexperia already owned a similar facility in Manchester, so evidently it was a comparatively well-known firm in the UK. Consequently, there were in the region of 100 redundancies at the Newport Wafer Fab, and lost order opportunities from both domestic and foreign clients.

---

22 BEIS (2022) National Security and Investment Act 2021 Publication of Notice of Final Order, 16 November 2022, available at https://assets.publishing.service.gov.uk/media/6375ef068fa8f5771111bd60/NWF_Final_Order_Public_Notice_16112022.pdf.

23 Reuters (2023) 'Netherlands to allow takeover of chip startup Nowi by Chinese-owned Nexperia', 27 November 2023.

Long-term damage included a lack of certainty over the future of the Newport Wafer Fab, including amongst US semiconductor firms. By which is meant US firms saw the opportunity to place orders with the Newport Wafer Fab, but in a post-Covid-19 climate of already constricted supply chains, rational strategic decision making led them to look elsewhere.

Undoubtedly, the final order made for Nexperia to divest from the Newport Wafer Fab was influenced by more than the application of the NSIA. Significant additional factors included international pressure from the US, Prime Minister as well as Secretary of State leadership changes in the UK over the investigation period and a lack of any detailed UK semiconductor strategy.[24]

Newport Wafer Fab is an example of a massive lost opportunity. The site has been owned by Dutch, Chinese and now US firms. It raises the question of why the UK Government has failed to provide a consistent semiconductor strategy that would have never allowed such a jewel in the crown to be passed around international buyers. Would that ever have happened in Austria, China, France, Germany, Japan, South Korea or the US?

The UK has been consistently open to long-term foreign direct investment (FDI). Foreign owners create innovation and demand from new markets. But the combined commercial opportunity and strategic importance of semiconductors makes domestic ownership or joint ownership a priority. To be master of your own destiny with profits flowing within the UK, combined with greater workforce stability and predictability of supply must be the ideal.[25]

---

[24] At the end of 2023, Pennsylvania-based Vishay Technology acquired the Newport Wafer Fab. See *Financial Times* (2023) 'Nexperia sells Newport Wafer Fab to US chip company for $177mn. Deal draws line under years of uncertainty surrounding fate of UK's biggest chipmaker', 8 November 2023.

[25] See Chapter 8 Contract law for alternative joint venture solutions that benefit both foreign and UK growth.

10.3 Multilateral support for supply chain resilience

To complement national security law and processes contained in the NSIA, there is a need for the right scale and proportion of multilateral support. For instance, the EU-US Trade and Technology Council is such an initiative that includes collaboration on semiconductor supply chain resilience. Specifically, the US Department of Commerce and the European Commission committed to implementing an early warning mechanism to address and mitigate semiconductor supply chain disruptions. This cooperation is committed to include:

- collaborating with industry on initiatives aimed gaining an accurate picture of demand for semiconductors;
- improving our understanding of forecasted global semiconductor demand, including the sharing of demand forecasting methodologies;
- exchanging information and best practices on investment approaches;
- exploring cooperative initiatives in research in semiconductors.[26]

Consistent with the explicit intentions of the EU-US Trade and Technology Council, in early 2023, to work with other like-minded international actors, there was an inaugural meeting of the 'US-UK Comprehensive Dialogue on Technology and Data'. This cooperation aims, among other things, to determine opportunities for cooperation within their respective semiconductor industries in the areas of investment, research and development (R&D) and skills.[27]

10.4 Semiconductor Five Eyes

During the House of Lords Select Committee on Semiconductors, the Bessemer Semiconductor Manufacturing Group floated the idea that that 'to strengthen its position, the UK could help coordinate a Five Eyes equivalent for the semiconductor and advanced electronics industry

---

[26] The White House, (2022) US-EU Joint Statement of the Trade and Technology Council.

[27] UK Government (2023) 'The Inaugural Meeting of U.S.-UK Comprehensive Dialogue on Technology and Data', Press Release, 12 January 2023, available at www.gov.uk/government/news/inaugural-meeting-of-us-uk-comprehensive-dialogue-on-technology-and-data.

which extends the traditional definition of national security beyond military defence into protection of the most sensitive parts of the economy'.[28]

This idea dovetails well with industrial policy protecting semiconductor supply chains relevant to defence applications. A secure database of semiconductor supply chain information could be accessed and developed across the intelligence agencies. Further, applying the Five Eyes history, the membership could be extended to provide levels of access to trusted third parties from the EU and Nordic countries.

However, given the global semiconductor supply chain is truly global in reach, for non-defence applications the approach would more logically follow a United Nations-type reach of allowing all nation-states to join if they follow the expected charter and detailed rules.

10.5 Policy analysis

The UK's NSIA, and arguably the EU and US equivalents, attempt to balance industrial policy and national security. In 2023, at a seminar in Oxford, Emeritus Harvard Professor Joe Nye,[29] presented a paper entitled 'How not to respond to a rising China'.[30] The main thrust of his presentation was that the China-US relationship had some of the hallmarks of a classic Thucydides trap. By which is meant the competition leads to war between an established and rising power.

The question I posed to Nye was is there a potential risk of greater instability if Chinese investment in the semiconductor sector is contained? He

[28] Business, Energy and Industrial Strategy Committee (2022), *The Semiconductor Industry in the UK*, Fifth Report of Session 2022–23, HC 291 (2022) (SEM0074) at 7(c), available at https://committees.parliament.uk/writtenevidence/109271/pdf/.

[29] Joe Nye is one of the greatest foreign policy scholars of the last six decades. A Harvard faculty member since 1964, and former Dean of the Harvard's Kennedy School of Government, he also served as Assistant Secretary of Defense for International Security Affairs in the Clinton Administration of 1994–95.

[30] Nye, J. (2023) 'How to respond to a rising China', Exeter College Oxford Seminar, 23 May 2023.

replied that the focus of US policy on restraining Chinese semiconductor activity was at the most advanced level – the 7nm or below level. That is partly the case, because the US Chips Act does not restrict Chinese semiconductor activity above 22nm.

What Nye's response underlines is two things. First, there is a wide technical difference between 22nm and the aspiring sub-7nm device. In a military conflict, which includes surveillance activities leading up to engagement, both drones and missiles made up of sub-7nm semiconductors, all other things being equal, will win. Therefore, a more nuanced NSIA can maximise economic activity and simultaneously achieve national security goals by acting as a protective filter on sub-10nm devices. That way 10nm devices and above can be more promptly assessed as lower threat economic activities. Currently, the NSIA does not explicitly adopt a quantitative level of nm as part of its decision making. A revised NSIA with specific nm metrics seems a logical improvement.

Second, the UK's industrial policy can most successfully be implemented by balancing international trade and security priorities around semiconductors. In short, while the NSIA explicitly concentrates on national security, this statute is in effect a fulcrum between commercial competitive advantage and security risk. Even by the close of the twentieth century, a Korean industrial policy expert, Professor Sung Gul Hong, had commented that perhaps the most important aspect of the semiconductor sector is its utility for military and strategic aims.[31] For all the commercial excitement surrounding advanced robotics and machine learning, the NSIA is a key risk filter concerning who is attempting to own which semiconductor firm or IP asset.

However, in my view, the NSIA can evolve with a detailed and transparent industrial policy that proportionally encourages and discourages foreign investment. UK industrial policy, and by extension the NSIA and amending statutory instruments, need to be simultaneously growth led and defensive in intent. Supporting low-risk commercial situations, for example mass production components, and deterring any involvement in cutting edge manufacturing or research that has clear military application.

[31] Sung, G.H. (1997) *The Political Economy of Industrial Policy in East Asia*, Cheltenham, UK and Lyme, NH, USA: Edward Elgar Publishing, at 10.

Legislative select committees focused on the NSIA will greatly benefit from industrial policy and military strategic expertise. Only then can the law be developed to mirror long-term policy outcomes. Part of any long-term policy outcome requires support from comparative investigations into what the UK structurally wants to achieve.

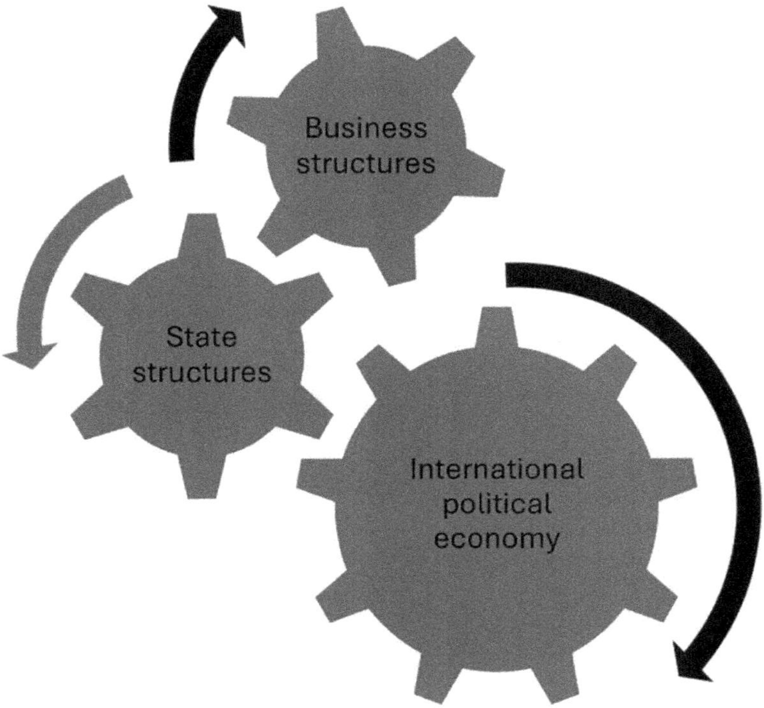

Source: © Iain Sheridan (2025)

Figure 10.2 Structural variables

As illustrated in Figure 10.2, the UK is balancing (a) business structures, (b) state structures, and (c) international political economy.[32] Statistical analysis can examine cause and effect in the UK semiconductor sector compared with leading semiconductor markets. For example, South

[32] Ibid at 10.

Korea. John Stuart Mill's indirect method of difference is one potentially insightful logical technique to be applied.[33] In essence, the indirect method of difference compares similar cases to explain differences. Hypothetically, imagine the UK has the same key variables as South Korea in terms of population (X_1), corporate taxation (X_2), rule of law (X_3),[34] access to engineering talent (X_4) and environment (X_5).[35] These five common variables can be eliminated from UK policy and legal outcomes.

South Korea has been assessed to apply unique policies. Its business structures (X_6) revolve around huge industrial groupings.[36] South Korea's state structures (X_7) have loose national level coordination of science and technology. Its international political economy (X_8) is seriously constrained by its security position and Mutual Defence Treaty with the US. These three dependent variables ($X_{6,}$ X_7, and $X_{8)}$, cause the effect of South Korea's global dynamic random access memory (DRAM) domination. Currently, South Korea produces more than 40 per cent of all memory chips.[37]

Turning to the UK, the indirect method of difference benefits comparative analysis in this way. If the UK's policy outcome is superior fabless design, pinning down the specific nature of UK business structures (X_6), state structures (X_7) and the nature of its international political economy (X_8) will provide remarkably valuable information. On reaching

[33] Ibid at 8–9. Mill's original explanation of the indirect method of difference is 'if two or more instances in which the phenomenon occurs have only one circumstance in common, while two or more instances in which it does not occur have nothing in common save the absence of that circumstance; the circumstance in which alone the two sets of instances differ, is the effect, or cause, or a necessary part of the cause, of the phenomenon': Mill, J.S. (1843) *A System of Logic*, John W. Parker, at 463.

[34] By rule of law that would include the consistent application of procedures. So not just the predictability of court decisions.

[35] Imagine that environment refers to just climate change transition costs, access to water and the cost of electricity. Further, factor in that the population of South Korea compared with UK is slightly different, and their physical environments quite different.

[36] Known in Korean as *chaebol*, these groupings include Samsung Group and SK Group.

[37] Korea Trade Investment Promotion Agency (KOTRA) (2024) 'Semiconductor Factsheet'.

that future level of understanding, a third way, between South Korean DRAM domination and the current superior fabless design, can be determined. That third way, from business margin and geopolitical supply chain viewpoints, will certainly include far more manufacturing activity across the UK. By which is meant making semiconductors for R&D and low-quantity high-quality or military applications.

10.6 Critical thinking and NSIA remedies

A valuable critical thinking technique is called fishbone analysis, invented by a Japanese engineer called Kaoru Ishikawa. Some readers, especially engineers, will be aware that this technique is especially strong when analysing how a product or service can be improved. In this context fishbone analysis is often integrated into the process of continuous improvement in manufacturing to dissect causes that contributed to an effect.[38]

Fishbone analysis is also a technique that can be of potential value for civil servants, legal counsel, and semiconductor sub-sector experts advising the Secretary of State in the Cabinet Office and the ISU. This manufacturing-anchored process can be adapted to analyse a completed investigation of a proposed acquisition. The Secretary of State in the Cabinet Office can determine what, if any, solutions exist for a managed conditional clearance. Put another way, what angle or angles avoid a prohibition of the transaction? Equally, who needs to be heard to avoid either opportunity group-think, or a group-think convinced low risk cannot be managed.

Breaking down the issue of an acquisition, as shown in Figure 10.3, into sub-branches creates the risk management elements independently but also interdependently. There will be situations, for example with less advanced semiconductor products, that allow for an acquisition based on corporate governance expectations or joint venture structure. For example, if the acquirer is controlled by a parent entity incorporated in a non-NATO country or incorporated in the UK or the EU with the controlling directors possessing less than ten years' residence in the UK that can be verified.

---

[38] Ishikawa, K. (1990) *Introduction to Quality Control*, Productivity Press.

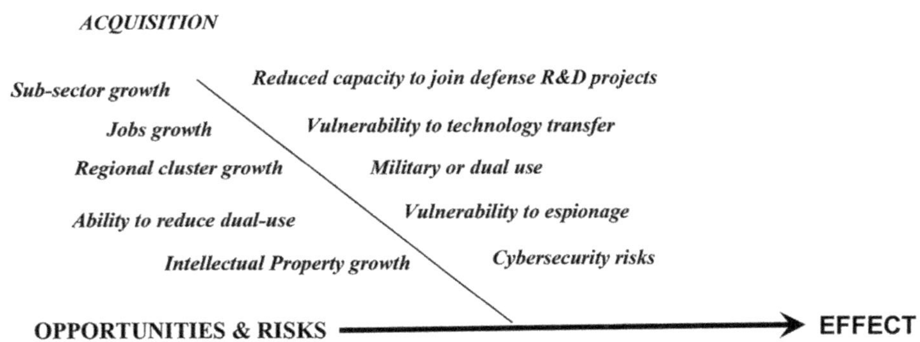

Source: © Iain Sheridan (2025)

Figure 10.3 What are the opportunities and risks of conditional clearance?

The NSIA already provides a supporting filter to deter foreign entities participating in Department for Business and Trade (DBT)-vetting processes to be accurate and clear in information they supply or are requested to provide. To deter the use of false or misleading information. All the contexts are covered, namely (a) a mandatory notice, (b) a validation application, (c) a voluntary notice, (d) a response to an information notice, and (e) in response to an attendance notice. The NSIA states that in all these (a) to (e) contexts 'Where a decision made by the Secretary of State…is materially affected by the false or misleading information, the Secretary of State may reconsider the decision and may affirm, vary or revoke it'.[39]

Cultivating the habit of including the fishbone analysis will benefit not only national security but also commercial growth. Civil servants, their legal counsel, and independent experts will incrementally be able to pinpoint and issue in writing the viable remedies. As the eminent Harvard cognitive scientist, Steve Pinker, put it 'none of us, thinking alone, is rational enough to consistently come to is sound conclusions: rationality emerges from a community of reason as is spot each other's fallacies'.[40]

10.7 Future decision making

Solution-driven quality decision making is the win-win part of any future NSIA quality framework. First, in my opinion quantitative metrics should play a significant role in determining if a foreign entity can acquire a UK semiconductor firm. Second, in my view, of most importance is conditionally permitting joint ventures based on minority shareholdings by foreign parent entities. That way the critical nature of the semiconductor sector is respected and in non-defence applications such conditions may work for some projects.[41] An interesting case is the fact that the UK's Competition and Markets Authority (CMA) has the power to propose undertakings which a party or parties to a proposed acquisition can choose to accept.

---

[39] Section 22(2) NSIA 2021.

[40] Pinker, S. (2021) *Rationality, What It Is, Why It Seems Scarce, Why It Matters*, Penguin, at 16.

[41] Joint ventures are considered in Chapter 5 Strategic issues, and Chapter 10 Contract law. They are also touched upon in Chapter 11 Taxation law.

Table 10.3 sets out a proposed quality framework. Both consistency of decision making and a prompt decision are important. There may also be a place for an appeal process based on unreasonable decisions. For instance, if the firm believes the DBT has included irrelevant considerations based on the use of semiconductors made at a particular factory.

Table 10.3 Proposed quality framework

Key characteristic	Explanation
Transparency	Providing ongoing communication to potential acquirers on the progress of the NSIA assessment. Further, to publish in real time the total time taken for each review.[1]
Quantitative and qualitative metrics	Publishing technical standards and thresholds that provide both domestic and foreign acquirers with a clear understanding of what is likely to be permitted. US statutory metrics that could be applied in the UK as published DBT guidelines for permissible acquisitions, with or without conditions are: • 28 nanometer generation or older logic semiconductors; and • memory technology, analog technology, and packaging technology relative to 28 nm generation logic semiconductors.[2] Guidelines might also include quality tolerances on products that are associated with defence or space applications.
Joint venture conditions	Fundamentally, the commercial opportunities of collaboration are balanced against the security risks by not permitting foreign shareholding around 33.3 per cent with no scope for future foreign control without further DBT review. See Table 10.4.

Key characteristic	Explanation
Other remedies	In any assessment, the government authority is to consider one or more of the following: • restricting sales by the target firm to foreign investors from high risk countries; • governance conditions that remove the ability of the parent firm to be represented on the target board; • restricting the shareholder ownership of a foreign investor to minority percentage at or below 33.3%.[3] • restricting the ability of the acquirer's parent firm to appoint key senior managers from the acquirer in the target; • appointing a government observer to the board of the target firm paid for by the acquirer firm; • appointing a third-party observer, such as a non-conflicted barrister or solicitor for a continuous term of at lease three years.[4]
Appeal processes	The right to challenge a DBT decision on the grounds of unreasonable decision making.[5]

Notes: [1] A positive indication of how transparency is likely to improve is the commitment by the UK Government to annually publish the average number of working days from receipt of a voluntary notice to notification of an approval or rejection decision. See UK House of Commons (2023) 'Memorandum of Understanding on Scrutiny of the Investment Security Unit', at 8, section 21(e). [2] Section 9902(a)(6) of the 2021 National Defense Authorization Act (NDAA). [3] A German Government decision concerning COSCO's investment in the Hamburg Harbour Terminal, restricted COSCO's shareholding to 24.9 per cent. The original plan was for COSCO to acquire 35 per cent. See Reuters (2023) 'China COSCO Shipping Subsidiary Climbs on German Nod of Port Terminal Deal', 11 May 2023. [4] In the US, CFIUS practice has already included the appointment of third-party observers. [5] Section 49 NSIA 2021 provides for a claim for judicial review of a relevant decision, but involving the administrative High Court is unlikely to answer the technical questions with consistency. Further, this court is inundated with multifarious applications.
Source: © Iain Sheridan (2025)

10.8 Joint venture conditions

There will be many future scenarios of foreign entities seeking to acquire semiconductor firms in the UK. Such scenarios can be both a security risk and a commercial opportunity. Consider, for example, there are already foreign firms that will seek to challenge Nvidia in the graphics processing unit (GPU) for AI markets. Further, there will be firms from many countries relying on British employed talent from GoogleMind and equivalent to advance neural processing units (NPUs). These GPU and NPU firms may come from Asia where business structures, state structures, and international political economy are all radically different.

As set out in Figure 10.4, in my view a viable joint venture structure would typically work with one participant taking the role of the operations manager subject to an operational committee made up of representative directors from all participants. In the following example a joint venture called Cardiff & Swansea Automotive Sensors Limited (C&S Sensors), based in Port Talbot, is formed. The land for the UK activity is provided by Neath Port Talbot Council, so the local government is the commercial landlord.

Turning to Table 10.4, it captures the division of interests and key benefits of each participant. Up to 10 per cent could be held by a Sovereign Wealth Fund (SWF) investor. The benefits of leadership and the sharing of time-consuming responsibilities are achieved by rotating the Chief Executive Officer (CEO) every three years.

Notably the change in participants would never affect the operation or strategic direction of the joint venture, because its constitution would forbid any single semiconductor firm from acquiring a 51 per cent controlling stake. This restriction functions to temper competition between the joint venture participants and is likely to prove favourable with DBT and competition law authorities.

In closing, it is evident the UK's NSIA is not only a new statutory framework, but also an evolving one, a key pillar for managing geopolitics and resurging industrial policy. For example, consider US General Motors (GM) has committed to selling only electric vehicles (EVs) by 2035. That challenge will require its legal team to construct many new contracts for batteries, charging infrastructure and semiconductors. Many of

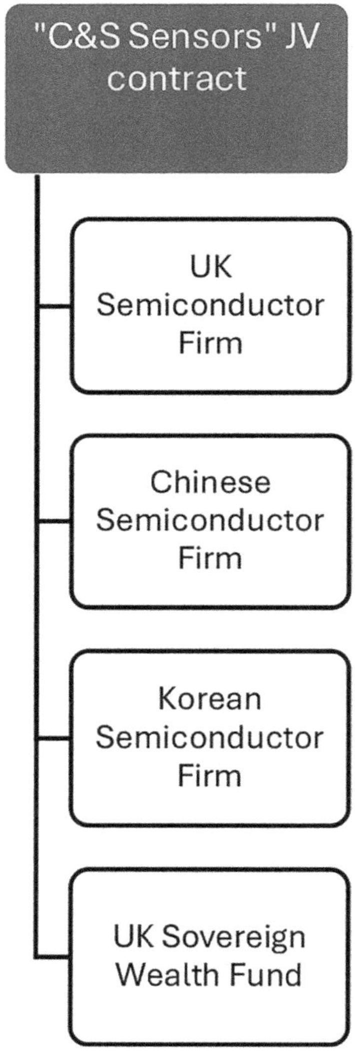

Source: © Iain Sheridan (2025)

Figure 10.4 C&S Sensors, an unincorporated joint venture

Table 10.4 *Obligations and rights under the Cardiff & Swansea Sensors UJV*

Entity	Parent entity country	Shareholding	Operational leadership rotation	Management committee representation
British firm	UK	30.5%	Y	30%
US firm	US	30.5%	Y	30%
Chinese firm	PRC	30.5%	Y	30%
SWF	UK or Norway or UAE or combined smaller percentages	8.5%	N	10%

Source: © Iain Sheridan (2025)

the decisions will be influenced by geopolitics. Craig Glidden, a general counsel at GM, has remarked that his legal team has 'to focus on not [just] the case law, but the current events that are actually going to determine the shape of the business in the future'.[42]

10.9 Balancing national security and business opportunities

The current commercial situation of the UK differs markedly from Germany, the Netherlands, and the US. Dutch-owned ASML is the largest global photolithographic equipment maker. However, often not highlighted in the media is the fact that three Dutch-owned manufacturers, ASM International, and BE Semiconductor (Besi) and NXP Semiconductors, are also all thriving. In Germany Infineon, is an established powerhouse, as is Intel in North America, in their respective areas of expertise.

[42] Lambert, Y. (2024) 'In-house lawyers pick up pace on generative AI and supply chains, Trends in geopolitics force faster responses from legal teams', *Financial Times*, 5 December 2023, available at www.ft.com/content/fb66799c-1ee8-45a2-8db4-072304278629.

Turning to Asia, Japan in the past had a far larger share of semiconductor manufacturing and now seeks to cooperate with other foreign firms and make long-term investments. In South Korea, Samsung and SK Hynix are global leaders. In Taiwan TSMC is the pre-eminent global leader. Both South Korea and Taiwan started with industrial leapfrogging strategies that have been so successful they are both now critical suppliers across global supply chains.

The UK is in catch-up mode. Because of the pre-eminence of ARM Holdings, the UK is an established regional powerhouse in fabless design. It has the potential to be even more dominant in design. The NSIA will directly and indirectly significantly influence a UK industrial policy that can widen growth to all other areas that are vulnerable to negative foreign behaviour.

For instance, while on its own the UK cannot enter the cutting-edge semiconductor market, in the long term, via collaboration with two or more other countries, it is possible to compete under 14nm. Mustafa Suleyman, co-founder of DeepMind, has remarked that the combined dominance of ASML, Nvidia and TSMC represent a 'choke point'.[43] Global market dominance presents a concentration risk that can only be mitigated by substantial industrial policy investment, long-term cooperation, and appropriate governmental protection.

[43] Suleyman, M. (2023) *The Coming Wave – AI, Power and the 21st Century's Greatest Dilemma*, Penguin, at 251.

11. Taxation law

When semiconductor entrepreneurs begin a start-up business, intuitively taxation is a strategic factor well down the list of priorities. Just one element of multiple factors that bear on long-term strategic plans. Tax can be a complex landscape to navigate across. Consequently, the risks, especially concerning patenting activity and research and development (R&D), make this chapter as important as all the others. As the much respected and quoted Chinese strategist Sun Tzu said, 'Grasp and win'.

11.1 Introduction

This chapter attempts to cover key issues and tax principles that are of recurring importance for semiconductor firms. Naturally, the analysis for a multinational cannot compare with a start-up. While readers are dedicated to analysing their own unique tax positions based on the scale of their operations, generally patent box, R&D activity, transfer pricing, and cost contribution agreements are all recurring significant topics.

The cross-border nature of semiconductor business makes the United Kingdom (UK) an attractive location for semiconductor growth whether independently or in collaboration with UK-established firms and start-ups. Policy makers from outside the UK should also appreciate its international insights. This includes references to Asia, Europe, and North America.[1]

---

[1] At the risk of appearing to be dry, my professional tax qualifications awarded by the UK Chartered Institute of Taxation include the jurisdictions of Australia, China, Hong Kong (SAR) and Singapore. Inevitably there are examples from some of these markets, but the focus remains on semiconductors. Given the importance of other semiconductor markets, especially the EU, Japan, South Korea, and the US, these are also referenced.

Government officials with the weighty challenge of contributing to national semiconductor strategy, must answer the following question: What does an optimum semiconductor tax regime look like? The combined policies in Figure 11.1 represent, in my view, the optimum long-term position for law makers and semiconductor producers.

At this intersection, the patent box regime is fully utilised, and relief for R&D expenditure continues. Tax laws are enacted covering both deterrence and incentives. Ideally, both patent activity and other R&D projects are supported by cost contribution agreements approved by the tax authorities.[2] It is notable that the UK's pre-2024 corporation tax scheme for small- and medium-sized enterprises (SMEs) has been described as 'world-leading'.[3] This trinity of laws supports the view that the UK offers a significant tax advantage to semiconductor firms.

11.2 Research and development taxation

R&D activity is essential for not only the growth of all start-up semiconductor firms, but also the sustained success of established businesses.[4] The UK Department for Science, Innovation and Technology guidelines

---

2 In the past, my research has addressed how tax can optimally manage taxing smartphone components, including the main central processing unit (CPU). See Sheridan, I. (2016) 'Smartphones, Research and Development and Corporation Tax: Current Treatment and Future Possibilities', *Intertax*, 44(11), 788–90.

3 HM Treasury (2021) *R&D Tax Reliefs Report*, at 13.

4 R&D is also defined under generally accepted accounting practice (GAAP), and international accounting standards (IAS). Notably, both UK Financial Reporting Standard (FRS) 102 and IAS 38 are broader than UK tax law definitions. Section 1042 Corporation Tax Act 2009 (CTA 2009) defines R&D to be '(a) related to a trade carried on by the company, or (b) from which it is intended that a trade to be carried on by the company will be derived'. The HM Revenue and Customs (HMRC) manual on Corporate Intangibles and Research and Development (CIRD) sets out detailed guidelines on what qualifies as R&D for UK corporation tax purposes. The R&D activities must relate to a project which represents an advance in science or technology knowledge (R&D guidelines, para.3). The judgment in *B E Studios Ltd v Smith & Williamson Ltd* [2005] EWHC 1506 (Ch) confirms that for UK tax purposes an R&D project must advance science or technology generally. It's insuffi-

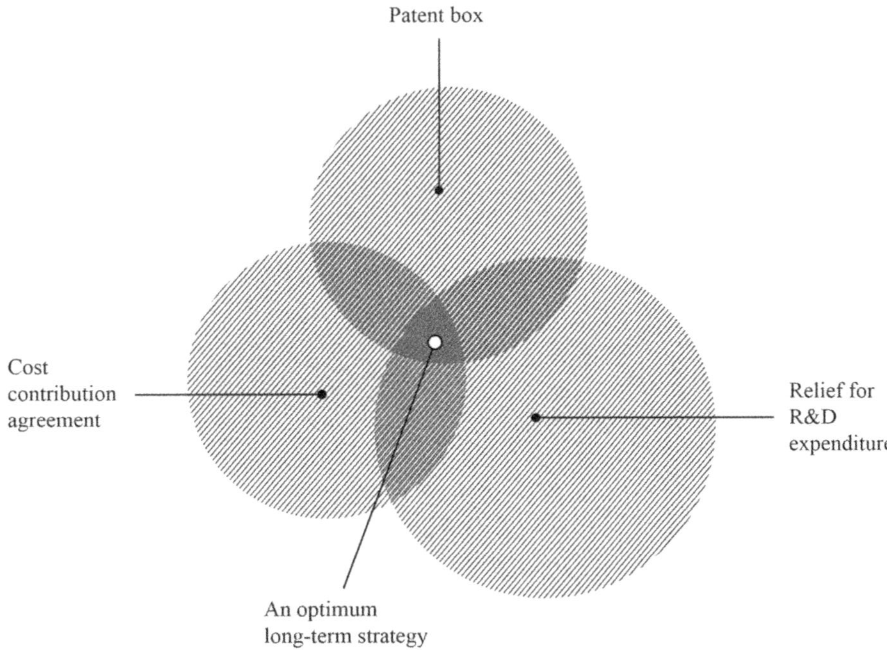

Source: © Iain Sheridan (2025)

Figure 11.1 An optimum long-term tax position

(the DSIT guidelines) are the initial point of analysis to confirm that an activity qualifies as R&D.[5]

Qualifying R&D must achieve an advance in science or technology. However, specified qualifying indirect activities linked to the project are also R&D.[6] Examples of qualifying projects in the DSIT guidelines include:

- extending overall knowledge or capability in a field of science or technology;[7] or
- creating a process, material, device, product or service which incorporates or represents an increase in overall knowledge or capability in a field of science or technology; or
- making an 'appreciable improvement' to an existing process, material, device, product or service through scientific or technological changes;[8] or
- exploiting science or technology to duplicate the effect of an existing process, material, device, product or service in a new or appreciably improved way.[9]

In the context of semiconductor advancement, a slight change/improvement in the degree of complexity of system interactions is likely to be qualifying R&D. For example, heterogenous integration research fits the DSIT guidelines' view that system uncertainty is R&D, because those

---

cient for a project to only advance a specific company's product, because it is 'cutting-edge' or 'innovative'.

5 UK Government (2024) 'Guidance Meaning of research and development for tax purposes: guidelines', available at www.gov.uk/government/publications/guidelines-on-the-meaning-of-research-and-development-for-tax-purposes/meaning-of-research-and-development-for-tax-purposes-guidelines.

6 Ibid, at sections 3 and 5.

7 Abortive projects still count as R&D for this tax relief. The crux is whether there is an intention to achieve an advance in science or technology.

8 The most important hurdle to clear is that of 'an appreciable improvement'. Under the DSIT guidelines the improvement must be more than a minor change. Additionally, it is something that a competent professional in the relevant field would judge to be a non-trivial.

9 UK Government (2024) 'Guidance Meaning of research and development for tax purposes: guidelines', at section 9.

involved in the activity are focused on finding improved ways to combine components.[10]

11.3 UK case law

There are several UK tax tribunal cases that deserve scrutiny. My approach here has been to attempt to present the most valuable guidance and rulings so that firms can reflect on the fine lines being drawn and caution required.

11.3.1 Compliance with DSIT guidelines

First, UK courts have confirmed that maximising the likelihood that a claim for relief is accepted by HMRC requires complying with all the DSIT guidelines. In short, 'the provisions form a detailed and meticulously drafted code, with a series of defined terms and composite expressions, and a large number of carefully delineated conditions, all of which have to be satisfied if the relief is to be available'.[11]

11.3.2 Must advance science or technology

Second, for UK tax purposes an R&D project must advance science or technology generally. It is insufficient for a project to only advance a specific company's product, because it is 'cutting-edge' or 'innovative'.[12]

11.3.3 Experimental development

Third, there is the issue of what constitutes experimental development. Judicial commentary makes clear that commercial product development is outside R&D.

> The basic rule is to look at the primary objective of the work undertaken. If the primary objective of the development is to test the viability of the R&D, or

[10] Ibid, at section 29.

[11] *Gripple Ltd v RCC* [2010] STC 2283, per Henderson J at [12]. The referenced R&D guidelines commented on by the High Court concerned the previous form under Sch 20 Finance Act 2000.

[12] *B E Studios Ltd v Smith & Williamson Ltd* [2005] EWHC 1506 (Ch).

> to make further technical improvements on the product or process, then the work comes within the definition of R&D (subject to the basic requirement that R&D has to include an appreciable element of novelty)...R&D would include novel work which draws on or creates a new source of knowledge which might lead to the breaking of new ground or a technical advance and which might subsequently entail the creation or development of a new or substantially improved product, process or service.[13]

11.3.4 Documenting evidence

Fourth, the detailed documenting of R&D is vital. The High Court has rejected a claim compiled by an R&D adviser, concluding:

> the product may have been bespoke and even innovative however the invoices which refer to 'designs' and 'drawings' did not provide any indication as to how the activities went beyond a competent professional readily deducing a solution and producing a design. Furthermore, the documentary evidence... failed to explain how the activities made a material change or advance in science or technology as a whole and in those circumstances, we could not be satisfied that the BIS [now DSIT] Guidelines were satisfied.[14]

11.3.5 Going concern status

Fifth, the High Court has held that a research and development expenditure credit (RDEC) cash payment claim will be denied if accounts are made up for a financial year in which a firm was not a going-concern basis.[15]

11.3.6 Competent professional

Sixth, competent professional. The High Court has previously agreed with HMRC views on the term 'competent professional'. While not a defined term, HMRC counsel have argued that:

> its natural meaning is self-explanatory, and that it goes beyond having an intelligent interest in the field...to be accepted as a competent professional, an individual would need to be able to demonstrate appropriate qualifications,

---

[13] Ibid, at [23].

[14] *Hadee Engineering Co Ltd v HMRC* [2020] UKFTT 497 (TC) (10 October 2020), at 266. The referenced BIS guidelines were the original R&D guidelines now contained in the DSIT guidelines.

[15] *MW High Tech Projects UK Ltd* [2024] UKFTT 9011 (TC).

> experience and up-to-date knowledge of the relevant scientific and technological principles involved.[16]

The High Court has recently underlined this stance in the context of a business owner who had applied for R&D tax relief, but in the view of HMRC had insufficient technical expertise. The applicant was judged to be competent in the information technology (IT) sector from costs, client, IT strategy, processes, and wider sector-specific strategy perspectives, however, he was not a competent professional in the context of making an R&D tax relief application.[17]

11.4 Indirect activity

As previously mentioned, specified indirect activities also qualify as R&D. These include:

- Administration, clerical activities, finance and human resource can be activities, maintenance and security in the context of R&D.
- Feasibility studies supporting strategic decision making on a specific R&D activity.
- Innovative testing, data sampling or survey methods, where this research is not R&D.
- Miscellaneous activities essential to R&D, for example computing resources, leasing laboratories, maintaining equipment and salaries.
- Research conducted at universities by students and researchers.
- Scientific and technical information services, for example the preparation of R&D reports on findings.
- Training required to support an R&D project.[18]

---

[16] *AHK Recruitment Ltd v HMRC* [2020] UKFTT 232 (TC) (*AHK*), per Judge Bedenham, at [29].

[17] *Flame Tree Publishing Ltd (FTPL) v HMRC* [2024] UKFTT 349 (TC) (25 April 2024), at [68].

[18] UK Government (2024) 'Guidance Meaning of research and development for tax purposes: guidelines', at section 31.

11.5 RDEC and SME specific schemes

Having determined the semiconductor activity qualifies as R&D, two distinct regimes are research and development expenditure credit (RDEC), and loss-making SMEs. From April 2024 there has been significant reform to UK R&D tax reliefs. First, firms of any size can claim under the RDEC regime. Subject to exceptional situations, such as a ring fence trade,[19] the available credit is 20 per cent of a firm's qualifying R&D costs.[20]

Second, a loss-making SME with the prerequisite R&D intensity can claim under the SME loss making regime.[21] In this scenario, a firm can claim (an additional) 86 per cent deduction for qualifying expenditure.[22] Alternatively, such SMEs can benefit from a tax credit of 14.5 per cent of its surrender loss.[23] There is also provision to claim a tax credit for deemed trading loss in the situation of R&D expenditure before a firm commences trading.[24]

Start-ups and established growing firms are categorised as 'SME' based on the qualifying limits of 500 employees, an annual turnover of €100 million and a balance sheet of €86 million. Many semiconductor firms in the UK will qualify as an SME. The HMRC SME tax relief manual contains a set of multiple choice questions to determine if a firm qualifies.[25] This

[19] Section 1042G(1)(a) CTA 2009 provides a 49 per cent credit for a ring-fence trade.

[20] Section 1042G(1)(b) CTA 2009.

[21] A qualifying SME needs to have: (a) less than 500 staff; (b) a turnover of under €100 million or a balance sheet total under €86 million; (c) a trading loss for tax purposes before relief is calculated; (d) R&D intensity of at least 30 per cent. See UK Government (2024) 'Claiming Research and Development (R&D) tax reliefs', available at www.gov.uk/guidance/corporation-tax-research-and-development-rd-relief.

[22] Section 1044(8) CTA 2009.

[23] Section 1058(1)(a) CTA 2009.

[24] Section 1045 CTA 2009.

[25] The detailed questions are set out in text format at the end of the HMRC CIRD manual. See www.gov.uk/hmrc-internal-manuals/corporate-intangibles-research-and-development-manual/cird100000.

online guidance is easily accessible and clearly drafted. It also includes a flowchart.[26]

11.6 Subcontracting R&D

Often throughout all early growth phases there can be exceptional gains made by including contractor talent. Equally the largest semiconductor multinationals benefit from innovative contract input. Even though, under UK R&D tax law rules, universities are ineligible to claim relief, expenditure by a semiconductor firm on R&D contracted out to it by a university may qualify for relief.

11.7 Venture capital company shareholdings

An additional important aspect for start-ups and established SMEs is existing or planned capital raising partners. There is a need to pay attention to the potential consequence of venture capital company shareholdings on a firm's ability to claim R&D tax relief.

An important UK First-tier Tribunal tax case on this point concerned the Siemens Technology Accelerator GmbH's (Siemens) ownership of greater than 25 per cent in Pyreos Ltd (Pyreos), a pioneer of thin film pyroelectric infra-red sensors.[27] Siemens' equity stake varied between 49 per cent and 36 per cent.

Under an EC Recommendation,[28] because Siemens held over 25 per cent of Pyreos' shares, the two companies would have ordinarily been considered partners. The Annex to the EC Recommendation provided that '"Partner enterprises" are all enterprises which are not classified as linked enterprises within the meaning of paragraph 3 and between which there is the following relationship: an enterprise (upstream enterprise)

[26] Available at www.hmrc.gov.uk/gds/cird/attachments/cird100000-eligibility-flowchart.pdf.

[27] *Pyreos Ltd v HMRC* [2015] UKFTT 123 (TC) (18 March 2015), available at http://www.bailii.org/uk/cases/UKFTT/TC/2015/TC04328.html.

[28] Article 3, paragraph 2, Annex to the EC Recommendation (EC) No. 2003/361.

holds...25% or more of the capital or voting rights of another enterprise (downstream enterprise).'[29] Therefore, applying this guidance, Pyreos would not be considered an autonomous SME entitled to the R&D tax relief sought.

However, the EC Recommendation also provides that a firm can still qualify as autonomous if the 25 per cent threshold is reached by investors that are not linked enterprises. Paragraph 3 defined 'linked' relationships to include majority or sole control of the shares or voting rights in the enterprise. Further, in this context 'investors' includes venture capital companies (VCCs).

The UK tax court determined that the phrase VCC was to be construed:

> in its dictionary sense of a company whose interest is in maximising the financial return on its investments in new businesses and speculative ventures. Matters of commercial risk will motivate it too, and no doubt the date of realisation of potential benefits. But the day-to-day executive management of the subject concerned in which it invests, would not. The nature and pattern of their trading, other than their profitability, would not ordinarily be a matter of concern. A VCC's interest is in short, in the balance sheet value and revenue generation of its investments, and the ability to realise these.[30]

An additional aspect of interest to semiconductor start-up readers will be the fact that Pyreos was licensing Siemens intellectual property (IP), an arrangement commonly found in spin-off arrangements. Indeed, the role of this specific Siemens company is to licence IP and other technological knowhow in which Siemens Group has no ongoing interest. Therefore, Pyreos was contracting with Siemens to licence IP. On this arrangement the UK tax court concluded 'any continuing commercial contact between Pyreos and the Siemens Group was at arms-length'.[31]

The SME was autonomous from Siemens because all IP was subject to contractual terms made at arm's length. In sum, the decision to allow Pyreos to claim R&D relief will be of significant value to some semicon-

---

29 Ibid, Article 3, paragraph 3.

30 *Pyreos Ltd v HMRC* [2015] UKFTT 123 (TC) (18 March 2015), per HHJ Mure, at [54].

31 Ibid, per HHJ Mure, at [56].

ductor SMEs with substantial existing or planned venture capital investment, including SMEs licensing IP from the same venture capitalists.

11.8 HM Treasury reports

In 2021, HM Treasury produced an *R&D Tax Reliefs* report.[32] Further, draft legislation to give effect to the changes was published in 2022. Responses from the UK Select Committee Semiconductor inquiry pinpointed two concerns. First, the view that the application process for claiming R&D relief was over-complex, and firms perceived they had to instruct agents to be sure the credits would be approved. Second, the view was expressed that the R&D tax credits should be broadened to cover capital expenditure on physical assets given semiconductor equipment is often incredibly high cost.

11.9 R&D tax incentives for cloud computing and data storage

Since 1 April 2023, firms are entitled to claim for most cloud computing and data licensing costs spent on R&D. Cloud computing includes data storage, hardware facilities, operating systems, and software platforms.[33] In part this updates UK R&D tax law to be congruent with the significant increase in data analytics, computer simulation, the Big Data revolution, and machine learning applied to innovation processes. The practical effect of this amendment is that it maintains consistency across UK tax law R&D definitions by including R&D expenditure on (a) cloud and (b) data licence costs within the R&D Fraction.

---

[32] HM Treasury (2021), *R&D Tax Reliefs Report*.

[33] Schedule 1 Finance (No.2) Act 2023, amending ss.1125–1126 of Chapter 9 of Part 13 CTA 2009 (additional relief for expenditure on R&D: supplementary).

11.10 Patent box

The UK patent box regime has been established for more than ten years.[34] In essence it allows qualifying patent-related IP profits to be taxed at a 10 per cent of the corporation tax rate. Given the main rate of corporation tax has increased to 25 per cent, the attraction of the patent box regime cannot be understated.[35] The regime's threefold aims are to incentivise businesses to:

(a) increase the level of patenting of IP developed in the UK, and ensure that new and existing patents are further developed and commercialised in the UK;
(b) manufacture and sell those innovative products and services from the UK;
(c) locate the high-value jobs associated with the development, manufacture and exploitation of patents in the UK.[36]

Based on UK HMRC statistics, on a consistent basis companies classified as manufacturing and those focused on 'professional, scientific and technical' activities, collectively make up more than 50 per cent of the total relief claimed on an annual basis.[37] Most if not all semiconductor firms would be part of one or both of these industry classification groups. Therefore, semiconductor firms are very likely to be already benefiting from the more than £1 billion tax relief claimed annually as part of regime.

The tax relief is highly attractive, because it has, historically, halved the rate of corporation tax paid to 10 per cent. However, because in recent years the main UK corporate tax rate has risen to 25 per cent, the patent

[34] The UK patent box was first introduced in the Finance Act 2012 and took effect from 1 April 2013.

[35] Sections 357A to 357GE Corporation Tax Act 2010 (CTA 2010) are entitled 'Profits arising from the exploitation of patents etc'. There is substantial detail in the patent box regime rules concerning where the patent features in a business.

[36] HMRC (2023) 'Patent Box relief statistics: September 2023', section 5, available at www.gov.uk/government/statistics/patent-box-reliefs-statistics/patent-box-relief-statistics-september-2023#annex-b-publication-tables.

[37] Ibid, at section 4.3.

box regime benefit has become even more generous for qualifying patent activity and commercial development.[38]

From a government policy-making angle, patent box tax incentives must play a part in either attracting new firms and incentivising existing firms to stay in the UK. It is notable that the patent box tax rates in several European jurisdictions with cutting-edge semiconductor activity are lower compared with the UK. For example, Belgium (3.75 per cent), Ireland (6.25 per cent) and the Netherlands (9 per cent).[39] Any greater difference in the UK tax rate compared with other European jurisdictions would be pose a risk.

Policy makers may be curious to know what convincing evidence exists that a patent box regime increases innovative semiconductor activity? Researchers have looked at all sector patent filings and R&D spending in several countries after the introduction of patent box rules, with inconclusive results. However, this analysis did not include data from the UK.[40] Future data on semiconductor firm sensitivity to differences in patent box rates across Europe would be valuable.

11.10.1 The essence of patent box rules

Three fundamental factors determine whether patent activity qualifies under the UK patent box regime:

- Patent ownership in the UK and many other European jurisdictions.[41]

[38] Under s.25(1) Patents Act 1977, a patent is protected for 20 years. This protection period takes effect from the publishing of the decision to grant, but the 20 years' protection begins from the date the application was filed. In the semiconductor sector the protective value is often far shorter because of the rapid technical progress. Therefore, tax revenues are generally higher in the first few years.

[39] Mengden, A. (2023) 'Patent Box Regimes in Europe, 2023', Tax Foundation Europe.

[40] Gaessler, F. et al (2019) 'Should There Be Lower Taxes on Patent Income?' National Bureau of Economic Research, Working Paper 24843.

[41] Section 357B CTA 2010 covering the meaning of 'qualifying company'.

- Qualifying development activity in the context of inventing, or significantly contributing to an invention's development, including its practical use.[42]
- Active ownership, meaning management decision making and planning for its exploitation.[43]

First, qualifying patents are patents that are owned, or an exclusive licence exists over the IP right in the patent. The patent must have been granted by the UK Intellectual Property Office (IPO), the European Patent Office (EPO), or specified European patent offices.[44] Such a wide European scope may surprise many readers, but the patent box regime was well established before Brexit.

Second, the pivotal qualifying development IP provision requires: (1) creating, or significantly contributing to the creation of, the patented invention; or (2) performing a significant amount of activity to develop the patented invention, any product incorporating the patented invention, or any process incorporating the patented invention. In short, significance can be measured in terms of cost, effort and time. Importantly, significant contributions include developing ways in which the invention may be used or applied.[45]

Third, active ownership requires significant 'management activity' concerning the qualifying IP rights, such as decision making and formulating plans linked to the development or exploitation of the rights.[46]

11.10.2 Patent box deduction formula

The patent box deduction is calculated in accordance with the following formula.

$$RP \times (AR - IPR/AR)$$

---

[42] Sections 357BC–357BD CTA 2010 covering the meaning of 'qualifying development'.

[43] Section 357BE CTA 2010 covering the meaning of 'active ownership'.

[44] The current list of eligible European patent offices is Austria, Bulgaria, Czech Republic, Denmark, Estonia, Finland, Germany, Hungary, Poland, Portugal, Romania, Slovakia and Sweden.

[45] Section 357BD(2) CTA 2010.

[46] Section 357BE(3) CTA 2010.

In the example below, imagine a semiconductor firm is specialising in photonic devices. The firm generates £1,000,000 in qualifying relevant IP profits (RP), chargeable to corporation tax. If all the profits of the company were non-IP related then the current AR, meaning the current main rate of UK corporation tax rate of 25 per cent, would apply.[47] Therefore, £250,000 corporation tax would be due. Under the patent box the qualifying IP profits deduction formula is applied before the standard corporation tax calculation. The patent box deduction is subtracted from the taxable profits before the main rate of corporation tax is calculated.[48]

Patent Box deduction =

Relevant IP Profits × Main Rate (AR) – IP Rate (IPR)

Relevant IP Profits = £1,000,000 × (25 – 10) /25) = £600,000

Corporation Tax payable = (Relevant IP Profits – Patent Box deduction) × AR

= £1,000,000 – £600,000 = £400,000

Corporation Tax @25% of £400,000 = £100,000

In sum, the patent box offers a substantial tax saving for qualifying activity. In the example just presented, £100,000 tax would be due compared with £250,000 of tax under the main corporation tax rate.

Patent box relief is restricted to profits generated from IP initially developed in the UK. Put another way, the focus is on all preferential treatment of IP based on the location of R&D activity. The R&D formula applied

---

[47] Under s.11 Finance (No.2) Act 2023, from 1 April 2023, the s.357A(3) CTA 2010 formula substitutes 'MR' with 'AR', where 'AR' is defined as a company 'where corporation tax is charged at the standard small profits rate on the company's taxable total profits'. This amendment ensures the correct patent box preferential rate of corporation tax is achieved when the Small Profit Rate of corporation tax applies.

[48] A decision to elect the patent box must be submitted to UK HMRC in writing. No specific format is required.

is based on allowing a fraction of total expenditure on qualifying IP to benefit from the substantially reduced corporation tax rate.

Calculating relevant IP profits requires applying an eight-step process.[49] The first three steps include dividing the income streams. At the outset, trade profits are divided into (a) relevant IP income stream, and (b) standard income stream made up of income irrelevant to IP income. Thereafter, the relevant IP income is divided into IP sub-streams, made-up of a (a) product sub streams or (b) process sub streams, or both. Additionally, expenditure is assigned to each sub-stream on a just and reasonable basis and deducted from that income.[50]

Once the sub-streams have been determined, routine deductions are made by the firm to each sub-stream based on 10 per cent. For example, routine deductions include premises costs, legal services costs, IP-related services, contractors, and permanent staff.[51] A fraction is calculated for each income stream by applying the R&D formula set out below. By which is meant, profit linked to a specific product or item.

IP-driven semiconductor firms may often have mixed IP expenditure based on in-house costs, connected company R&D, third-party outsourced IP costs and the cost of acquiring IP. The R&D formula is nuanced to their real circumstances to establish how IP is created and acquired.

11.10.3 R&D formula

$$(D + S1) \times 1.3$$

$$D + S1 + S2 + A$$

In the R&D formula, D equals direct *in-house* expenditure on R&D. Qualifying in-house expenditure may include contractors, cloud com-

[49] HMRC (2024) Corporate Intangibles Research and Development Manual – CIRD220100 – Patent Box, available at www.gov.uk/hmrc-internal-manuals/corporate-intangibles-research-and-development-manual/cird220100.

[50] Ibid, Steps 1–3.

[51] Ibid, Step 4; then Step 5 requires removing marketing assets concerning marketing or branding.

puting services, consumable items, software and staffing costs. S1 equals expenditure on *external* R&D subcontracted to third parties; S2 equals expenditure on R&D subcontracted to *related parties*; and A equals expenditure on *acquired* IP.[52]

In effect, the 1.3 multiplier applies a 30 per cent uplift to the numerator. This 30 per cent cap means that R&D costs by connected parties and the acquisition of patents are permitted, but the total expenditure cannot exceed 30 per cent of the costs from in-house and third-party subcontracted R&D.[53]

Cost sharing agreements (CSAs), or cost contribution arrangements, have specific R&D fraction rules.[54] Importantly for start-ups and other early phase SMEs, the definition of a CSA does not require one of the parties to the CSA to either own a qualifying IP right or possess an exclusive licence. Therefore, for one party entering into a CSA to develop IP there is no pre-existing IP ownership requirement.[55]

The nexus fraction is calculated by allowing an uplift of 30 per cent because there will be miscellaneous IP costs that are allowed to benefit from preferential treatment under the patent box – hence the numerator includes the multiplication of 1.3. Conversely, the nexus approach does not allow a company to ignore the costs of (1) R&D conducted by connected parties; and (2) the cost of acquiring IP. Therefore, the denominator includes these two variables. For example, if we return to the earlier hypothetical example of the photonic firm, if this UK business merely acquired IP from a competitor, it's logical to factor in that expenditure as a variable which reduces the amount of qualifying IP.

[52] Ibid, Step 6; then Step 7 requires adding the relevant IP sub-streams to obtain a total relevant IP profit; and Step 8 is relevant to profits, if any, from inventions awaiting grant of a patent if the patent is then awarded in the accounting period.

[53] In situations where the fraction does not properly reflect the firm's contribution to intellectual property, there is an application procedure to increase the R&D fraction based on 'exceptional circumstances'. See s.357BLH CTA 2010.

[54] CSAs are discussed in detail later in this chapter.

[55] Section 357GC CTA 2010.

Patent strategies are covered in the intellectual property law chapter. Although the value of granted patents for firms varies enormously, UK firms involved in or planning to manufacture semiconductors may also potentially benefit from the patent box regime. For instance, a firm's engineers may be adept at solving production challenges that include inventing patentable manufacturing solutions.[56]

11.11 Enterprise Investment Scheme

In existence since 1994, the Enterprise Investment Scheme (EIS) is a series of tax benefits that makes investing in UK SMEs a highly attractive opportunity. More than 53,000 firms have received EIS investment and more than £33 billion of funds have been raised.[57] The qualifying SME must have a permanent establishment in the UK and cannot be listed on the London Stock Exchange.[58]

From an investor viewpoint, the key benefits of the EIS are:

- 30 per cent upfront income tax relief;
- 100 per cent capital gains tax relief;
- capital gains tax deferral;
- up to 45 per cent loss relief on each investment;
- inheritance tax relief.

Most semiconductor firms would qualify for the EIS 'knowledge-intensive company' status, because IP is central to the business. A key criterion is having 20 per cent of the firm's full-time 'skilled' employees engaging in research for a period of at least three years from the date of investment.[59]

The Achilles heel of the EIS for knowledge-intensive firms is that the rules impose a lifetime limit on a firm raising more than £20 million,

---

[56] For more details, readers can refer to the section on patenting in the intellectual property law chapter.

[57] UK Government (2023) 'Accredited official statistics: Enterprise Investment Scheme: Commentary 2023' (17 May 2023).

[58] Notably, some alternative investment market (AIM)-listed firms would qualify under the EIS, so it is important to seek professional advice.

[59] Section 252A Income Tax Act 2007. Available at www.legislation.gov.uk/ukpga/2007/3/section/252A.

with a maximum investment per individual of £2 million. In the UK, as elsewhere in many of the G20 countries, rentier capitalism is creating greater inequality. Thomas Piketty concludes that the central contradiction of capitalism is $r > g$. By which is meant a destabilising force is that the private return on capital (r), can be far greater for long periods of time compared with the rate of income plus output (g). The seminal point made is that because r is greater than g, many entrepreneurs transform, in the long run, into rentiers.[60]

One positive initiative would, in my view, be to increase g by making the EIS lifetime limit for knowledge-intensive firms a different order of magnitude. For example, raising the maximum lifetime limit from £20 million to £200 million, and increasing the maximum investment per individual from £2 million to £20 million. A certain path leading back to less inequality is for tax law to reward risk in the form of investment in technology. That would include many growing semiconductor firms.[61]

11.12 Entrepreneurs and pension funds

Arguably the most important initiative will be changes to incentivise more entrepreneurs to operate in the UK semiconductor sector because of pension fund capital. In France, the 'Tibi' initiative and subsequent regulation makes that economy a more founder-friendly place for growth firms compared with the UK. Encouragingly, in 2024 the UK Labour Party published a paper confirming its intention to establish a British version of the Tibi regulation with the aim of increasing defined contribution pension fund investment in both small cap growth and venture capital equity.

---

60 Piketty, T. (2017) *Capital in the Twenty First Century*, The Belnap Press of HUP, at 746.

61 Further, given 65 per cent of all recent EIS investment went to Southeast firms, that statistic raises the issue of how policy makers can constructively assist in growing all regions of the UK: UK Government (2024) 'Accredited official statistics: Enterprise Investment Scheme: Commentary 2023' (23 May 2024).

11.13 Transfer pricing

Transfer pricing is the method by which pricing transactions between connected or related parties are calculated. To avoid tax authorities challenging such intra-group arrangements, the arm's length principle is applied. By which is meant the connected parties' pricing needs to be comparable with the market prices that would have been charged if independent, unrelated parties had carried out the transactions.[62]

For large multinationals, the UK has adopted the Organization for Economic Cooperation and Development (OECD) Base Erosion and Profit Shifting (BEPS) Country-by-Country (CbC) Reporting standard as a legal framework. To date, over 100 jurisdictions have domestic laws in place introducing a CbC reporting obligation. The CbC covers all key semiconductor markets, including China, Germany, Japan, and South Korea. The OECD publishes aggregated and anonymised data from CbC reporting, together with information on the global tax and economic activities of nearly 7,000 multinational groups operating in more than 100 jurisdictions.[63]

Qualifying CbC multinationals fill in an annual template for each tax jurisdiction in which they do business.[64] Each CbC report is filed by the parent entity and made available to all the relevant tax administrations. The reporting parent entity is expected to list, on a tax jurisdiction-by-tax jurisdiction basis and by legal entity name, all the entities in its corporate group. Information is also required concerning the jurisdictions where all activities and assets are taxed. This includes sections covering R&D, as well as all IP ownership.

---

62 The UK HMRC manual on transfer pricing can be accessed at www.gov.uk/hmrc-internal-manuals/international-manual/intm410000.

63 OECD (2024) 'Action 13 Country-by-Country Reporting', available at www.oecd.org/tax/beps/beps-actions/action13/.

64 The CbC reporting applies to all multinational groups with annual consolidated group revenue of at least €750 million: OECD (2015) *OECD/G20 Base Erosion and Profit Shifting Project Transfer Pricing Documentation and Country-by-Country Reporting ACTION 13: 2015 Final Report*, at 21, para.52, available at www.oecd.org/tax/transfer-pricing-documentation-and-country-by-country-reporting-action-13-2015-final-report-9789264241480-en.htm.

Transfer pricing arrangements are more likely to be challenged at every size of multinational operation.[65] The great majority of semiconductor firms will not be affected by this reporting requirement because of the BEPS CbC €750 million annual revenue multinational group threshold. While SMEs are usually exempt from transfer pricing requirements, the global point is that tax authorities have increasing amounts of data on semiconductor operations across borders. The OECD application of transfer pricing approach to hard-to-value intangibles (HTVI) may be of special importance to some firms.[66]

If a semiconductor firm grows without a thoroughly assessed, detailed transfer pricing policy supported by contemporaneous documentation there are potentially diverse consequences. These include high litigation costs, wasted board level time, recalculated tax bills with interest, and fines. Depending on individual circumstances, a semiconductor firm growing internationally with R&D facilities may choose to submit an advance pricing agreement to the relevant tax authorities.

11.14 Cost contribution arrangements

The sharing of costs between connected and unrelated parties is typically recorded in a cost contribution arrangement (CCA).[67] For example, R&D costs between joint venture partners or between intra-group entities. Another example is sharing the costs associated with semiconductor patents.[68] A CCA can have multiple benefits beyond R&D costs and spreading the risk of innovative projects which may have a high chance of failure. Additional benefits can include using the talents of engineers from

[65] The OECD provides an online tool to determine which countries have, among other things, adopted the CbC reporting regime, available at www.oecd.org/tax/beps/international-tax-co-operation-map.htm.

[66] Available at www.oecd.org/tax/transfer-pricing/guidance-for-tax-administrations-on-the-application-of-the-approach-to-hard-to-value-intangibles-beps-action-8.htm.

[67] A CCA is also widely termed a cost sharing arrangement or cost sharing agreement (CSA).

[68] HMRC (2024) INTM421090 – Transfer pricing: Methodologies: OECD Guidelines: Cost contribution arrangements, available at www.gov.uk/hmrc-internal-manuals/international-manual/intm421090.

different entities, and economies of scale savings on hardware or software or both. The OECD devotes a whole chapter of its latest Transfer Pricing Guidelines to CCAs.[69]

11.14.1 *Altera Corporation & Subsidiaries v Commissioner* – case study

The long running litigation between Altera, a manufacturer of programmable logic devices, and the United States (US) Internal Revenue Service (IRS) highlights how rigorously complying with tax rules can save immense amounts of money and wasted time.[70] Readers would be forgiven for thinking Altera, acquired by Intel in 2015, is a historical example. Yet the importance of semiconductor firms implementing tax law-compliant CCAs cannot be understated.[71] In short, the timeframes of such cases highlight the unpredictable costs and uncertainties of conducting tax litigation.

The facts of the Altera case revolved around Altera Corp, a parent company incorporated in Delaware. From 1997 to 2007, Altera Corp and its subsidiary, Altera International, a Cayman Islands corporation, made a technology R&D CCA with the aim of pooling their resources for R&D projects. Additionally, in the tax years 2004–07 Altera Corp gave stock options to specified employees who performed R&D activities under the CCA. The employees' cash compensation was included in the cost pool under the CCA, but their stock-option compensation was not. The IRS challenged this omission claiming insufficient tax was paid in the US for the years 2004–07.

The key arguments made by the IRS included the fact that the arm's length standard was only reached by increasing Altera International's cost-sharing payments. Altera Corp was breaching US tax law by omitting

[69] OECD (2022) 'OECD Transfer Pricing Guidelines for Multinational Enterprises and Tax Administrations 2022', Chapter VIII.

[70] *Altera Corporation & Subsidiaries v Commissioner*, 926 F.3d. 1061 (2019).

[71] Prior to the *Altera* case, the main US high court litigation concerning CCAs revolved around the field programmable gate array (FPGA) pioneer Xilinx Corp. See *Xilinx, Inc. v Commissioner*, 598 F.3d 1191 (9th Cir. 2010).

to share the cost of the stock-option compensation required for inclusion in all intangible development costs.[72]

In 2019, after four years of litigation, the US Court of Appeal held that a regulation requiring cost sharing of stock-based compensation was valid.[73] However, another year passed before the case confirmed this decision because of an unsuccessful appeal application made to the US Supreme Court.[74]

11.15 International strategies

In an era of increasing attention focused on semiconductor sector expansion as part of national industrial policy, there is still sense in considering the strategic options for expanding into markets that provide additional tax benefits. A number of important semiconductor markets have government tax policies to assist foreign direct investment. These include Japan, South Korea and China. However, given the potential scale of expansion in the European Union (EU) and the US, these two markets require detailed coverage on how the EU Chips Act and the US CHIPS Act benefits foreign semiconductor firms.

11.15.1 The US CHIPS Act

The Creating Helpful Incentives to Produce Semiconductors and Science Act of 2022 (CHIPS Act), effective August 2022, aims to act as a catalyst for investment in the US semiconductor sector. The first part of the CHIPs Act promotes and supports semiconductor manufacturing in the US, including the provision of funding. The CHIPs Act also expands on the semiconductor manufacturing incentives provided in the William M.

[72] Section 482 US Internal Revenue Code (IRC). The IRS approach is set out in www.irs.gov/pub/int_practice_units/ISO9411_07_01.pdf.

[73] *Altera Corporation & Subsidiaries v Commissioner*, 926 F.3d. 1061 (2019). On 22 June 2020, the United States (US) Supreme Court announced that it was denying the petition for certiorari for *Altera Corporation & Subsidiaries v Commissioner.*

[74] On 22 June 2020, the US Supreme Court announced that it was denying the petition for certiorari for *Altera Corporation & Subsidiaries v Commissioner.*

(Mac) Thornberry National Defense Authorization Act for Fiscal Year 2021 (the NDAA 2021).

An initial reading of the CHIPS Act reveals the fact it is nearly 400 pages of immense detail that aims to make the US a leading semiconductor manufacturer. Over a ten-year period, of the total $278.2 billion expenditure $24.2 billion is allocated to advanced manufacturing tax credits. Based on US Treasury projections, Figure 11.2, shows the estimated expenditure.[75]

The tax element of the CHIPS Act is termed an advanced manufacturing credit. The CHIPS Act does not define 'semiconductor', so US statutory interpretation rules would apply in the event that the manufacturing activity or manufacturing equipment was challenged to be inapplicable.[76] However, in such a situation, given the Semiconductor Industry Association (SIA) is a leading industry body with wide participation, its definition and views are likely to be persuasive.

The credit is set at 25 per cent of a 'qualified investment'.[77] The type of qualifying investment is a 'qualified property'.[78] forming part of an 'advanced manufacturing facility', primarily used in the 'manufacturing of semiconductors or semiconductor manufacturing equipment'.[79]

To clarify, the scope of a 'qualified property' includes any advanced manufacturing facility 'constructed', 'reconstructed', 'erected' or 'acquired'.[80] What cannot be claimed is a building or part of a building used for

---

75 Congressional Budget Office (2022) 'Estimated Budgetary Effects of H.R. 4346'. See www.cbo.gov/system/files/2022-07/hr4346_chip.pdf.

76 See *McDermott International, Inc. v Wilander*, 498 U.S. 337, 342 (1991); *Old Colony Railroad Co.*, 284 U.S. 552, 560 (1932) ('The legislature must be presumed to use words in their known and ordinary signification. … This rule is applied to taxing acts.').

77 Section 107 CHIPS Act amending, by inserting Section 48D(a), the Internal Revenue Code of 1986.

78 Ibid, amending, by inserting Section 48D(b)(2)(A), the Internal Revenue Code of 1986.

79 Ibid, amending, by inserting Section 48D(b)(3), the Internal Revenue Code of 1986.

80 Ibid amending, by inserting Section 48D(2)(A)(iii)(I-II), the Internal Revenue Code of 1986.

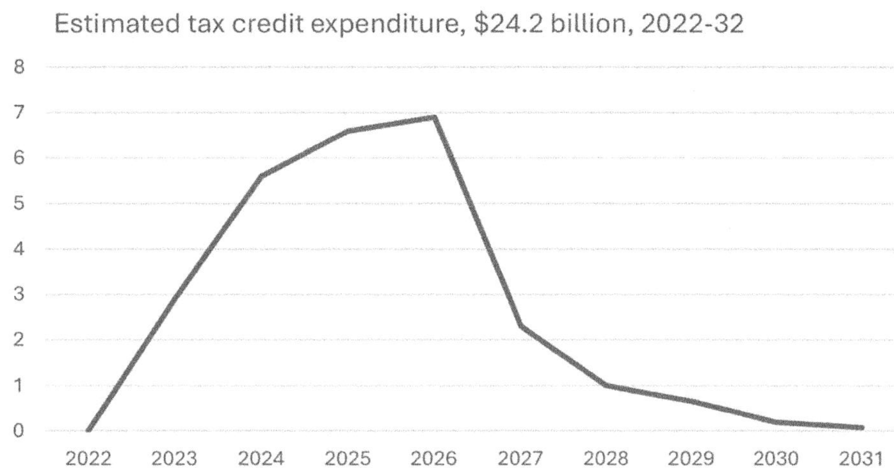

Source: Congressional Budget Office (2022) 'Estimated Budgetary Effects of H.R. 4346'. See www.cbo.gov/system/files/2022-07/hr4346_chip.pdf

Figure 11.2 *Estimated CHIPS Act tax credit expenditure*

administrative functions.[81] Further, equipment used to manufacture semiconductor equipment integral to the manufacturing process would also qualify. For example, photolithographic machines.

An important date to bear in mind is 1 January 2027, because to qualify for this tax credit the construction work must start before then. If significant physical work has not started by that date, there is the possibility of providing documentation to the IRS to prove that at least 5 per cent of the total cost of the property has been paid – a 5 per cent safe harbour rule.[82]

Building manufacturing plants typically costs billions of dollars, the massive savings to be made have already attracted TSMC and IDM expansion in the US. However, there is no minimum amount to claim, so there is no reason why SMEs cannot equally benefit by collaborating to build relatively lower budget, smaller manufacturing or packaging facilities.

11.15.2 Applicable transactions

It is positive that the CHIPS Act offers foreign firms an opportunity to gain tax credits when they expand existing manufacturing facilities or build new ones. Yet it equally offers opportunities for foreign semiconductor firms.

However, a key issue for strategic tax planning assessment is the geopolitically linked provisions. Specifically, a firm is ineligible for the advanced manufacturing tax credit if it has made an 'applicable transaction'.[83] The definition of an 'applicable transaction' is determined by several US federal government departments as, 'involving the material expansion of

---

[81] Ibid amending, by inserting Section 48D(2)(B)(ii), the Internal Revenue Code of 1986.

[82] IRS (2013) Notice 2013-29, Section 5. This IRS Notice applies to a different tax credit scenario, but it provides valuable detail on IRS expectations. Note especially, that after making payment thereafter, the taxpayer is expected to make continuous efforts to advance towards completing the construction.

[83] Ibid amending, by inserting Section 48D(2)(c)(2), the Internal Revenue Code of 1986.

semiconductor manufacturing capacity of such applicable taxpayer…in a foreign country of concern’.[84]

The NDAA 2021 specifies each foreign country of concern to be any listed elsewhere in United States Code (USC).[85] Logically, as international relations change, so may this list of countries expand or contract.[86] However, in 2024 the list included North Korea, China, Iran, North Korea and Russia.[87]

There is an important exception relevant to any foreign country of concern. Namely, any ‘legacy semiconductor’ transactions will not qualify as a significant transaction. As long as the legacy semiconductors involved are not critical to US national security, as determined by the US federal government, a permissible ‘legacy semiconductor’ includes:

- 28nm generation or older logic semiconductors;
- relative to 28nm generation logic semiconductors, all memory technology, analog technology, packaging technology, and any other relevant technology, as determined by US federal government departments; and
- any additional semiconductor technology identified by the US Treasury Secretary in a public notice.[88]

---

[84] Ibid amending, by inserting Section 50(a)(6)(D), the Internal Revenue Code of 1986.

[85] Section 2553c, Title 10, USC.

[86] Section 9901(7) of the William M. (Mac) Thornberry National Defense Authorization Act for Fiscal Year 2021.

[87] The CHIPS Act refers separately to China when addressing foreign countries of concern, given it is the nation-state perceived as the greatest threat from a technological supremacy viewpoint. However, it is likely, especially if Sino-US relations improve, that the scope of legacy semiconductors will expand below 28nm. In turn that may allow many international semiconductor firms to expand operations in both China and the US.

[88] Section 9902(a)(6) of the NDAA 2021.

11.15.3 The European Chips Act

The EU Chips Act has aspects in common with its US counterpart, although the total amount of funding offered exceeds €43 billion.[89] What is important to highlight is that the EU has approached its collective semiconductor planning with humility. Perhaps setting an example that the UK Government can follow. In its communication, which proposed the EU regulation, it succinctly summarised Europe's vulnerabilities and aims in these terms:

> Europe has limited chip manufacturing capabilities, mainly in mature production nodes (at 22 nm and above), and none in leading-edge chips (at 7 nm and below).7 It has also strong dependencies in design, packaging and assembly.[90]

It concluded that its objective:

> will require building balanced semiconductor partnerships with like-minded countries. The aim of these partnerships would be to set out cooperative frameworks on initiatives of mutual interest and seek a commitment to ensure continuity of supply in times of crisis…As a first step, the above will be explored – using existing or new fora – with like-minded partners, such as the United States, Japan, South Korea, Singapore, Taiwan and others.[91]

In sum, sensible, logical planning on how to improve its collective position.

The EU Chips Act mirrors the US CHIPs Act at an albeit radically smaller scale. There is 25 per cent tax credit benefit. From one viewpoint the EU Chips Act seeks to grow EU member states' global share of semiconductor manufacturing. However, from a global viewpoint it shows that the semiconductor sector is a priority within the EU, and that it has all the same benefits for any semiconductor firm as the US.

While the 25 per cent tax credit would not be available to UK semiconductor firms, the EU Chips Act does provide these benefits for joint ventures. Therefore, a joint venture or other innovative initiative between a UK and German or Belgian firm would be one opportunity. Another

[89] European Commission (2022) A Chips Act for Europe, COM/2022/45, at 11. The European Chips Act entered into force on 21 September 2023.

[90] European Commission (2022) A Chips Act for Europe, COM/2022/No 45.

[91] Ibid, at 21.

opportunity would be for a UK firm to establish a wholly owned subsidiary in any EU member state country.[92]

While the gargantuan challenge of establishing a new fabrication plant would undoubtedly benefit from the 25 per cent tax rate, it is less certain that such a benefit would be pivotal for an SME seeking to provide design or manufacture specialist advice. What must certainly be powerful is the combination of both tax credit and punctual grants on offer for conductor activity within the EU.

In sum, the EU Chips Act is a catalyst to build stronger eco-semiconductor subsectors in both regions. Put another way, if Intel has a manufacturing facility in Dresden, in the medium and long term the additional supply chain infrastructure, local labour talent supply and university spin-out activity are the effects of tax. In short, but for such tax policies, the semiconductor sector would grow slower and in a less coordinated way. Furthermore, there is a high likelihood of future tax reform in the EU to support technical innovation.[93]

For all SME firms, the short-term value of the EU Chips Act includes increasing data on where other semiconductor firms plan to innovate and grow. For that reason alone, there is value in keeping up to date with this taxation policy. Further, to understand what national and local EU member state tax laws provides additional benefits.

11.15.4 The South Korean K-Chips Act

South Korea's dominance in memory chip manufacturing has been bolstered by the Korean Government's introduction of its K-Chips Act. Effective from Q1 2023, this legislation provides Korean-based firms with a 25 per cent tax credit if they are classified as a small- and medium-sized enterprise (SME), and a 15 per cent tax credit if a firm is classified as either a middle-standing or larger enterprise. For foreign firms there is also the opportunity to benefit from the K-Chips Act through their Korean

---

[92] In this book Chapter 5 Strategic issues, includes UK-EU possibilities.

[93] Ebrahimi, A. (2024) 'Groundbreaking Chip Sovereignty Europe's Strategic Push in the Semiconductor Race', IFRI, 31 May 2024.

subsidiaries or via portfolio companies making eligible investments.[94] In the past, South Korea has not been the easiest jurisdiction in which to conduct business, however, in recent years, their approach has been more open to foreign direct investment.[95]

11.15.5 The Japanese Tax Reform Act 2024

Japan's long mastery of quality control gives this economy realistic potential to revitalize its semiconductor sector. The Japanese Government's industrial strategy is supported by its Tax Reform Act 2024. Under this legislation, a maximum 20 per cent tax credit in each year applies to semiconductors. This credit is based on the smaller of (a) the quantity of components produced within ten years of the business plan certification date, or (b) the acquisition cost of any manufacturing equipment.[96] This tax credit applies to a business plan approved by the Ministry of Economy, Trade and Industry (METI) before 31 March 2027.[97]

Historically, Japan has shown resistance to foreign business investment, which could justifiably make Chief Executive Officers (CEOs) sceptical about the benefit of this tax credit. However, their ambitions to regain a leading position in the semiconductor sector requires openness to both international cooperation and foreign direct investment. To date, Japan is collaborating with IBM, Micron, and Western Digital.

11.16 Concluding remarks

To build the next Intel, Samsung or TSMC requires ambition, creativity, error, risk taking – and huge amounts of money. Over 15 years ago,

---

[94] Kim & Chang (2023) 'Enactment of the K-Chips Act – Government's Support and Regulatory Policies for the Semiconductor Industry', 22 May 2023, available at https://www.kimchang.com/en/insights/detail.kc?sch_section=4&idx=27331.

[95] For more details, please refer to the section on South Korea in Chapter 5 Strategic issues.

[96] Ministry of Finance (2023) 'Financial Year 2024 Tax Reform (Proposals)', available at www.mof.go.jp/english/policy/tax_policy/tax_reform/fy2024/06keyhighlight.pdf.

[97] Article 9(1) Industrial Competitiveness Act, No. 98 of 2013 (as amended).

Chinese tax law offered considerable incentives for firms setting up fabrication plants. The thinner the wafer the greater the tax reduction. Clearly the Chinese Government understood the importance of encouraging semiconductor manufacturing – the more cutting edge the better. China as an economy is 'catching up' and has for many decades been acutely aware of the importance of a semiconductor sector to that goal.

In the competitive global semiconductor sector, the EU countries, the US and the UK have all fallen behind South Korea and Taiwan. At different scales, all Western economies are 'catching up'. Only in recent years has the US and the EU followed suit and started to support semiconductor activity, including creating favourable tax laws. In the UK, ongoing government industrial policy is likely to at least acknowledge the semiconductor strategy and include tax incentives.

In the medium- to long-term future, governments can also develop sophisticated taxes that do not impede semiconductor growth at the cutting-edge, but gain tax revenues from advancement in transistor density. My past research included considering how, in the manufacturing of a smartphone, each CPU can be a measurable tax point metric for fiscal authorities.[98] All businesses value a phone that has the potential to work as quickly as a smartphone can at each evolution of CPU power.[99]

As all technical readers know, CPU processing speed is measured by 'clock rate'.[100] Currently, a smartphone with a 2.5GHz processor is considered fast. Accepting that the CPU is a vital part of a high-performance smartphone and that GHz is a specific internationally accepted unit of measurement, there is logic in partly taxing smartphones based on GHz.[101] Additionally, higher tax bands could be applied to cutting-edge transistors based on their nanometer (nm) architecture. For example, all

---

[98] Sheridan, I. (2016) 'Smartphones, Research and Development and Corporation Tax: Current Treatment and Future Possibilities', *Intertax*, 44(11), 788–90.

[99] Ibid, at 835.

[100] The clock rate refers to the clock cycles per second or its equivalent. The clock rate unit of frequency in the International System of Units is hertz (Hz). There are 1,000,000 Kilo Hertz (kHz) in one Giga Hertz (GHz).

[101] For example, each 500,000 *k*Hz could be charged at half a percent smartphone corporation tax. So a 1 Ghz increase would result in a corporate tax increase of 2 per cent.

semiconductor designs below 3nm would be subject to an extra 5 per cent tax payable by the designer.

The CPU tax idea is not to encourage UK HMRC to give with one hand and take away with the other. The consistent more important aim is to encourage and support research on sustainable semiconductors. However, smartphones are a logical source of tax with many measurable variables that would make for clear, predictable taxation. They are also ubiquitous. As remarked upon in a US Supreme Court case they 'are now such a pervasive and insistent part of daily life that the proverbial visitor from Mars might conclude they were an important feature of human anatomy'.[102]

11.16.1 Future 3D semiconductor tax

Taxing the density of 3D semiconductors presents another future opportunity for governments to provide a win-win scenario of development phases with tax breaks followed by manufacturing phases taxed on output. For example, as Moore's Law comes to a halt, an expert group that included TSMC's former CTO Chenming Hu, have considered an alternative metric that combines the densities of logic (DL), memory (DM), and connections between them (DC).[103] The expert group called this combined metric LMC. Importantly, they reasoned that LMC was of increasing relevance because it acknowledged both speed and energy efficiency.[104]

IMEC in Belgium, France's CEA-Leti and Intel are developing technology that would build n-channel metal-oxide semiconductor (NMOS) and p-channel metal-oxide-semiconductor (PMOS) transistors that combine to form complementary metal-oxide-semiconductor (CMOS) logic, one

[102] *Riley v California*, Case No. 13-132 (2014). See www.law.cornell.edu/supremecourt/text/13-132.

[103] The expert group also included all three co-inventors of the FinFET, namely Chenming Hu (former CTO of TSMC), Tsu-Jae King Liu, and Jeffrey Bokor. See Moore, S. (2020) 'A Better Way to Measure Semiconductor Progress', IEEE Spectrum, available at https://spectrum.ieee.org/a-better-way-to-measure-progress-in-semiconductors.

[104] Ibid. See also Chapter 6 of this book covering sustainability.

on top of the other.[105] Such a direction is likely to have support from industry leaders. Consider, a former chair of the Institute for Electrical and Electronics Engineers International Roadmap for Devices (IRDS) has proposed that the sector specifies levels of 3D semiconductor advancement by adopting a three-number metric that combines contacted gate pitch (G), metal pitch (M) and, crucially for future semiconductor advancement and potential taxation, the number of layers, or tiers, of devices on the chip (T).[106] For example, the IRDS provides the example of 5nm semiconductors: these could have a contacted gate pitch of 48nm, a metal pitch of 36nm and a single tier – making the metric G48M36T1.

Whether the LMC metric or the IRDS three-number metric provide better performance measurement, the fiscal point is that legislators are well placed to support and tax future semiconductor innovation. Taxing semiconductors' cutting-edge technology maximises the long-term growth of the sector. All current proposed metrics may be incisive on performance measurement but have flawed taxation methods. Often significant technical innovative breakthroughs derive from error. Perhaps future taxes may be stimulated by erroneous first attempts that need revision. All too often UK tax reform has been too slow to innovate. Let great tax innovations from small errors grow.[107]

The measurable degree of benefit of tax credits is complex. For large manufacturing firms such as Intel, Samsung and TSMC, the benefits may be expressed in the very long term, over at least a decade or more. For SMEs seeking to enter a niche market with a unique contribution, tax benefit may make the short-term difference of continuing to the next accounting period. If Moore's Law is to continue, the energy of trying new ways, such

[105] IMEC was originally established with government funding and still receives more than 15 per cent of its monies from the Belgian Government.

[106] Moore, S. (2020) 'A Better Way to Measure Semiconductor Progress', IEEE Spectrum. 21 July 2020, available at https://spectrum.ieee.org/a-better-way-to-measure-progress-in-semiconductors.

[107] A viable future semiconductor tax in the context of smartphones could focus on, among other things, taxing CPU clock rate based on GHz. For example, a CPU with a clock rate of 2GHz would require an additional corporate tax charge of 2 per cent. A clock rate of 4GHz would mean 4 per cent extra, and so forth. See Sheridan (2016).

as 3D stacking and chiplets or tiles, requires continuous R&D. Taxation plays a role in supporting such initiatives.

11.16.2 Future targeted higher education course incentives

Other future possibilities include that potentially valuable tax incentives could be provided for both electrical and electronic engineering, and business management courses.[108] Many great entrepreneurs have increased their knowledge and contacts by attending business schools that support their early start-ups.

It is notable that for both electrical and electronic engineering, and business management the UK has, at least for the moment, a substantial global competitive advantage, based on the number of top 100 ranked courses. UK university fees are now a considerable debt burden for graduating students from both the UK and abroad. That is an obvious barrier to entry that government policy makers can change. Allowing students on these courses to receive a tax credit of 150 per cent for any summer placement work carried out in a semiconductor firm could be a beneficial addition.

As Table 11.1 indicates, the UK has a substantial competitive advantage based on these high-ranking courses relevant to the semiconductor sector. Accepting the logic and experience of Professor Fitzgerald of the Massachusetts Institute of Technology on the need for Technology, Market, and Implementation awareness,[109] both these specific engineering courses and business management are the most relevant. Pricing out domestic students would be a long-term mistake. It makes sense to have tax policies they are beneficial to both domestic and international students.[110]

---

[108] The statistical rankings for electrical and electronic and business management courses derive from the QS University Rankings: QS University Rankings (2024), available at www.topuniversities.com/university-rankings.

[109] Chapter 4 in this book on strategy frameworks provides a detailed explanation of the Technology ↔ Market ↔ Implementation insight.

[110] There are many other universities that are pockets of excellence developing engineering students with high-quality semiconductor training. My own visits to Cardiff University, Kyungpook National University and Swansea University revealed resources, teaching excellence and student talent to match any institution.

Table 11.1 *University rankings relevant to the semiconductor sector*

Country	Population (millions)[1]	Number of universities in global top 100 for Electrical and Electronic Engineering[2]	Number of universities in global top 100 for Business and Management Studies[3]	Annual R&D expenditure as % of GDP[4]
China	1 424	8*[5]	5	2.43
Germany	83	3	2	3.14
Japan	125	3	1	3.3
Korea	51	5	3	4.93
Taiwan	23	1	0	3.77
UK	68	8	15	2.91
USA	341	22	23	3.46

Notes: [1] *The Economist* (2025) 'The World in 2024', World Health Organization data at https://data.who.int/countries. [2] QS University Rankings (2025), available at www.topuniversities.com/university-rankings. [3] QS University Rankings (2025), available at www.topuniversities.com/university-rankings. [4] The Global Economy.com (2024), 'Research and development expenditure - Country rankings for the year 2021', available at www.theglobaleconomy.com/rankings/research_and_development/; and UK Government (2024) 'Science and Innovation Snapshot - Taiwan', available at https://assets.publishing.service.gov.uk/media/65dd5105b8da630011c8625a/UK_Science_and_Innovation_Network_Snapshot-_Taiwan.pdf. [5] Notably, Hong Kong (SAR) also has four universities with electrical and electronic engineering courses in the top 100 global rankings.
Source: © Iain Sheridan (2025)

Tax regulation could be based around a combined salary and payment of tuition fee debt for sandwich course students. Looking at the R&D expenditure as a percentage of GDP, there would be scope to make the industry year component of a sandwich course part of R&D tax credits on condition that the student contributed to commercially focused research within the sponsoring employer.

12. Conclusions on achieving growth

Our doubts are traitors and make us lose the good we oft might win by fearing to attempt.[1]

Foreign direct investment (FDI) has played a valuable part in economic growth. The involvement of internationally experienced entrepreneurs has also deeply enriched the United Kingdom (UK) semiconductor sector. But, for the British people, as a predominant pattern of entrepreneurial growth, that cannot be the best or only path.

On many occasions British university research teams have their spin-outs funded by foreign venture capitalists. The mature firm, the one that has scaled-up from being a new venture, is then sold to a foreign firm. Does this pattern happen as much in Austria, China, France, Germany, Japan, South Korea, Taiwan or the United States (US)? The related question is how can the UK reduce over reliance on international venture capital? The same questions are of equal relevance to other ambitious medium-sized countries. There is a need to be simultaneously more patriotic and consistently open to international investment.

12.1 Introduction

The concepts of mapping and dashboards are well established as both quantitative and visual tools for coordinating complex strategies. The 3D figure presented in Chapter 1 and the strategic lens in Chapter 4, can both assist corporate strategists. However, specifically for policy makers, a useful structure to apply is set out in Figure 12.1. The idea of this strategic

1 Shakespeare, W. (1603) *Measure for Measure*, Act 1, Scene 4, https://shakespeare.mit.edu/measure/measure.1.4.html.

compass germinated from a very detailed process diagram produced by Korean Government planners. The context was the Korean Government's strategy to become an advanced power by 2030. Impressively, this plan was first drafted in the noughties.[2]

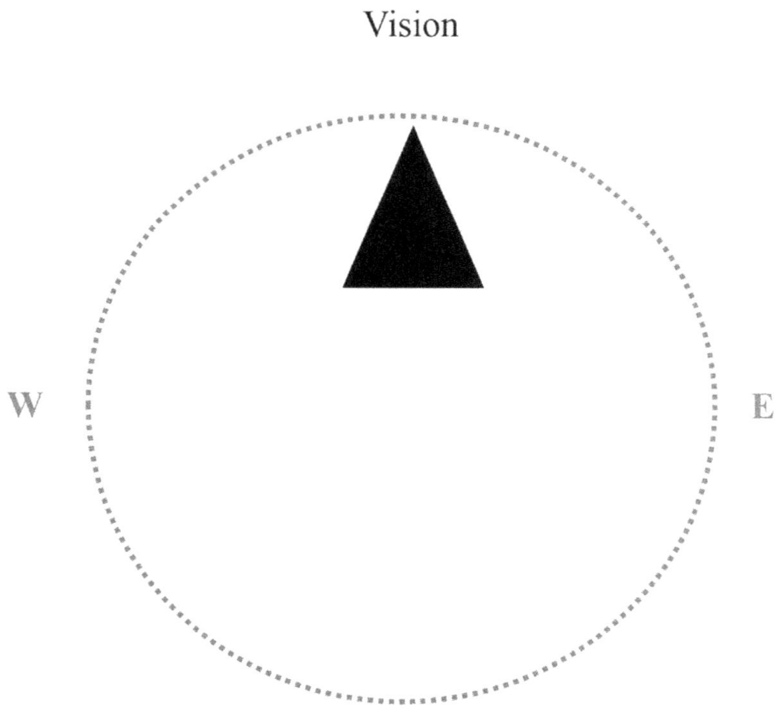

Source: © Iain Sheridan (2025)

Figure 12.1 A policy maker's strategic compass

Rather than adapt the original Korean process diagram, which was made up of more than 20 boxes, a compass is both a more memorable and practical tool. It provides, in my view, a cerebral portability.

---

[2] Korean Presidential Commission on Policy Planning (2008) *Korea's Future: Vision and Strategy, Korea's Ambition to Become an Advanced Power by 2030*, Seoul Selection Publishing.

First, the directional compass tip is the vision. For the UK this could be ‘ambition’, ‘focus’, and ‘innovation’ on semiconductors. Second, progress towards the vision requires agents. These agents of progress would include government policy, increasing the number of citizens with varying levels of electrical engineering competence and capital raising from diverse sources.

Third, major policy tasks as well as documented detailed commitments, provide the discipline and momentum to maintain a consistent bearing towards the vision. Finally, the means of realisation of all these policies and strategies will include not only substantial financial commitment and tax law changes, but also institutional reform to ensure technology-facing ministers contribute long-term service to the vision. In sum, there is the committed bearing towards a vision, which is supported by policies, finance and institutional reform.

A recent UK Government document provides a wider science and technology framework with the aim of delivering higher productivity. The framework is based on the ten levers set out in Table 12.1.[3] If applied in the context of the Figure 12.1 strategic compass, all ten levers are sensible. Especially so given semiconductors are vital components for diverse businesses, including those competing in advanced manufacturing, artificial intelligence, clean energy industries, defence, life sciences, quantum technologies and telecommunications.

At an illuminating strategy event hosted by the Resolution Foundation, Dame Ottoline Leyser, Chief Executive Officer (CEO) of UKRI, presented the three corners model found at Figure 12.2.[4] She argued that success is achieved by the integration of these ten levers into these three corners. The three corners being productivity, skills in the sense of highly qualified prospering people and innovative growth firms offering high quality jobs.

---

3 UK Government (2023) Department for Science, Innovation and Technology, ‘The UK Science and Technology Framework’, at 6, available at https://assets.publishing.service.gov.uk/media/6405955ed3bf7f25f5948f99/uk-science-technology-framework.pdf.

4 The Resolution Foundation (2023) ‘Inventing a better Britain: how does R&D fit into a new UK economic strategy?’ Seminar, 15 November 2023.

Table 12.1 UK Government levers to achieve higher productivity

No.	Significant intervention	Explanation
1	Identifying critical technologies	After assessing 50 technologies, five critical technologies have been identified. These are (i) semiconductors, (ii) engineering biology, (iii) artificial intelligence, (iv) quantum technologies and (v) future telecommunications. While the UK Government intends to review this list on an annual basis, it is highly likely that semiconductors will remain on it. The broadest aim is for the other nine levers listed below to enable these five critical technologies to grow.[1]
2	Signalling the UK's strengths and ambitions	The vision here is for consistent messaging concerning the UK Government's science and technology priorities. The title is aptly entitled signalling strengths and ambitions, because there is an intention to follow narratives akin to China's 'Made in China 2025', and even the US Apollo programme's 'we choose to go the moon' narrative.[2]
3	Investment in research and development (R&D)	The R&D plans are diverse and include raising domestic public investment outside the greater Southeast by at least 40 per cent, as set out in the UK Government's 'Levelling Up' white paper.[3] There is also an intention to reduce bureaucracy surrounding research and innovation funding.[4] In the UK there are increasing efforts to improve innovative research that becomes a commercial product. UK Research and Innovation (UKRI) is the UK's largest public funder of research and innovation. Charlotte Deane, its Executive Chair, commented that research 'has to show ROI, that there is a societal benefit rather than providing money for wacky ideas'.[5] In effect a lens that includes real innovation thinking is evident at the earliest stages of public research funding. In the long term this will impact the commercialisation of semiconductor initiatives.[6]

No.	Significant intervention	Explanation
4	Talent and skills	To expand the number of workers in science, technology, engineering and maths (STEM) sectors, which would clearly include semiconductors. Domestically there are innovative initiatives such as the Lifelong Loan Entitlement allowing new and returning learners to borrow money for STEM training.[7] To attract international workers the UK benefits from the Global Talent visa as summarised later in this chapter.[8] There is also the high-skilled visa system.[9]
5	Financing innovative science and technology firms	The aim is to ensure there is a sufficient supply of capital at all stages of each firm's growth. Encouragingly, there is a plan to increase the supply of UK institutional investment for scaling UK science and technology firms. There is a specific intention to examine the barriers that prevent defined contribution pension schemes from investing in innovative UK firms.[10]
6	Procurement	The UK Government intends to form a variety of partnerships with innovative high growth firms. They also intend to learn from valuable procurement experiences gained during the Covid-19 pandemic in the context of vaccines and ventilators.[11] From a legal and regulatory viewpoint, the most significant initiative is to reform government procurement by making the process, especially for new entrants, a consistently faster experience. This is being achieved by introducing The Procurement Act 2023.[12]

No.	Significant intervention	Explanation
7	International opportunities	The aim is, by 2032, among other things, to have developed a wider range of international partnerships. Encouragingly, in the context of semiconductors there do seem to be more UK Government initiatives to increase partnerships with the European Union (EU), Japan, South Korea, and the US.[13] However, there is a risk of lost opportunities by overlooking partnerships with other nations. In 2024 I had the opportunity to ask Ronald Lamola, South Africa's newly appointed foreign affairs minister about semiconductors. He was acutely aware it was a technology with increasing global demand.[14] South Africa is just one example.[15]
8	Access to physical and digital infrastructure	The range of initiatives included publishing the Independent Future of Compute Review in 2023.[16] Thought-provoking recommendations in the Compute Review included increasing public cloud computing access that is interoperable with private clouds and on-premises compute.[17] Further, there was a sensible recommendation for government procurement to support innovative sustainable computing by acting as the 'buyer of first resort'. This may present commercial opportunities for semiconductor firms.[18]

No.	Significant intervention	Explanation
9	Regulation and standards	Regulators will have the mandate to support regulatory sandboxes. This concept is already well established in the financial services sector. The UK Government's Regulators' Pioneer Fund (RPF) has helped regulators and local authorities to test new regulation that encourages business innovation and investment. For example, as part of the UK Government's response to the Pro-Innovation Regulation of Technologies Review, it pointed out that the Civil Aviation Authority (CAA) has already completed sandboxes that explored how aviation regulation would need to adapt to accommodate drones. In short, regulatory sandboxes responsible for different sectors may present commercial semiconductor opportunities.[19]
10	Innovative public sector	This lever may be described as increasing STEM skills and literacy across all levels of government. Most pivotally the UK Government has recognised the need to nurture a culture within the public sector that supports and rewards innovative approaches. One of the most ambitious action plans includes increasing the number of STEM graduates in the UK Civil Service Fast Stream to 50 per cent.[20]

Notes: [1] UK Government (2023) Department for Science, Innovation and Technology, 'The UK Science and Technology Framework', at 7, available at https://assets.publishing.service.gov.uk/media/6405955ed3bf7f25f5948f99/uk-science-technology-framework.pdf. [2] Ibid, at 9. [3] UK Government (2022) 'Levelling Up the United Kingdom'. This 332-page document has important material for semiconductor entrepreneurs in the context of freeports and enterprise zones. [4] Ibid, at 10. [5] UKRI, Engineering and Physical Sciences Research Council (2024), 'A Community Forum with our Executive Chair', seminar, 25 April 2024. [6] As part of its steps to improve understanding of the Technology ↔ Market ↔ Implementation interaction, UKRI has published 'Commercialising your research with UKRI'. This summary aims to help researchers and businesses quickly absorb how UKRI can support them in research commercialisation. See UKRI (2024) 'Commercialising Your Research with UKRI', available at www.ukri.org/publications/commercialising-your-research-with-ukri/. [7] UK

Government (2024) 'Lifelong Learning Entitlement overview', 22 March 2024. [8] See www.gov.uk/global-talent. [9] See www.gov.uk/skilled-worker-visa. [10] UK Government (2023) Department for Science, Innovation and Technology, 'The UK Science and Technology Framework', at 12. [11] Ibid, at 13. [12] The Procurement Act 2023 entered into force in October 2024. [13] UK Government (2023) Department for Science, Innovation and Technology, 'The UK Science and Technology Framework', at 14. [14] Chatham House (2024) 'The future of South Africa's foreign policy', discussion, 16 July 2024. [15] Other ambitious countries to assess partnering with include Estonia, Latvia, and Malaysia. [16] UK Government (2022) 'Independent Review of the Future of Compute', 13 June 2022. [17] Ibid, section 6.1, recommendation 5. [18] Ibid, section 6.1, recommendation 7(b). [19] UK Government (2023) 'Response to Professor Dame Angela McLean's Pro-Innovation Regulation of Technologies Review Cross Cutting', section 16, at 11. [20] UK Government (2023) Department for Science, Innovation and Technology, 'The UK Science and Technology Framework', at 14.

Source: UK Government (2023) Department for Science, Innovation and Technology, 'The UK Science and Technology Framework', at 6, available at https://assets.publishing.service.gov.uk/media/6405955ed3bf7f25f5948f99/uk-science-technology-framework.pdf

Beyond these ten levers, Ottoline remarked there was a positive role for tax revenues to be channelled into R&D. Specifically, she said 'I would argue very strongly that public investment in research innovation is another critical way in which you can invest tax spend much more wisely to drive the three corners up, rather than suck things down'.[5]

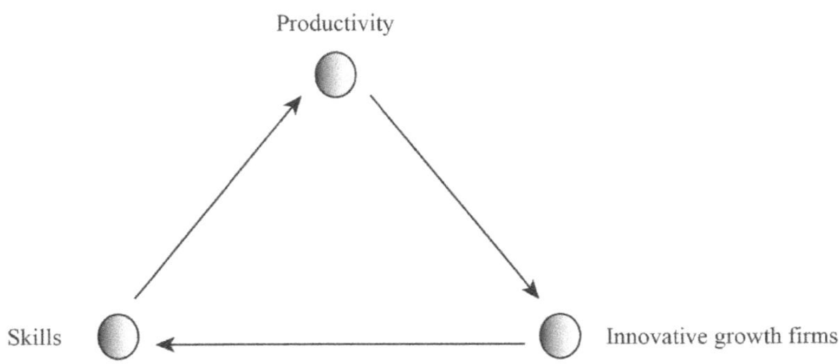

Source: © Iain Sheridan (2025)

Figure 12.2 Three corners model

12.2 Importance of mapping

Chapter 3 provided a survey of major semiconductor clusters throughout the UK. The risk for governmental policy makers is having excellent mapping of several subsector revenue areas, but weaker analysis and ground truths on other subsectors. For example, knowing everything about what exists or is researched in South Wales but less so for Northeast England and Scotland which have indisputably harsher winter climates and longer distances from London. As mentioned in the Chapter 1 introduction, experts who provided evidence to the House of Commons select committee on semiconductors pointed out that a full picture of the supply chain allows for a quality strengths, weaknesses, opportunities and threats (SWOT) analysis.[6]

---

5 Ibid.

6 UK House of Commons (2022) *The Semiconductor Industry in the UK*, Fifth Report of Session 2022–23, HC 291, at 27.

12.3 Software niches

The challenges of hardware are often interlinked with the challenges of software. For example, graphics processing unit (GPU) architectures require different tools, such as Compute Unified Device Architecture (CUDA), open computing language (OpenCL) and the high level programming model called SYCL. In the current global artificial intelligence (AI) hardware competition, the tools used play a significant role. There is an opportunity for the UK, with its mature programming sub-sector, combined with decades of experience in diverse sectors, including automative, defence and financial services.[7]

To give an example of how important software development can be for GPU development, since the acquisition of DeepMind by Google in 2014 for the bargain sum of £400 million, the second largest acquisition has been AMD's purchasing of Finnish start-up Silo AI for $665 million in 2024.[8] Silo AI's expertise is open-source AI models. AMD's strategy is to compete with Nvidia's CUDA software by offering open-source alternatives. Ultimately, AMD in collaboration Google, Meta and Microsoft, is developing OpenAI software called Triton, that will allow code to run on a wide range of semiconductors.[9]

12.4 Building the skills pipeline

During the 1990s, what really caught the imagination about Estonia was the fact that its government implemented an effective industrial policy to make technology a national priority. Called Project 'Tiger Leap' this policy

---

7 For financial services sector readers specifically interested in asset manager, bank, or Fintech firm AI risks, see Sheridan, I. (2022) *Financial Regulation and Technology*, Cheltenham, UK and Northampton, MA, USA: Edward Elgar Publishing.

8 Since the purchase of Deep Mind, the largest acquisition has been Nvidia's purchase of Run:ai for $700 million, which was approved at the end of 2024. Run:ai provides management software that speeds up GPU initiatives by pooling available resources. See Silicon Republic (2025) 'Nvidia to make Run:ai open source following acquisition', 2 January 2025.

9 *Financial Times* (2024) 'AMD to buy Finnish start-up Silo AI for $665 million in drive to compete with Nvidia', 10 July 2024.

included access to the Internet for all primary schools. Decades later this policy has certainly played a positive role in the now technology-dynamic Estonian economy. From primary school, Estonian pupils become familiar with computers, programming and the resources of the Internet.

For the UK to maximise its semiconductor sector potential it seems that the return on investment (ROI) on electronics courses and kits provided to secondary schools would, in the long term, be astonishingly positive. An example of a company providing the established courses and hands-on kits purchased by schools and universities across Europe is VUB Photonics. Available online, this firm provides 33 photonics workshops for three different target groups: 10–14-year-olds, 15–18-year-olds and 18-plus-year-olds.[10] If such initiatives were combined with encouraging girls to become interested in electronics then the growth rate might be beyond what anyone can envisage.[11]

12.5 Increasing the number of engineers

A UK innovation report published by Cambridge University and produced by its Industrial Innovation Policy group did not specifically analyse the semiconductor sector, but it did provide many thought-provoking comparisons with Germany, South Korea and the US.[12]

In the year 2018, 44.2 per cent of UK total graduates studied STEM disciplines.[13] This compared favourably with the US (36.8 per cent). However, the total number of engineering, manufacturing and construction grad-

---

[10] https://www.b-photonics.eu/en/photonics-explorer.

[11] A promising initiative is the UK Electronic Skills Foundation (UKESF) 'Girls into Electronics' initiative developed by the UK Electronics Skills Foundation. The UKESF is a charity. Its committed leaders include the founder Neil Dickins, and its CEO Stewart Tomlinson. See https://www.ukesf.org/what-we-do/girls-into-electronics/.

[12] Cambridge Industrial Innovation Policy (CIIP) (2021), *The UK Innovation Report 2021*, 'Introduction and Overview', available at www.ciip.group.cam.ac.uk/innovation/introduction-and-overview/.

[13] In the Cambridge Industrial Innovation Policy report STEM was defined to include: medicine and dentistry, subjects associated with medicine, biological sciences, veterinary science, agriculture and related subjects, physical sciences,

uates was relatively low at 8.4 per cent. Contrast this with Germany (23.4 per cent) and Korea (20.7 per cent).[14]

The existing total numbers of UK engineering graduates also requires further dilution, because of the high numbers of foreign students taking undergraduate engineering courses. While some of these foreign students will stay permanently in the UK, many will return to their home country or emigrate to a third country. Part of the solution is to support the financing of engineering degrees so that more UK residents can choose this path. Another financially supportive aspect is to increase the total number of undergraduate sandwich courses.

There is also value in a far higher number of firms inviting graduates to gain industry experience for a couple of months. The elephant in the room is that industrial policy could logically pay for half of the placement costs, including contributing to paying the internee a market level salary for the duration of the placement. An interview with a talented British engineer based in the northwest of England led me to this conclusion. By way of brief background, Alex Skelton is an engineering graduate with both hardware and programming experience. His career to date includes working for Dyson near Bristol, Siemens in Manchester, and Infineon in Graz. Infineon had tasked Skelton with completing sensor projects for the automotive sector.

First, I asked him 'what is a successful work environment for graduate engineers?' He was quick to focus in on culture. Skelton pointed to the Germanic 100 per cent trusting performance-based management style. If an engineer can do their job they are most effective and innovative when left alone to get on with it.

Second, he specifically noted that Infineon invested in regular intakes of placement students from universities. The combination of engineering graduates with semiconductor masters degrees and industry experience is accelerating the number of engineers into the Central and Eastern European semiconductor workforce.

---

mathematics, computer science, engineering and technology, architecture, building and planning. CIIP (2021) at 62.

14 Ibid, at 63.

The potential to increase the number of engineers is also facilitated by entrepreneurial immigration initiatives such as the Global Talent visa.[15] This visa provides maximum flexibility for international technical talent, including not only hardware engineers and individuals with Chief Technology Officer (CTO) or Vice President (VP) engineering experience, but also founders to work in the UK for up to five years. No job offer is required and, once granted, the individual can change firms or start their own venture.[16]

Successful applicants can also bring their families. There are two categories of Global Talent visa applicants, namely Exceptional Promise and Exceptional Talent.[17] The UK firm Tech Nation is an endorsing body of the UK Home Office and plays a supportive role in the maximising the chances of an applicant succeeding.[18]

Once settled in the UK, the vital issue is what will make exceptional talents choose to stay? Based on many benchmarks, the UK's soft power attributes, including art, film, and music, consistently maintain global appeal across age generations. Additionally, spectator sports opportunities, especially English Premier League teams and international cricket matches are unique attractions. Astonishingly for a small island, there are also more than 1,300 weekly park runs, 400 climbing walls, 15 national parks, and 450 wild swimming sites.

---

15 See www.gov.uk/global-talent.

16 For readers seeking legal advice on detailed immigration rules, the leading law firm Fragomen is fully aware that the semiconductor sector's skill shortage requires balancing grassroots development with international talent immigration. For example, Charlotte Wills, a partner in its London office has contributed the following short article: Wills, C. 'The UK's Semiconductor Moment: Why Immigration Policy Must Keep Up', 25 March 2024, available at www.fragomen.com/insights/the-uks-semiconductor-moment-why-immigration-policy-must-keep-up.html.

17 Many successful applicants under the Exceptional Talent category have patents.

18 See https://technation.io/global-talent-visa/.

12.6 Familiarising people with semiconductor fabrication

Readers who have worked in a fab, or currently do so, are aware that there is so often a gap between what people think about semiconductor manufacturing and the reality. In the context of clean rooms that has an extra challenge because of wearing protective clothing. Astronauts, fighter pilots and surgeons all wear protective clothing, but I can never remember that being mentioned as an inconvenience. Part of the solution lies in school and high school familiarisation visits to semiconductor manufacturing units. It is likely that once an individual understands what manufacturing semiconductors entails, bias will be significantly reduced.[19]

12.7 Increasing holistic understanding and systems thinking

It is notable that Siemens has become an important catalyst for creating more STEM talent with systems thinking awareness in the context of an increasingly data-driven workplace.[20] Siemens provides a teaching programme 'Connected Curriculum' in collaboration with at least five UK universities.[21] Their platform combines advanced industrial tools, data and analytical approaches across apprenticeship, undergraduate and master's level courses.

Facilitating technical understanding can be largely university based with some components delivered online. However, a practical appreciation

---

[19] The Institute for Manufacturing (IfM) has produced a useful two-minute animation entitled 'Perceptions of Manufacturing' that could form part of any pre-familiarisation briefing. Available at www.ifm.eng.cam.ac.uk/news/tackling-manufacturings-image-problem-through-policy/. The firm Pragmatic also provides an impressionable two-minute video introducing its FlexIC foundry that produces 200mm or 300mm wafers. Available at www.pragmaticsemi.com/foundry.

[20] Siemens (2019) 'Siemens launches Industry 4.0 curriculum for universities', 19 June 2019, available at https://news.siemens.co.uk/news/siemens-launches-industry-4-0-curriculum-for-universities.

[21] Currently, the collaborating universities include the universities of Liverpool John Moores, Manchester Metropolitan, Middlesex, Newcastle and Sheffield.

of how all elements of the sector interact requires face to face communication. In my view, a recurring pattern of how innovation is practically achieved, is liquid networks. By which is meant there is a proven pattern of innovation occurring at informal researcher gatherings. As Figure 12.3 proposes, a dynamic liquid network for the semiconductor sector could also include capital raising experts and entrepreneurs able to crystallise how best to turn R&D into a product that buyers want.[22]

12.8 Enterprise zones

It is evident from the incredible growth of China in the 1990s and 2000s that enterprise zones were often highly effective catalysts. They produced collaborative and hiring synergies between firms given these geographical areas encouraged businesses to be clustered together. Semiconductor manufacturing also benefited from attractive tax benefits.

With its seeds in the previous UK Government's levelling up white paper, enterprise zones have been promoted as ways to grow a more balanced share of industry across England, Wales, Northern Ireland and Scotland. For the semiconductor sector, competitive advantages could flow from enterprise zones that are in or near already established clusters. For example, Cardiff, Glasgow, or Newcastle.

Torsten Bell is the former CEO of the think tank Resolution Foundation. Bell published a thoughtful book that reflects on the UK's decades of economic decline. He prescribes long-term investment across a range of issues.[23] Bell's key statistical analysis is that average wages in 2023 were below 2008 levels.[24] This contrasts with Americans in their early thirties who currently have 21 per cent higher wages compared with 2007. In the UK that specific age group's income decreased by 1 per cent.

In my view, the fact that semiconductor wages are double the average wage presents a strong case for increased investment in the sector. Especially so in the established clusters. Coincidentally, in July 2024 Bell

---

[22] Johnson, S. (2011) *Where Good Ideas Come From – The Seven Patterns of Innovation*, Penguin, Chapter 2, at 61.

[23] Bell, T. (2024) *Great Britain? How We Get Our Future Back*, The Bodley Head.

[24] This wage comparison factors in inflation.

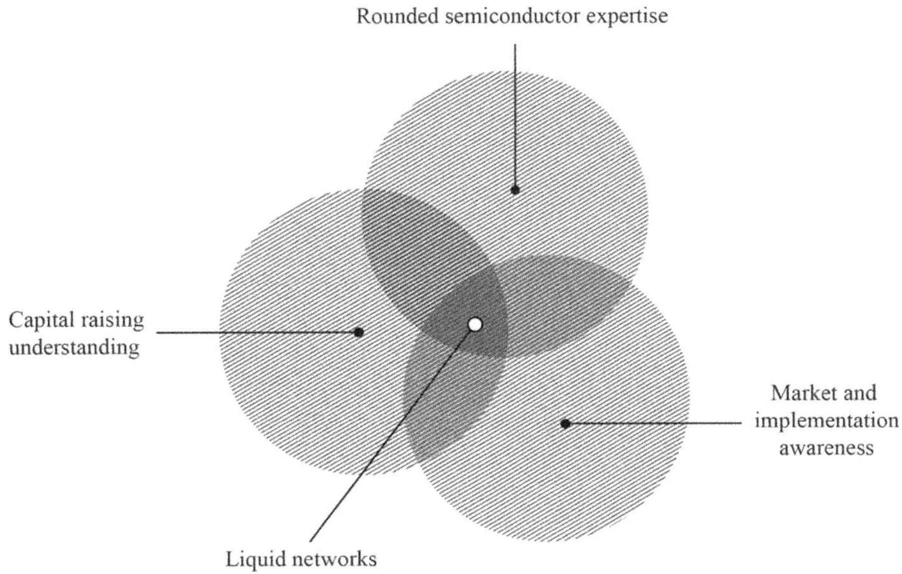

Source: © Iain Sheridan (2025)

Figure 12.3 *Liquid networks*

became the MP for Swansea West, a constituency that forms part of the important South Wales cluster, arguably the jewel in the UK's long-term semiconductor strategy crown. Since January 2025 he is also the UK's pension minister.

There is currently a Labour Government in power. However, the Conservative Party has invested in understanding enterprise zones and would have some valuable insights to contribute. There would be logic in returning to 'Butskellism'.[25] By which is meant a consensus-style working relationship between the Labour Government and Conservative Party; pooling knowledge, collaborating across social classes and bringing MPs together on semiconductor industrial policy issues.

At the beginning of 2025, Vince Cable, former UK Minister for Business, directly put it this way:

> British politics is adversarial, tribal and inimical to long-term business decision making. Industrial strategy won't work if it becomes a political football. Labour [the Labour Government] can only make a success of it if it treats it as a practical, non-partisan initiative, not a performative exercise.[26]

12.9 Heterogeneous integration

At the annual UK semiconductor conference hosted by Sheffield University, the veteran semiconductor leader Sean Redmond provided an excellent presentation on where the semiconductor sector is going. Perhaps the most memorable slide was the one entitled the four horsemen of the apocalypse. Redmond was referring to the challenges of scaling from the perspectives of central processing unit (CPU) single core performance, drum density roll-off, transistor power, and CP density roll-off.[27]

---

[25] Butskellism refers to the combination of R.A. Butler (Conservative) and Hugh Gaitskell (Labour), the successive Chancellors of the Exchequer.

[26] *Financial Times* (2025) 'Industrial policy must be practical not performative – New structures and pronouncements mean little unless business takes them seriously – there is no appetite for talking shops', 2 January 2025.

[27] Redmond, S. (2023) 'EGG and CHIPS', Presentation, UK Semiconductor Conference, 14 July 2023.

One of the solutions to the challenge of the four horsemen lies in 3D chiplets, the heterogeneous integration of logic and memory functions. The UK has an incredible track record in being technically innovative so it is realistic for its universities and subsequent spin-outs to be at the forefront of this advance. But so will many other leading economies.

As just one example, a former Japanese foreign minister speaking at Chatham House had 20 minutes to summarise Japanese ambitions mixed with diplomatic intent. One of the main points he raised on technology was that the Japanese planned for more than Moore. Part of the Japanese solution is a need to make 3D semiconductors.[28] The 3D semiconductor race will be a competitive one. UK Government funding support will prove to be a valuable supporting element.

12.10 Packaging

The UK has established firms carrying out the packaging element of the manufacturing process of semiconductors. In the past there was a trend for large volumes of packaging to be completed in Asia. However, the pandemic has highlighted the flaw in adopting a non-diversified strategy. There is a growing demand for packaging in Europe. A recent example is the funding by UK Research and Innovation (UKRI) of exploratory research into the best strategies for packaging in heterogeneous integration. Led by BAE Systems, the research team is made up of experts from established UK firms and Southampton University.

In 2024, I also had the opportunity to attend an event that brought together firms, government departments and universities to discuss recurring issues that would further stimulate 3D chiplet growth. It was agreed, among other things, that government support to make electronic design automation (EDA) software licensing more accessible and long-term government investment, would both be effective initiatives.[29] The demand is there – it just needs to be matched with vision.

---

[28] Chatham House (2023) Hayashi Yoshimasa, Japan Foreign Minister, Japanese-UK relations, 21 June 2023.

[29] iMAPS UK (2024) 'Heterogeneous Integration – Silicon and Glass Interposer Workshop', Gaydon, Warwickshire, 27 November 2024.

As a memorable example of what can be achieved, Ian Burnett, an industry veteran from Inseto UK, presented on how future 3D chiplets would make cardiac pacemakers much thinner and therefore far less visible to the human eye. Further, benefits would include lower production costs, more flexible production processes and the lack of need for lithographic processes.[30]

12.11 Lesson from the Newport Wafer Fab

National security law, as covered in Chapter 10, is a vital framework for ensuring enemy states and other actors do not weaken the UK's sovereignty. That significant challenge needs to be balanced with a reputation for expediting FDI that can choose to go somewhere else.

Reputational damage to UK plc was caused by the UK Government's protracted investigations in the case of Newport Wafer Fab. The time between when the acquisition was announced to the final Department for Business, Energy and Industrial Strategy (BEIS) notice order prohibition amounted to 15 months.[31] Consequently, there were in the region of 100 redundancies at the Newport Wafer Fab. Long-term damage included a lack of certainty over the future of the Newport Wafer Fab, which certainly put off US semiconductor firms and other foreign order buyers.

A crucial procedural factor to manage in all future cases is when components have a dual use. In all such instances it is realistic to expect a lengthier vetting process. If the applicant acquirer of an asset or entity is permitted to proceed to make, own or research dual-use components, the most sensible option or undertaking is for the UK Government to require ongoing independent supervision. Lawyers are well suited to such supervisory roles.

---

[30] Burnett, I. (2024) '3D Integration of ICs for next generation applications', presentation, 27 November 2024.

[31] In February 2023, BEIS was superseded by the Department for Business and Trade (DBT).

12.12 The impediment of balkanization

Dame Ottoline Leyser, CEO of UKRI, has highlighted that in her experience the main weakness in the UK is a balkanisation between research and investment. She encapsulated the issue in this way:

> people go to university and never leave. If they do leave, they go to a business and stay in that business... We need much more movement of people between the academic, business, policy, and investor sectors. If we had a proper churn of people, the whole thing would be better connected. Everybody would feel more confident and know more people ... They would know people to pick up the phone to and say what do you think about this? That is a key opportunity for the UK.[32]

Part of the solution is to understand that the UK, in educating its workforce, at some point expanded universities with insufficient focus on how degree courses can increase economic productivity. If you go to Boston and visit the Massachusetts Institute of Technology (MIT) what you absorb is, in effect, an elite polytechnic. By which is meant it is an extremely solvent higher education institute that sits within industry to serve industry. Imperial College London has followed suit. The raison d'etre of MIT is technology for industry. Many engineering professors sitting inside MIT have professional networks that extend across pure research, market research, start-up scaling, and, ultimately, capital markets listing.

12.13 Societal problem solving

The strategic frameworks in Chapter 4, presented three models, namely real innovation, value-based strategy and risk, all backed up with supporting evidence. Currently, business need only be lawful not moral. Yet the trend of environmental, social and governance (ESG) points to societies around the world expecting more from firms, including moral responsibility. Professor Colin Mayer of Oxford University emphasises that all firms should be committed to problem solving in the context of societies,

---

[32] The Resolution Foundation (2023) 'Inventing a better Britain: how does R&D fit into a new UK economic strategy?', Seminar, 15 November 2023.

solving problems concerning people and planet. That all profits should derive from producing solutions not problems.[33]

Mayer's most recent book, built on over three decades of analysing firms, offers a moral filter for capitalism extending well beyond sustainability. Like a polarising sheet of film, it blocks out business decisions that create problems – only the light of problem-solving actions passes through the filter. As Mayer succinctly puts it, each company should be expected:

> to identify where its activities as a producer, employer, purchaser, neighbour, or consumer of public goods and ecosystem services are having a detrimental effect on the interests and well-being of others. It must then be determined how it can best mitigate, remedy, rectify, or compensate for the detriments it is causing.[34]

Only a few years ago in private equity and venture capital (VC) circles there was an entrenched view that, subject to compliance with law and regulation, making profit gave rise to no obligation to stakeholders beyond shareholders. Climate change and general sustainability issues such as the use of plastic are acting as the most prominent catalysts to change even the most ruthless of business cultures.

Societal problem solving is a renewed argument in the sense that Adam Smith's primary influence on capitalism has been *The Wealth of Nations* (1776).[35] However, his first work, *The Theory of Moral Sentiments* (1759), has been ignored. *The Wealth of Nations* focused on self-interest.[36] In contrast, *The Theory of Moral Sentiments* emphasised that societal interests have a higher priority compared with individual private ones. In short, there is a renewed argument for firms, including semiconductor product and service providers, to maximise profits responsibly as a moral obligation to society.

---

33 Mayer, C. (2024) *Capitalism and Crises – How To Fix Them*, Oxford University Press, at xiii.

34 Ibid, at 107.

35 Smith, A. (1776) *An Inquiry into the Nature and Causes of the Wealth of Nations*, University of Chicago Press.

36 Smith, A. (1759) *The Theory of Moral Sentiments*, Cambridge University Press.

12.14 Pension fund investment in semiconductors

At a UK semiconductor strategy evening hosted by the Foundation for Science and Technology, many if not all the salient issues to make the UK semiconductor sector successful were discussed publicly in front of a nucleus of the industry's leaders. In the context of long-term investment, it was memorable that several of these leaders expressed the view that the UK was not tuned into long-term investment. The contrast was 'Silicon Valley vision' versus the more conservative British way of worrying about the bottom line. This dichotomy could be encapsulated as 'US vision versus UK positive cash flow'. Dr Jalal Bagherli, former CEO of Dialog Semiconductor and current co-chair of the UK Government's Semiconductor Advisory Board incisively said, 'UK pension funds would bring massive injection of patient capital'.[37]

In my view, this was a light bulb moment. Demographic projections point towards smaller families. There is also the challenge of turning the UK into a 'friends and family' start-up funding culture. Altering pensions law to make semiconductors an accessible investment is a brilliant possibility.

Dr Hermann Hauser, Co-Founder of Amadeus Capital Partners, and co-founder of Acorn the precursor to ARM, has pointed out that, in 2000, UK pension funds used to fund 39 per cent of the London Stock Exchange, but that has plummeted to only 4 per cent. He has observed that UK pension funds are too conservative, choosing government bonds instead. Hauser concludes 'getting pension funds to invest in the UK economy, and changing legislation so they can take these risks, is crucial'.[38]

Future regulation that permits defined contribution (DC) funds to invest in private businesses that need long-term capital, is an obvious UK Government policy improvement. Yet there are logistical challenges, not least that many DC schemes have insufficient expertise and resources to efficiently invest in private assets. Further, money redirected to private assets will deplete both listed equities and government money from

---

[37] Foundation for Science and Technology (2023) 'The UK Semiconductor Strategy', 24 May 2023.

[38] Founders Forum Group et al (2024) *Beyond Returns Report*, at 25.

bonds. As head of strategic research at Schroders, Duncan Lamont, put it 'you can't whack all the moles at once'.[39]

Encouragingly, the Capital Markets Industry Task Force (CMIT), a monthly gathering of top executives from across the financial services sector, is advocating for pension system reform to allow an increase in pension fund allocation to unlisted assets. That would be a significant benefit for semiconductor start-ups. Only established in 2022, CMIT has been a positive influence focusing on the need for UK capital markets to be more competitive.

Influencing an accelerated reform of pension funds' allocation to unlisted assets could be an important catalyst in not only providing more VC funds for start-ups to reduce UK firms moving to the US, but also in creating greater citizen-level awareness of the relevance of capital markets to the UK's collective wealth.

However, an obvious weakness of CMIT is that it attempts to solve too many issues, with the risk of solving none of them, even on a multi-year basis. One member of CMIT has even commented that they are 'frustrated that we [CMIT] still don't know what we're all aiming at and what we think the problem is that we're trying to solve'.[40] In my judgement, there is a need for CMIT to focus on just two issues at once and effect change as quickly as possible. When solution to those two issues are successfully implemented, CMIT is then better placed to concentrate on another two new issues, and so forth.[41]

There is also the reality that many high-net-worth individuals are logically attracted to the stable revenue streams achieved from commercial and residential property portfolios. Taxation changes that encourage these individuals to be more entrepreneurial and invest in private long-term capital for semiconductor firms would be beneficial.

---

[39] *Financial Times* (2023) 'Stop blaming everything on pension funds!', 24 March 2024.

[40] *Financial Times* (2024) 'The club of City executives plotting a revival of the UK's capital markets – CMIT is pushing for reform in a bid to end malaise engulfing London market', 24 June 2024.

[41] There would also be value in CMIT expanding to have at least two semiconductor entrepreneurs, for example one from silicon and one from photonics.

When looking at the UK from the outside, some foreign leaders have remarked that the British landlord culture borders on 'feudal', because English law permits wealthy people to reduce the supply of residential properties for sale to individuals, and earn rents based on minimal labour, and low risk. Many landlords are getting richer, and young people are less able or unable to save for a deposit because a high percentage of their net income is spent on rent. Does it really need to be like this? Landlords will always seek to rationalise their choices, but English law currently incentivises them to act against their own younger citizens.

Ironically, a British culture that values investors committed to entrepreneurs sounds more innovative and noble – more British. Such a shift could reward high-net-worth individuals with tax incentives to invest in start-ups, including semiconductor firms, which has an obvious win-win benefit. English law could be reformed to incentivise the rich to act in the interests of their own younger citizens. In so doing, communities throughout the UK would be more harmonious, with no doubt increased productivity.

12.15 The UK National Centre for Semiconductors

The establishment in May 2024 of a UK Semiconductor Institute to support the UK semiconductor sector is encouraging. If there was a common denominator across leading figures in the semiconductor sector, it was their call for such a UK national coordinating centre. To name just two influential experts, the photonics pioneer, Sir David Payne of Southampton University and Professor Rachel Oliver Director of the Cambridge Centre for Gallium Nitride.

In late 2024, I met Charles Sturman, CEO of TechWorks. My first question to him was 'how can coordination across multiple expert semiconductor manufacturing and packaging trade associations be maximised?' He reflected that 'In the UK we are good at arguing amongst ourselves, with too many people in a small boat, fighting over the one oar. What we need to do is work together to build a bigger vision for the country and that's what TechWorks is aiming to do'.

In my view, such a situation needs a rapid change in mindset if the UK is to maximise the sum of its parts. Other countries are better at national level coordination of their semiconductor sector. The UK needs to learn from other economies. The US leads in fabless chip and systems companies, Europe in integrated device manufacturers (IDMs). The list of countries would also include Belgium given the incredible success and ongoing importance of IMEC.

The second question put to Sturman was 'what do you think is the best location for the UK National Centre for Semiconductors?' Sturman did not offer a best location but he indicated that prioritisation should be on the right non-partisan remit and with the right governance structure. Crucially, the remit must include creation and management of supporting infrastructure and distribution of funding around the UK.

12.16 The US National Semiconductor Technology Center

Given the significantly greater budget of the US Government, its newly formed National Semiconductor Technology Center (NSTC) will be a source of ideas and initiatives to avoid money wasted in the UK on reinventing the wheel. The goal of the NSTC is similar to that of the UK National Centre for Semiconductors; to act as a collaborative platform for semiconductor firms, entrepreneurs, government agencies, investors, national laboratories, customers, suppliers, educational institutions and workforce representatives.[42]

The US Department of Commerce has committed to investing $250 million in the NSTC's Workforce Center of Excellence (WCoE) over ten years. Additionally, the NSTC has already allocated $11 million in awards across more than a dozen states through the NSTC Workforce Partner Alliance (WFPA) programme to further support workforce development initiatives. For example, an award to Texas A&M University means that that institution can implement its WAVE-CHIP project which aims to equip more than 7500 individuals in the semiconductor sector with hardware verification skills. Further, this project's impact will extend far

[42] NSTC (2024) 'The National Semiconductor Technology Center, The vision for 2024', available at www.nist.gov/system/files/documents/2024/05/24/NSTC%20Roadmap_FINAL.pdf.

beyond its immediate participants by training 109 community college and university-level instructors. Consequently, this will ensure a diverse long-term supply of verification engineers.[43]

12.17 Building a mental map of the landscape

Semiconductors are an established technology developed with increasing power over more than six decades. In Tony Blair's recent book on leadership, the former prime minister mentions that the explosive interest in generative AI means for the government 'not just a step change in understanding but a preparedness to master and harness what AI can do'.[44] Yet the greater strategic priority is to be part of the design and manufacturing of semiconductors that power not only AI but also all future electronic devices. In my view, politicians and civil servants forget that at our collective peril. It is the compass pointing towards long-term forward-thinking strategies as implemented in South Korea and Taiwan.

Leadership from politicians and civil servants requires a commitment to understanding the semiconductor sector, something that requires dedicated learning over many months. The right level of strategic understanding, combined with the self-discipline required to keep up to date with the sector, may be the most important leadership action by politicians and government officials.

It is memorable that one of the UK's dedicated leadership experts has observed 'learning is one of the defining habits of leadership, and even the most seasoned leaders should continue to draw insight from new experiences, challenge themselves with new perspectives, and ask themselves

---

[43] NIST (2024) 'Biden-Harris Administration Launches NSTC Workforce Center of Excellence with Expected $250 Million Investment – Includes an anticipated $11.5 million for the first workforce development awardees to address critical U.S. job and skill gaps across semiconductor research, design, manufacturing, and production. CHIPS for America', Press Release, 25 September 2024.

[44] Blair, T. (2024) *On Leadership – Lessons for the 21st Century*, Hutchinson, at 162.

how they should adapt to changes to context'.[45] In the second quarter of the twenty-first century the context is semiconductors.

12.18 Maintaining a long-term heading

Government funding of semiconductors requires billions not millions of pounds. It remains to be seen if the current generation of political leaders are prepared to make brave, long-term decisions that could release large sums to channel into the sector. Making semiconductors the first priority makes 100 per cent sense, given it is the enabler, the common denominator of all other technologies, especially AI, automotive, aviation, defence, health, renewables, space and telecommunications. If this heading is maintained for 10 to 15 years, we'll start to see a significant change in the UK economy.

It seems, for political leaders and civil servants, there are three challenges. First, relying on semiconductor sector experts to clarify the areas for growth and explain the global supply chain. As mentioned, this requires initial and ongoing learning of the landscape. Second, communicating to the electorate the opportunities of direct employment growth, indirect employment growth, and higher salaries.[46] Third, implementing short-, medium- and long-term funding.

12.19 Work culture change as a catalyst for growth

While work culture cannot be quickly altered, there are additional challenges that cannot necessarily be solved by the government taking the lead. First, in Chapter 9 Intellectual property law, there was passing

---

[45] Sharp, L. (2022) *The Habit of Excellence – Why British Army Leadership Works*, Penguin, at 244.

[46] Evidentially, that communication can be backed up by the CS Connected annual report on the South Wales cluster. In its latest annual report, direct and indirect jobs supported in Wales is expected to exceed 4,000 by 2025. Further, in 2023 average salaries in the cluster were in the region of £61,000, and with a range of £46,700 to £74,800. Source: Cardiff University and Welsh Economy Research Unit (2024) *CS Connected Annual Report: Compound Semiconductor Cluster in South Wales*, Draft, at 26.

reference to many employers dampening the motivation of employees with employment contracts that essentially close off worker opportunities to get involved with other out-of-office innovative projects. If the UK is to maximise its creative culture, employers should tolerate second jobs or involvement in external pilot projects that might lead to a new venture. Today's employee could be tomorrow's client or joint venture partner.

Second, British work culture needs to promptly shift to viewing entrepreneurial failure as an attribute. Andrew McAfee of MIT has observed that when comparing Europe with Northern California, Europeans seem to retain some stigma from being part of an unsuccessful start-up. In contrast, start-up failure was an experience of the great majority of McAfee's Northern California friends.[47] Early career entrepreneurs grow by learning from mistakes. In contrast, many corporate ladders are climbed with a risk aversion mindset.

What solutions might accelerate this change in attitude? In the future, all firms with more than 20 employees could be encouraged to implement start-up returnee policies that offer any former employee whose start-up has failed an automatic interview for a new role. In the past, I recall that the Swedish technology firm Ericsson adopted such an attitude.

12.20 Ambition, eating bitterness and government support

A practitioner book follows a predictable structure so that its utility as a source of professional reference is maintained. There are logical points of coverage for law, tax and strategic frameworks, so that potential advantages can be explored. This book focuses on rules and strategies that matter to semiconductor firms, so philosophy is, at first glance, a misplaced addition.

There is one philosophical aspect, based on my experience dealing with Chinese and Korean business professionals that merits highlighting. The

[47] *Financial Times* (2024) 'European Competitiveness and How Not to Fix It – The Draghi Report Gets a Lot Right and the Main Thing Wrong', 4 December 2024.

use of the phrase 'eating bitterness' which derives from these four Chinese characters:

吃苦耐劳

The full phrase can be translated as 'to eat bitterness and endure hard work'. By which is meant to persevere through hardships because challenging experiences make any individual better equipped to continually face other challenges. Ambition is sustained by a tolerance to endure.[48] It is interesting that Jason Huang of Nvidia has emphasised how much he values the experience of bitterness in his career. A point mentioned by Stan Boland when presenting to UK semiconductor start-ups in the context of his four successfully acquired scale-up firms.[49]

Creating and sustaining competitive advantage is also about ambition. Technical competence, the discipline to tolerate routine tasks and resilience to bounce back from setbacks in innovation are omnipotent. If you think this is a dated view of Chinese people, and East Asians generally, a former TSMC manager and semiconductor expert recently made the following comment:

> Taiwan and South Korea are the two places that have the perfect work culture for developing semiconductor manufacturing...You need to have this group of trained professionals with solid engineering training and you need them to be willing to follow orders and willing to work overtime to get things right.[50]

Contractual certainty, allowing for the unforeseen, protecting intellectual property (IP) and training workforces are all important, but each is eclipsed by ambition. Competition driven by ambition can be a significant determinant of survival, from the established multinational to the start-up. Ultimately it is the ability to endure that has kept US, Asian and European semiconductor leaders at the cutting-edge. A commitment to do more, a willingness to suffer the vicissitudes of market cycles, and win. A habit, a hard-working mindset and a spirit of ambition.

---

[48] Similarly, in Korean culture people communicate to each other that hardship is good.

[49] Boland, S. (2024) 'Building a successful scale-up', Presentation at ChipStart UK Conference, 13 June 2024.

[50] Li, L. and C. Ting-Fang (2024) '"Confucian culture" gives Asia edge in chipmaking, former TSMC exec says', *Nikkei Asia*, 28 May 2024.

A strategy for growth across the whole UK semiconductor sector includes a balanced government semiconductor industrial policy as a core ingredient. As James Ashton puts it:

> for a country that has got by for decades with no semiconductors strategy to speak of, mixing just enough cash, decades of experience, and the exuberance of youth is the recipe to begin with... But ministers might lay the groundwork with training and skills...they [ministers] could foster more understanding investors offering patient capital when small firms need space and time to scale up.[51]

When the UK Government published its intention to provide £1 billion over the next decade to the semiconductor sector, the view expressed by Amelia Armour, partner at Amadeus Capital Partners and current member of the UK Semiconductor Advisory Panel, was that the plan lacked ambition.[52] Many semiconductor experts throughout the UK from many different specialisms would be inclined to agree with that assessment. It would be unrealistic for the UK to match the €43 billion investment made by the EU to support its Chips Act until 2030.[53] Yet that figure can stimulate more 'what if' assessments on a viable British investment level.

12.21 Quantum computing investment

It is notable that £2.5 billion of UK Government funding has been committed to quantum computing R&D for the period 2024–32.[54] There is the risk of potentially flawed government thinking about funding for quantum computing or semiconductors. It is not an A or B assessment.

---

[51] Ashton, J. (2023) *The Everything Blueprint – The Microchip Design That Changed the World*, Hodder & Stoughton, at 391.

[52] *Financial Times* (2023) 'UK government unveils long-awaited £1bn semiconductor strategy', 19 May 2023, available at www.ft.com/content/757cfa86-adeb-4d8e-ad71-034c9a4d2f7d.

[53] European Commission (2023) European Chips Act, available at https://commission.europa.eu/strategy-and-policy/priorities-2019-2024/europe-fit-digital-age/european-chips-act_en.

[54] UK Government, Department for Science, Innovation & Technology (2023) 'National Quantum Strategy', at 12. This quantum computing budget builds on an existing ten-year investment made in 2014.

While quantum computing holds huge promise, current investment is speculative given there is not practical proof-of-concept. By which is meant that, to date, because of noise and error correction challenges, there has been no quantum computer that has come close to being a practical, reliable product. Further, even with proof-of-concept accessible quantum computing, perhaps in five or ten years' time, application will be extremely limited.

12.22 Semiconductor investment

Policy makers need, in my view, to prioritise the certainty of investment in semiconductors. Four arguments point to more semiconductor funding. First, the semiconductor sector has existed for decades and provides proven cutting-edge products. Multiple practical devices have semiconductors in them. There is also the fact that hardware plays a central future role in progressing different types of machine learning and robotics.

Second, it is evident that the UK's annual defence budget exceeds £50 billion per annum. Given the reliance on defence and dual-use semiconductor components across Ministry of Defence procurement, a semiconductor strategy budget of £5 billion does not seem too high.

Third, the right level of ambition is vital. There is a risk that a modest public and private investment by the UK, relative to its direct competitors, especially Germany, Japan, or South Korea, will leave the UK further behind. Investment ambition requires confidence and foresight as the logical foundations for success.

Fourth, the UK has a competitive advantage from its track record of developing extraordinary STEM talent. For instance, the UK has been the training ground of innovative chemists, engineers and physicists, including Jalal Bagherli, Sir Tim Berners-Lee, Stan Boland, Professor John Goodenough, Professor Owen Guy, Sir Denis Hassabis, Simon Knowles, Drew Nelson, Sir David Payne, Andrew Rickman OBE and Nigel Toon.

The opportunity is a calculated risk that requires truly ambitious decisions – to invest now for the future. Long-term growth requires patient, long-term investment. The long-term investment should be, in my view, at least Cardiff-Compound Valley, Glasgow-Silicon Glen, and

Southampton-Photonics Valley. Whatever the precise future locations of UK semiconductor firms, there is the potential to compete or cooperate with the established clusters of Stanford-Silicon Valley and MIT-Greater Boston. Clusters whose talented staff have so often been British or UK-educated engineers or both.

There are also many possibilities to cooperate with spheres of growth across the EU, such as Dresden and Leuven. In March 2024, the UK became a 'Participating State' in the EU's 'Chips Joint Undertaking'. Consequently, UK semiconductor researchers can access funding backed by the UK Government and Horizon Europe. Jalal Bagherli, Chairman, PTSL, Chair, Williams Advanced Engineering and Co-Chair UK Semiconductor Advisory Panel, said he believed that 'this initiative is the next major step enabling engagement with our global partners to advance the state of the art in chip development and innovative packaging technologies in the UK'.[55]

Further, the ChipStart UK initiative has already taken on its second cohort of potential new semiconductor firms. Led by industry veterans, such as Ross Addinall, Russell Haggar and Sean Redmond, new entrepreneurs are mentored and gain unique access to potential VC backers. Equally important, their ambitions are fuelled by the experience of meeting highly experienced engineers, such as Janet Collyer MBE. ChipStart UK is partly funded by the UK Government, but it also relies on the generosity of established EDA firms to provide free software design tools.[56]

The first UK Government semiconductor strategy is positive because, as Moore's Law diminishes, many British cutting-edge disruptive firms can add value by being innovative. Firms must be dedicated to establishing cost-saving opportunities, thinking through strategic protection of innovation and understanding how different governments or other public sector actors support growth in the sector. Law, regulation, and policy also contribute to the long-term success of the semiconductor sector.

---

[55] UK Government (2024) '£35 million boost for British semiconductor scientists and businesses on international chip research', Press Release, 13 March 2024, available at www.gov.uk/government/news/35-million-boost-for-british-semiconductor-scientists-and-businesses-on-international-chip-research.

[56] Available at www.siliconcatalyst.uk/chipstart-uk.

The UK can grow its share of the global semiconductor market. Both gifted foreign and home-grown talent can undoubtedly achieve more with appropriate industrial policies and supportive regulation. Many readers will be aware that government policies are often compromised by a focus on the short- and medium-term forces of election cycles. The UK semiconductor strategy, established in 2023, provided the roots of a collective ten-year vision for any elected government to grow.

In recent years, some British politicians at the ministerial level have been shortsighted and self-serving.[57] It is difficult to break these selfish habits and serve the country by becoming commercially patriotic. Semiconductors are the linchpin sector for automotive, data management, defence, health, space and many other sectors. When politicians are thinking about the many potential areas for business growth, they are directly or indirectly assessing semiconductors.

The key issue is ministerial competence. What is a professional formula for success? Part of the formula should include their educational backgrounds, patience to understand perhaps the most complex of sectors, length of time in the role (as an absolute minimum two years) and ability to achieve a rounded understanding. Additionally, at the end of each service term an absolute minimum hand over period of one month. The complexity of the semiconductor sector may mean it is the least attractive subject for policy makers to make decisions on. Even a STEM-educated minister of uncharacteristically long-term tenure would struggle to build insights.

Given the challenge facing any future minister to successfully grasp the opportunities and risks, the UK Semiconductor Advisory Panel is pivotal to supporting ministerial understanding. The composition of that panel needs a balance of compound, photonics and silicon industry expertise.

---

[57] Interestingly, former UK prime minister Theresa May, a Member of Parliament for 27 years, said the following in her final speech to the UK Parliament: 'I worry…that too many people in politics today think that it is about them, their ambitions, their careers, and not about the people they serve. Being a Member of Parliament is a public service. We are here to serve our country and our constituents', available at https://hansard.parliament.uk/Commons/2024-05-24/debates/5DAFA076-1E8A-4498-8BCE-E3BFA7C8D725/details#contribution-933B8DCE-7F8D-449A-87D1-AE51FCB64E49.

Rory Stewart, a former minister and popular broadcaster is valued as a pragmatic thinker. Recently, Stewart has commendably focused on the issue of ignorance, arguing that recognising gaps in our knowledge makes humans humbler, more innovative and wiser.[58]

In the semiconductor sector many of the key participants have first-class honours engineering degrees. They will explain that it is probably impossible to 100 per cent understand all aspects. Trusted advisers from compound, photonics and pure silicon will be required to provide evidence-based detail. Indeed, given the risk of an individual consultant lacking objectivity on such high-cost issues, it will be rational to duplicate trusted advisers from each specialism – law, strategy, tax and technical. Semiconductor strategy implemented by ministers requires trusted advisers that seek to broaden and deepen the sector across the UK.

Ultimately, government commitment must include cautious but significant investment. In June 2024, Japan's Leading-edge Semiconductor Technology Center (LSTC)[59] announced it was committed to start sending engineers to Tenstorrent. A total of 200 Japanese engineers will be trained over five years. Japan's Ministry of Economy, Trade and Industry is contributing many millions of pounds in subsidies toward the initiative, paying for pre-departure training and living costs overseas. The UK would be wise to follow this long-term investment initiative.[60]

The allocation of government funds to the most promising disruptors requires a challenging variety of decision making. That mix includes championing various areas of technology as well as diversifying across compound, photonics and pure silicon. Additionally, to concentrate activity in clusters, as well as adapting to emerging architectures and materials.

---

58 BBC Radio 4 (2024) 'The Long History of Ignorance', Podcast, 11 July 2024.

59 The LSTC is a research consortium formed by Rapidus and the Japanese Government in 2022. Members include the University of Tokyo, along with other national universities and research institutes.

60 Mukano, R. (2024) 'Japan to send 200 engineers to U.S. for AI chip training at Tenstorrent – Rapidus-led group seeks to revive semiconductor industry with new talent', *Nikkei Asia*, 15 June 2024.

In November 2024, the Labour Government published the first draft of an industrial policy entitled 'Invest 2035'.[61] After seeking consultation, the intention is to implement a final plan in 2025. Yet evidenced on the direction taken by other countries, such as Japan, South Korea and Taiwan, sustainable success is a long-term plan. Their future mindset is 'Invest 2045' or 'Invest 2055'.

Encouragingly, 'Invest 2035' commits to learning what works in other economies. In my view, the industrial policy gold dust for the UK derives from examining how similar countries achieve industrial policy aims. John Stuart Mill's indirect method of difference is one potentially insightful logical technique to apply. The indirect method of difference analyses similar cases and explains the cause of different performance levels. Given the complexity, the task needs a comparison for each sector that is thriving in a comparable country.[62] Thereafter, ministers can prioritise two or three broad sectors as viable 20- or 30-year priorities.

In his thought-provoking book *The World in 2050*, Hamish McCrae, an economic journalist and global trends speaker, there is a chapter on technology subtitled 'The Big Questions for the Next Thirty Years'. In my view, his key observation is that incremental technological advances are highly significant.

For example, McCrae mentions that it is unclear if healthcare is becoming generally more efficient. Given many populations are ageing, medical costs will be a rising share of gross domestic product (GDP). He predicts that technical breakthroughs will play a transformative role in meeting

---

[61] UK Government (2024) 'Invest 2035: the UK's modern industrial strategy', available at www.gov.uk/government/consultations/invest-2035-the-uks-modern-industrial-strategy/invest-2035-the-uks-modern-industrial-strategy#executive-summary.

[62] Mill's original explanation of the indirect method of difference, as summarised with a memorable example in Chapter 10 National security law, will assist the process of elimination. The essence of Mill's indirect method is 'if two or more instances in which the phenomenon occurs have only one circumstance in common, while two or more instances in which it does not occur have nothing in common save the absence of that circumstance; the circumstance in which alone the two sets of instances differ, is the effect, or cause, or a necessary part of the cause, of the phenomenon': Mill, J.S. (1843) *A System of Logic*, John W. Parker, at 463.

this challenge, especially for incremental advances.[63] Semiconductors are the technology that will deliver lower cost diagnostics and medical intervention for the NHS.

What is the probability of economic success? The variables include the fact that semiconductors enable nearly all other cutting-edge sectors. AI, cars, drones, health service technology, satellites, smartphones, and wearables. The UK is an established world leader in CPU design. The largest percentage share of revenue across the complex jigsaw of semiconductor production goes to the owner of the design IP. Based on this evidence the right semiconductor strategy has a high probability of success.

Practical, continuously adjusted real innovation strategies, fuelled by self-belief, will provide the best formula for success. Dedication has taken Chinese, German, Japanese, Korean, Taiwanese and US semiconductor firms incredibly far. To varying degrees, each of these countries underline that semiconductor success is possible from modest starting points. More British firms, supported by government actors, can choose the same direction. To take less travelled entrepreneurial paths, eating bitterness along the way. To be ambitious, innovative and resilient.

[63] McRae, H. (2023) *The World in 2050 – How to Think About the Future*, Bloomsbury, at 141–9.

Index